75

Curriculum Improvement
for Better Schools

Curriculum Improvement
for Better Schools

Jack R. Frymier
Ohio State University

Horace C. Hawn
University of Georgia

Charles A. Jones Publishing Company
Worthington, Ohio

1 2 3 4 5 6 7 8 9 10 / 74 73 72 71 70

Library of Congress Catalog Card Number: 78–116550
Printed in the United States of America

To
Kimball Wiles
who lived and worked
for "better schools"

Preface

Education and educators are on the move. Those who have thought about, argued for, pleaded, and cajoled for movement within the system all agree that important changes are underway. The slow but steady and dependable giant is showing remarkable signs of vigor and life. Change is actually becoming the byword in education today.

This book has been written with that reality of change in mind. It is intended for advanced students in professional training, and for teachers, supervisors, curriculum workers, and administrators who function as practitioners in the field.

All of the illustrations and theoretical propositions in this book are real. Nothing is contrived. Every incident, every set of data, every problem identified is reality-based. This book is an attempt to set forth a theoretical framework and series of specific case examples which will be vivid, concrete, and real. Maintaining fidelity with the educational reality has been a primary goal.

The authors of this book feel very strongly that persons responsible for curriculum development in local schools can and must assume primary responsibility for initiating and continuing curriculum improvement efforts in their schools. For too long those of us who are curriculum workers have taken our cues from persons who function outside the field. For too long we have been reacters to external events rather than purposeful actors in our own professional sphere. This book urges teachers, supervisors, administrators, and curriculum workers to unite in their conviction that curriculum can be improved for more effective learning in better schools.

And what should be the basis for curriculum change? "Hard" data and "soft" data generated from careful evaluations of curriculum changes undertaken within the local district which is involved. Responding to the demands of outside "experts" or "national programs" or "local tradition" is no substitute for valid information produced as a result of studying teaching and learning in one's own school. This book outlines general principles and specific procedures to help practicing school men go about the business of comprehending and modifying the curricular reality with which they work.

Part I explores the theoretical and practical considerations which are involved in curriculum development efforts, and sets forth principles of curriculum improvement which are based on actual experiences in local school districts.

Part II describes a series of research and evaluation approaches which were aimed at improving curriculum in a variety of ways. Each chapter represents a "case study" of sorts, but the examples cited are meant to be illustrative rather than definitive, and it is the spirit rather than the letter of the endeavor which should be inferred and then applied.

Part III attempts to make such inferences and draw them together into a meaningful whole. In responding to the question "Can we learn from the experiences of others?" the authors of this book have articulated in precise detail a set of theoretical conceptualizations drawn directly from the experiences and processes described. We have, in fact, attempted to learn from our experience, and to share those learnings with others in the curriculum field.

Many of our colleagues in the public schools and in the university community have contributed immeasurably to the development of ideas in this book. To the students, teachers, supervisors, and administrators in Orange County, Florida; Franklin County, Ohio; Hamilton County, Ohio; and Richland County, Ohio we are particularly indebted. Without their energies, enthusiasm and participation in these ventures, the publication of this book would never have been realized. Rhea Anderson, John Burrows, O. R. Davis, Louis Edwards, Betty Hoyle, James Jacobs, Alice Johnson, Mills Lord, Eddith Montgomery, Audrey Norris, Richard Porter, Jane Scroggs, and Mary Thomason have all contributed greatly. Paul Klohr, Kelly Duncan, and Bill Williams entered into penetrating dialogue with us as we tried to "think the ideas through." Harry Passow, O. L. Davis, Jr., and Paul Halverson, all read portions of the manuscript and made critical and extremely helpful suggestions. And to Ruthann Reed for typing the manuscript and Grace Van Atta for editorial assistance throughout, we shall be forever grateful.

Before his untimely death, Kimball Wiles read part of the manuscript and made many constructive suggestions regarding content and organization. Kim was also directly instrumental in encouraging us to complete the manuscript, so we have taken this opportunity to dedicate this book to him.

Jack R. Frymier
Horace C. Hawn

Columbus, Ohio
Athens, Georgia

January, 1970

Contents

3

Establishing Relationships for Change, 35

4

Devising a Structure for Change, 51

Curriculum Improvement in Practice, 63

5

Curriculum Studies Involving the Community, 65

6

Curriculum Studies Involving Students, 83

Curriculum Improvement
for Better Schools

Introduction

American people are concerned about their schools. This commitment and concern has been noticeably expressed in recent years in terms of greater financial support, increased dialogue, extensive legislation, and obvious belief in education as a means to improve the quality of life for all persons in the United States. In response, those whose duty it is to coordinate, administer, and improve education have been stimulated to expand and extend their efforts to change education for the better. These efforts have taken many forms.

Some changes have attempted to upgrade the content or subject matter. Others have been directed at modifying the organizational components of education (time, space, staff, resources, etc.) or have focused upon the methodological aspects of education (language laboratories, teaching machines, etc.). There have also been improvements in teacher preparation programs, inservice education endeavors, and teacher certification requirements.

Many observations might be made about these change efforts, but two seem especially significant. First is the insistence that evaluative data be employed as the basis for decisions regarding curriculum change. Second is the assumption that local school districts are not capable of initiating curriculum improvement efforts comparable in quality to those developed at the "national" level. The authors believe that the first point is valid, but that the second point is not. We maintain that persons responsible for curriculum improvement activities in local school districts not only can but also must assume *primary* responsibility for beginning and continuing curriculum development efforts. Furthermore, we maintain that such efforts can only be effective if they are predicated upon information generated from careful evaluations of curriculum changes undertaken within the district.

The task is difficult, to say the least. John I. Goodlad outlines the very real problems inherent in any major effort to improve curriculum in local schools:

Our schools have a long, hard road ahead if they are to become stimulating places for the good work of those who reside in them. Unless schools become significantly more intense, they will fall by the wayside as other institutions and media become the prime educational influences. I do not believe any single innovation to be sufficiently powerful to provide the panacea. *And I certainly do not believe that the rhetorical appeal to educational leadership on which we have largely depended is of much use in effecting change.*

If I were to prepare "a state of the schools" message today, the topic sentences would read somewhat as follows:

First, there is an enormous gap between our concept of what schooling could be, circa 1968, and what it is.

Second, a substantial number of principals and teachers want to know much more about the newer ideas and concepts and especially how to implement them. There is, in other words, a critical mass of personnel positively oriented toward change.

Third, we have left the reeducating of these personnel largely to a process of osmosis. If school personnel can listen and read, we assume they will change their conceptual and performance behavior.

Fourth, and closely related, there are few comprehensive conceptual, simulated, or real models of what redesigned schools might look like.

Fifth, the norms of and expectancies for schooling are so built in to the total structure that the prospect of redesigning any significant part of the whole is discouraging, if not frightening.

Sixth, upward mobility for individuals in the system depends not only on learning its nature but also on reinforcing the system. Consequently, to ask middle management leaders—the leaders closest to the point where change ultimately must occur—to be countercyclical to the system is to ask them to be exceedingly divergent in their leadership behavior.

Seventh, because of most of the above, significant educational change can only result from a comprehensive attack on the whole. But such an attack, if overt, is likely to alert the system and to strengthen the very mechanisms which are to be the focus of attack.

Eighth, and perhaps most critical, we are not at all clear on how to go about effecting this comprehensive attack on the whole, in spite of our diversified experience with programs designed to bring about educational change.*

---

* John I. Goodlad, "Educational Change: A Strategy for Study and Action," *The National Elementary Principal,* XLVIII (January, 1969), pp. 8 ff. Copyright 1969, Department of Elementary School Principals, National Education Association. All rights reserved.

Because many curriculum workers seem to feel that local school districts cannot realistically hope to compete with the foundation-supported, government-sponsored, or university-backed curriculum development projects, they have gradually come to accept unquestioningly the idea that "somebody else" will *develop* curriculum, and that they will *consider* and *adopt* the programs which others develop. Persons at the local level often do not perceive that the local district either can or should serve as the driving force and organizing center for curriculum ventures of all kinds.

This book sets forth an alternative to that kind of thinking. Our intentions are to outline how people who are working in a local school district can go about the business of improving the quality of educational programs in their schools. We also believe that unless local instructional leaders use evaluative techniques to determine the effectiveness of all kinds of innovations, the curricula for young people in American schools will probably become more uniform but less effective.

In general, the position described in this book is similar to the "alternative model" described by Donald T. Campbell and Julian C. Stanley in their classic chapter on experimental design.

The present authors are gradually coming to the view that experimentation within schools must be conducted by regular staff of the schools concerned, whenever possible, especially when findings are to be generalized to other classroom situations.

At present, there seem to be two main types of "experimentation" going on within schools: (1) research "imposed" upon the school by an outsider, who has his own ax to grind and whose goal is not immediate action (change) by the school; and (2) the so-called "action" researcher, who tries to get teachers themselves to be "experimenters," using that word quite loosely. The first researcher gets results that may be rigorous but not applicable. The latter gets results that may be highly applicable but probably not "true" because of extreme lack of rigor in the research. An alternative model is for the ideas for classroom research to originate with teachers and other school personnel, with designs to test these ideas worked out cooperatively with specialists in research methodology, and then for the bulk of the experimentation to be carried out by the idea-producers themselves. The appropriate statistical analyses could be done by the research methodologist and the results fed back to the group via a trained intermediary (supervisor, director of research in the school system, etc.) who has served as intermediary all along. Results should then be relevant and "correct." How to get *basic* research going under such a pattern is largely an unsolved problem, but studies could become less and less ad hoc and more and more theory-oriented under a competent intermediary.*

This book represents one attempt to implement these ideas in a public school setting.

---

* Donald T. Campbell and Julian C. Stanley, "Experimental and Quasi-Experimental Designs for Research on Teaching," N. L. Gage (ed.), *Handbook of Research on Teaching* (Chicago: Rand McNally and Co., 1963), p. 191.

Throughout the book, we ask that the reader "role play" as he reads and assume that he is the Curriculum Director or Assistant Superintendent in Charge of Instruction working out of the central office of a medium-sized school district. He is interested in education and curriculum improvement, in acquiring new techniques and in developing these skills. He also has faith in the power of ideas and in the importance of learning as a way to improve the quality of life for all mankind. We assume these things. We also think that putting these assumptions into practice in local schools is intellectually fascinating and professionally fun. We do not presume that this is the only way to work at curriculum improvements. There obviously are many other approaches, but this book describes one approach that we feel is effective. In essence, that approach involves using curriculum evaluation and curriculum research as a vehicle for deliberate, thoughtful curriculum change.

Curriculum Improvement in Perspective

Chapters 1 through 4 outline in theoretical and practical terms a framework for improving curriculum in a local school situation. Several assumptions are inherent in these chapters: curriculum improvement requires curriculum change; change should be predicated upon good information, good relationships, and a good rationale; and being a curriculum change agent requires sensitivity, intelligence, experience, and skill.

Chapter 4 describes an organizing structure which might serve as a vehicle for curriculum improvement. Before organizing a local school district or particular building or group for curriculum improvement efforts, however, many other considerations are identified. The press and tenor of the times is one consideration. What has been going on in education? How have these activities affected local schools? What are the basic assumptions implicit in prevailing practice, whatever that practice might be? What constitutes a reasonable approach to curriculum improvement? How much of the "whole" should be dealt with at any one time? Who are the central persons who ought to be involved? Those and other questions are explored.

Practical problems abound. Do the conditions under which one accepts a position make a difference in his ability to bring about positive curriculum change? How does one know when to "go fast" or "go slow?" What are the theoretical assumptions inherent in "good practice," and how can one operationalize sound theory in practical ways?

Part I deals with questions such as those posed above. Because this book represents "a point of view," the answers to such questions are pragmatic, but the general principles are also described. Curriculum improvement is a "people problem," because people are so intimately and so extensively involved. "Improving curriculum" means developing and nurturing, broadening and enriching, altering and adding, and uplifting and revitalizing the lives and minds of those who implement curriculum and instructional decisions every day. That is no simple chore.

Furthermore, it is not a responsibility which dare be assumed without the wholehearted cooperation and participation of all of those who are involved. "Changing curriculum" does mean "changing people," and unless those who are to be affected and to be changed are intelligent participants throughout the entire process, it becomes both authoritarian and a sham. The nature, direction, and the decision to change must be arrived at openly and without coercion, but change must occur if the educational enterprise is to improve.

We live in changing times and in a new era. The intellectual and emotional diet (i.e., the "curriculum") which we provide young people in schools must be improved. Part I deals with the general and specific problems involved in moving toward major curriculum improvement efforts in local schools.

1 Curriculum Improvement in Perspective

The Importance of Evaluation

Every model for curriculum development includes the concept of assessment or evaluation. From a theoretical point of view, evaluation plays an
important part in improving programs in several ways (1). Purposes can
be selected, for example, on the basis of good data about the nature of
society or the nature of the learner. Or, content, experiences, organization,
and methodology can be set forth in testable form. For instance, rather
than assuming any particular selection of content or sequence of experiences or methodological approaches or organizational stratagems is effective, one can hypothesize about these things, and put these hypotheses to
an empirical test. Over a period of time such evaluative and assessment
techniques should enable steady progress in terms of improving programs.

Talk of "national assessment" and the requirement for evaluation built
into the Elementary and Secondary Education Act programs are the
major developments of prominence that are forcing curriculum workers
to reexamine these notions as they apply to curriculum development
today.

Any view of the educational scene suggests that programs are changing

dramatically. At no time in the history of American schools have curricular changes been so widespread or so intensive as in the past decade.
Modifications of course content, organizational structures, methodological approaches, evaluation procedures, and even purposes themselves have
been instituted. Changes in curriculum have been extensive and many
have been positive, but few people are satisfied with the state of affairs in
American curriculum today; the inadequacies are all too obvious.

Curriculum workers are dissatisfied, and they are continuously struggling to find new and more powerful ways to improve programs. This is
partly because of a kind of gnawing professional perspective which says:
"No program is perfect. We must improve." But they are dissatisfied most
of all because of the very real fact that too many children hate the very
thought of having to learn in school.

Too many children find school a boring, unexciting place to be. Too
many are unsuccessful in acquiring ways of behaving which seem appropriate and desirable to people responsible for their learning. Why? Many
factors probably account for such a state of affairs today, but two are
suggested here. We can ask the wrong questions in curriculum, and we
can use assessment ineffectively as part of the total educational scheme.

In curriculum development, we often ask the *frequency* question or the
efficiency question rather than the *effectiveness* question. We say, "How
many schools are using language laboratories?" "How many schools have
PSSC physics this year?" "How many classrooms are non-graded?"
"How many teachers utilize generative grammar or structural linguistics
in their language arts programs?" The assumption underlying these
questions is that if more schools are using a particular program, it must be
better, which obviously is an inappropriate assumption. Frequency is not
an appropriate criterion at all. For instance, even though more than half
the youngsters studying physics in our secondary schools are in the PSSC
physics program, the proportional overall enrollment in physics actually
was steadily decreasing during the same period of time that the new
program came into being (2).

Consider another example. Judgments about a program might be made
in terms of money. "How much will it cost?" "How efficient will it be?"
"Can we afford such an innovation?" These questions presuppose that the
basic purpose of education is to save money. The fact remains that if we
ask an economic question, we can only get an economic answer.

If schools exist to save money, there are many ways to reduce expenditures. We can lower teachers' salaries, increase class size, or eliminate expenditures for instructional materials, and we will save a lot of money. The purpose of education is not to save money, but to help children learn.

We must always focus upon the *effectiveness* question. Does the new program, do the new materials, will the new techniques enable students to learn more, better, faster, than some other approach? Does it make a significant difference in the lives and minds of those we teach? If it does, the program is effective. If it does not, the program is ineffective. Whether it costs more money or less, or whether it is widespread or not in any other school is immaterial. We must learn to ask the effectiveness question every time.

A deeper, more elusive problem affecting program development, however, stems from the fact that education is a social system with a conceptual flaw. Every effective social system reflects three phases of operation which accomplish separate functions that enable the system to maintain itself in a dynamic way.

Phase one includes the intellectual activities: planning, policy-making, and hypothesizing. Phase two, the doing, accomplishing, and effecting. Phase three, the evaluating, assessing, reflecting, and judging. Taken together, they represent various aspects of social undertakings designed to allow the system to accomplish the objectives toward which it is aimed, and at the same time to keep improving. These three phases are most clearly illustrated in our concept of government. The planning phase is represented by the legislative branch. The doing phase by the executive branch. The evaluating or assessing phase by the judicial branch. In industry the model still applies; somebody plans, somebody produces, and somebody judges the effectiveness of activities in a realistic way.

Any careful study of social systems other than education suggests that these three functions are relatively discreet, and that they are accomplished by different groups, each one of which has a realm of power. That is, the Congress, the President, and the Supreme Court are distinct entities. The same notion applies at the state and local level of government.

A significant point rests on the fact that fully-functioning social systems in an open society actually depend upon the third phase of the operation to assure improvement and intelligent change. When the courts decide that a particular law is constitutional or unconstitutional, or that a particular action by the executive branch of the government either is or is not appropriate, they feed back into the system new data which guarantee that the enterprise will be able to change itself and to improve. In industry the same thing is also true. Planning and producing a new product or service represent the first and second phases of that social system in operation. Once the product goes on sale, however, evaluation must occur. If the general public buys the product or service, what they really do is feed back into the system new data that indicate to those responsible for planning and production they have done the job well. Or, if the public refuses to buy, corrective feedback indicates that a product or service is not satisfactory and must be changed. In either event, *evaluation plays the critical role of providing corrective feedback to the other parts of the system so that the entire operation can be improved.*

Two things are important about our discussion thus far. One is that the concept of corrective feedback, which is performed during the evaluation phase of the social systems operation, represents the precise point at which improvement can be assured. Second, it is also evident that the assessment or evaluation effort is best accomplished by a separate group which has appropriate influence of its own. Congress cannot decide the constitutionality of its own laws, for example, nor do manufacturing companies have the ultimate decision about the worthwhileness or value of the products they produce. These decisions are reserved for other groups.

The power of evaluation rests in part upon the nature of the feedback information which is generated by the process, and in part by the fact that the evaluation group has an authority of its own. Our system of government and our system of economics, at least, presume that when the evaluation group makes its decision known, *the rest of the system will have to pay attention to the feedback.* The rest of the system is not free to ignore the data, whether they are positive or negative.

Looked at in terms of such a social systems model, education obviously has a conceptual flaw. School boards accomplish the policy-making role. Professional persons undertake the effecting, implementing, doing role. But no special group's responsibilities encompass the assessment function in any meaningful way. The general public passes judgment on the effectiveness of schools, of course, but seldom do they have a way of communicating their concerns with precision and dispatch to assure improvement in schools. They may vote down a bond issue, but no one really knows what this negative vote precisely means.

Advisory councils and curriculum councils often attempt to perform the evaluation role. However, because their recommendations are *advisory*—no one has to pay attention to the feedback.

No aspect of the educational system regularly generates evaluative-type data; nothing in the concept requires that those within the system pay attention to the feedback data if they should appear (3). Education cannot improve as presently conceptualized, and as it presently functions. By maintaining that "education cannot improve" as it is presently conceptualized and as it presently functions, we do not by any means intend to foster pessimism or to arouse fear. Nevertheless, in terms of our experience and our observations the reality of education is actually as described.

This description of the *reality,* though, suggests exactly where we need to apply our energies if we really want curricula to be improved: program evaluation. Some might suggest an "outside" evaluation agency or group, such as "national assessment" or "statewide testing" to fill the void described. Our position is that local districts can and must undertake the evaluation activities themselves (4).

Educational professionals, working together in local districts, must devise concepts and procedures for evaluating the programmatic activities in local schools. This book describes in specific terms many approaches to that problem area which one might follow, but the point is, either local schoolmen must *generate* and use evaluative-type data to improve the program in schools, or accept *on faith* the many curriculum materials and projects which appear.

One may want to argue with that statement, because he thinks that "somebody else" has done or will do the time-consuming and difficult chore of necessary research. However, the history of curriculum development activities in the last ten years suggests that very few innovations are evaluated empirically either during development or after they appear fairly widespread on the educational scene. Further, evaluative data typically comes from those who have participated in the development of the new materials or new organizational or new methodological approaches, and utility of these data must be questioned in other situations with other teachers and other youngsters than those originally involved.

Evaluative data are essential if people in local schools hope to improve their educational programs, but data will have greatest utility and greatest impact if they concern teachers and students in their own schools.

The Trend Toward National Programs

Education in the United States has traditionally been a function of the states. Over the years, some curriculum projects or movements have assumed a "national" character of sorts, but with few exceptions (for example, vocational education programs in the high schools), they were generally sporadic and seldom widely adopted. "Progressive Education," "Life Adjustment Education," "the Core Program," and "the Community School" are all illustrations of some which became fairly well "known" but not very widely "adopted." The "graded school" and "objective testing," for instance, are still widely used curriculum concepts. Some textbooks were so popular that they constituted a kind of "national curriculum" on their own (e.g., *McGuffey's Readers*). However, these curriculum changes did not have the same kind of "attractiveness" or the same kind of "authoritativeness" many national curriculum projects have today.

The "national" concern and "national" effort to improve the programs in the American public schools have been generated by two recent historical events—the Supreme Court decisions related to school segregation and the launching of Sputnik.

The preoccupation of the United States with Communism meant that when the Russians launched a satellite into orbit before the U.S. did, something had to be changed. That "something" became the curriculum in our schools. Spurred on by Congress and various philanthropic groups, the public became concerned about and committed to improving curricula in public schools. "The new mathematics," "modern physics," and "team teaching," for example, all appeared in the professional literature and in the schools. "Experts" from the disciplines worked with classroom teachers on new and better instructional materials, organizational schemes, or methodological devices, and they were almost always backed up with government or foundation financial support. Grants-in-aid to local school districts were made for mathematics and science equipment, language laboratories, guidance institutes, and desegregation workshops, to mention only a few. Grants went to universities to develop new textbooks and teacher's manuals, research pertaining to educational programs, teacher training institutes which taught teachers to use "the new mathematics" or "the new biology," and to pay teachers and counselors to learn these new subject matter and teaching methods.

Because of the apparent urgency, the funding by the federal government, and the participation in many of these ventures by "experts" from fields other than education, an aura of respectability developed around the new programs.

"The new textbook must be good or else the government wouldn't spend all that money developing a new curriculum if they weren't certain that it is better than what we now have."

"This program has been developed under the direction of Dr. _____ who is an outstanding authority in the field of _____."

"If he says the old curriculum needs updating and if his committee has developed these new materials, they must really be the latest things. These curriculum materials just have to be good."

"The guidelines from the federal government only permit the expenditure of funds for certain things. Those fellows in Washington probably have a better overall picture of developments at the national level. This science equipment, which meets the USOE specifications, certainly must be better than that other equipment, which we cannot get reimbursed for anyway."

These kinds of statements have been very common. By adopting "the new mathematics," educational television, language laboratories, "modern biology," educators could get both more money and less criticism simultaneously. Because the national curriculum projects had been developed by experts in the disciplines, local curriculum leaders could show everyone that they were committed to "good" education, "hard subject matter," and "modern" approaches.

Many efforts have been made to sample teachers' opinions about the "new" programs; but, since those surveyed typically received seventy-five dollars or more a week for many weeks to learn the "new" program, one would be surprised that most did not "feel" that the old program was better than the new. If the new program is better, however, and if students do learn more, better, faster, and forget less than students in the traditional programs, then a careful evaluation will demonstrate that point. Merely *presuming* that a national curriculum project is better than an existing or a locally devised program without testing that presumption is a professional error of the most serious order.

The forces attracting curriculum workers to the national curriculum projects are powerful and real. Our concern is not to disparage these programs in any way, but to encourage curriculum workers to employ the power inherent in evaluation as a major means of improving the curriculum in their local schools. Before we proceed with an elaboration of what we think can be done, we feel it would be useful to give a brief overview of what various other people say regarding educational change.

The Concept of Educational Change

Curriculum improvement is a linear concept; it involves modification of curriculum over time. Changing anything for the sake of change is pointless, and changing education for its own sake is costly, frustrating, and senseless in every way. If one is concerned about working to bring about improvements in curriculum, he will inevitably be working to bring about change. If this change is to be meaningful and positive, one needs to understand the dynamics and the problems inherent in change.

Egon G. Guba (5) maintains that educational change involves four stages: research, development, diffusion, and adoption; while Everett M. Rogers (6) suggests that the adoption process itself has five separate stages: awareness, interest, evaluation, trial, and adoption. Breaking the change process down into these stages demonstrates the point that change involves modifications over time. Whether these change "models" depict changes in education as they typically *do* occur or as they *should* occur is not at all clear. If Rogers means "consideration" of the innovation when he says "evaluation," that would seem sensible, but in terms of our experience, "trial" would of necessity be followed by "evaluation" or "assessment" before "adoption" should occur. Rogers evidently means that "trial" should include assessment-type efforts. This part of the change process is too crucial to be included merely as an implicit aspect of any stage; it should be *explicitly* set forth as an important stage of the change process, and it should, in our opinion, come after "trial" but before "adoption."

From case studies included in a larger report, Harold J. McNally and A. H. Passow (7) list ten principles inherent in the curriculum improvement efforts. These principles may be helpful to the curriculum worker as he approaches his responsibilities in this area.

(1) Curriculum improvement was viewed as a process of changing teachers' behavior.

(2) Extensive participation of teachers in curriculum development could be encouraged by committee organization.

(3) A free flow of communication was necessary so that proposals for change might emerge from almost any place in the system and community.

(4) The local school building was viewed as the basic unit of participation.

(5) The responsibility for curriculum change was assigned to one person, but leadership within the organization was encouraged to emerge.

(6) System-wide coordination was essential for curriculum improvement.

(7) The organization for change in each system was determined by its own particular purposes, size, and resources.

(8) Participation of lay persons in the community was encouraged.

(9) Experimentation was an integral part of the process of curriculum improvement.

(10) It was a major responsibility for the school administration to provide time and resources.

While educators have begun to make progress in their efforts to understand what the concept of "change" in education really means, change is really only part of any curriculum worker's responsibility (8).

Ben N. Harris makes this point very clear when he distinguishes between "dynamic" and "tractive" supervision (9). "Improving" educational programs is one task curriculum coordinators must work at; and "maintaining" them is another very important professional activity. Effectiveness as an instructional leader depends in part upon one's understanding and skill in "maintaining" the educational enterprise (procuring books, letting contracts, preparing reports, ordering supplies, orienting new teachers, developing policy procedures, etc.) and in part upon one's understanding and skill in "improving" the program (conducting inservice workshops, introducing innovative ideas to professional staff, establishing "experimental" programs, etc.). As a matter of fact, most of the instructional leader's time will probably be spent in "maintenance" type activities, which is perfectly all right. Nevertheless, one must allocate certain portions of one's own professional time to "improvement" or "change" efforts, too.

Such an obvious point does not necessarily need emphasis. However, our experience suggests that not much change happens unless persons responsible for "improving" curriculum work deliberately and regularly allocate certain portions of their work time for "improvement" undertakings. There are always reports to be prepared, teachers to be hired, parents to be heard, phones to be answered. The point is that such "maintenance" responsibilities will take *all* of a curriculum worker's time, if he allows it. The only way to avoid this dilemma is to *plan* activities so that *some* energies are devoted to curriculum improvement every day.

In the chapters which follow we have set forth a number of specific suggestions which may be helpful in meeting responsibility for improving the curriculum in particular schools. Throughout these chapters we have assumed that responsibilities extend system-wide; we have made this assumption simply for logical consistency and writing style. We could have written this book from the perspective of a building principal, elementary supervisor, or superintendent because the principles of improving curriculum are the same for all. The specific activities or organizational structures or problems encountered would vary according to position, of course, but we strongly feel that program improvement must be approached head-on by people who work regularly in local schools.

Notes

1. Ralph W. Tyler, "The Function of Measurement in Improving Instruction," E. F. Lindquist (ed.), *Educational Measurement* (Washington, D.C.: American Council on Education, 1951), pp. 47–67.

2. John Walsh, "Curriculum Reform," *Science*, CXLIV (8 May 1964), pp. 642–646.

3. Jack R. Frymier, *Fostering Educational Change* (Columbus, Ohio: Charles E. Merrill Publishing Company, 1969).

4. *Ibid*.

5. Egon G. Guba, "Methodological Strategies for Educational Change," a paper presented to the Conference on Strategies for Educational Change. (Washington, D.C., 1965), Mimeographed.

6. Everett M. Rogers, *Diffusion of Innovations* (New York: The Free Press, 1962), p. 81.

7. Harold J. McNally and A. H. Passow, *Improving the Quality of Public School Programs* (New York: Teachers College, Columbia University, 1960).

8. The following are illustrative of the literature on "change" which has appeared in recent years: H. S. Bhola, "Implications of New Democratic Theory for Planned Educational Change," *Newsletter of the Conference on Strategies for Educational Change* (The Ohio State University, November, 1965), and "Categories of Social Change," *Newsletter* (January, 1966); Richard O. Carlson, *Adoption of Educational Innovations* (Eugene, Oregon: Center for Advanced Study of Educational Administration, 1965); Robert S. Gilchrist (ed.), *New Curriculum Developments* (Washington, D.C.: ASCD, 1965); John I. Goodlad, *School Curriculum Reform in the United States* (New York: Fund for the Advancement of Education, 1964); Paul R. Klohr and Jack R. Frymier, "Curriculum Development: Dynamics of Change." *Review of Educational Research,* Vol. XXXIII, No. 3 (June, 1963); Francis A. J. Ianni, "Appraisal of Changes in Education," *North Central Association Quarterly,* XL, No. 2 (Fall, 1965); Matthew B. Miles, (ed.), *Innovation in Education* (New York: Bureau of Publication, Teachers College, Columbia University, 1964); Daniel L. Stufflebeam, "The Use and Abuse of Evaluation in Title III," *Theory Into Practice* (June, 1967), and "Evaluation as Enlightenment for Decision-making," a paper presented at ASCD Conference on Assessment Theory (Sarasota, 1968); Kimball Wiles and Robert R. Leeper (eds.), *Strategy for Curriculum Change* (Washington, D.C.: ASCD, 1965).

9. Ben M. Harris, *Supervisory Behavior in Education* (Englewood Cliffs, N.J.: Prentice-Hall, Inc., 1963), Chapter 1.

2 Basis for Curriculum Change

These are exciting days for school-men. We now know more about how to improve education than ever before. We have available at our command more research data about how children learn and about how to manipulate the conditions to optimize this learning. But we seem to follow archaic traditions and outmoded concepts of teaching methods and school organization, perhaps because any opportunity for change is accompanied by increased responsibilities and added burdens.

Because schools have never had enough financial or moral support to make changes as they really should be made, schoolmen have come to cling to a "something less than best" philosophy. The task of providing optimum educational chances for all children is admittedly a mammoth undertaking; so is getting to the moon. As a nation, we have embraced the one job reluctantly and the other enthusiastically. More and better schools would without question actually help us reach the moon or Mars or anywhere more quickly, but the American public expresses its wishes in paradoxical ways.

One of the major challenges of the curriculum worker will be to tackle that big problem of public faith and belief in education, and to organize his energies in such a way that he actually attempts to reverse the present trend. The immediate problem is to help the instructional leader in his role for the months to come so that his day-to-day activities reflect an awareness of and congruence with the total situation, while at the same time changing that situation slowly but deliberately into dynamic change for educational improvement. Changing curricula is now the instruction leader's role so that more and more children will have ever increasing opportunities to experience and benefit from rejuvenated and revised educational programs.

One major thesis of this book is: "We do not need more of the same, but more of the different in our schools today." School people say "If we only had more money" or "If we only had more books," or similar comments. For example, administrators obsessed with the problems of increasing enrollments assume that children learn more and better in smaller classes than they do in larger ones. From a logical point of view, theirs is a tenable position, but the problems in education are only partly logical. Educational problems are predominantly psychological. Some data, in fact, do support smaller classes, especially for very young children; however, to find more and more teachers to preserve a constant teacher-pupil ratio ignores the fundamental problem of how youngsters learn. Actually, 25 or 30 is too many for genuine discussion and far too few for imparting information by telling or showing in other ways. Even if most research indicated classes should be large or small, they will stay about the same. The existing classrooms dictate class size, regardless of what research or authorities might say. But we still have to change.

The present situation in American education has been compared with the problem once faced by farmers growing corn. Farmers and their eager helpers in universities and experimental stations tried manipulating, one by one, all of the variables involved in farming to increase the production of corn in bushels per acre. Over a period of time the soil content, fertilizer, moisture, tilling, etc. were varied thoughtfully and deliberately to see what effect they had on corn production. Slowly at first, and then more rapidly, production went up and up, and then it slowed. Then there came a leveling off; production stayed about the same regardless of further research. Doing more and more in the same old way did not increase the production of corn. Finally, someone considered changing the very structure of the corn itself, and hybrid corn was born. With this basic, genetic change, new advances were made in corn production immediately.

The point of the example is this: there comes a time for those who strive to improve any situation when more of the same is not enough. Certain basic changes in the fundamental structure must be accomplished. If education is ever to become what it might really be, drastic changes in the basic policies must be achieved. Mere tinkering with the educational enterprise is not enough. This is the problem of the curriculum worker: to help those with whom he works come to conceive of education in terms of *what it could be.*

If the people of this nation ever decide to support education like they do the missile race, schools will be able to help children grow to educational heights unknown. One of the responsibilities of the curriculum worker, then, will be to find more and effective ways of mobilizing public opinion or better schools. Unless this is done, the minor changes in the educational situation are comparable to varying only the fertilizer content or depth of the plow in corn production. The very heart of the entire enterprise must be changed, not just a little, but a lot.

Where does one begin? Avoid perseveration in trying to solve a problem by repeating the same incorrect effort. The child who tries to put a square peg in a round hole over and over again is perseverating. Doing the same wrong thing again and again makes sense to no one, and yet a careful look at the educational scene shows one instance after another in which professional educators have repeatedly refused to grapple with new problems by seeking a new solution. Teaching more mathematics is not the same as teaching better mathematics. Neither is teaching better mathematics the same as teaching mathematics better. Given the explosion of knowledge and the limited staff and facilities available for educational activities today, H. G. Wells' often quoted statement that education is a race with catastrophe is probably more true today than ever before. We have to change our way of working in schools if we hope to solve our problems.

Consider a parallel situation. Some time ago the American telephone industry was confronted with deciding whether to go to the dial telephones or to retain women switchboard operators to place calls. Fortunately, the industry chose to use dial phones. There are not enough young women alive today in the United States, even if every single one of them worked at a switchboard, to handle our present flow of telephone traffic. We must change the basic structure of education if we hope to keep up with the great demand.

Demands are being made. Industry expects more of schools. Colleges expect more. Parents, government, the armed services, even children themselves expect more. But these demands carry with them hopes and expectations. The American public is actually far out in front of the profession in demanding change and progress. What they are expecting is not for the sake of change; they want schools to do more for the youth of today. Their concerns have many origins but most arise from their awareness of the increased tempo of life in general and the increased proficiencies demanded of people in particular. Unless young people are adequately equipped with the skills, knowledge, and attitudes to take their place in the world today, the schools have failed. Certainly, educators must pose these questions. Does learning to diagram sentences really help people communicate? Does doing two hours of "hard" homework on "tough" subjects every day make youngsters more intelligent? Does more science and mathematics in our programs encourage more persons to make careers in these areas? Will a person be a better doctor if he has more science or more art? Does forcing youngsters to know the first amendment to the constitution really make people more free?

In our earnest desire to help youngsters learn, we have neglected helping ourselves do the same. Our professional posture must be evaluated—thoughtfully and critically. Those who work in schools to improve instruction must conceptualize their efforts in such a way that entirely new ways of working and new ways of viewing education are involved.

This is a book of action. Ideas in education are worthwhile, if and when we can find ways of translating them into curriculum change. The pages which follow are outlined, in considerable detail, with specific suggestions for action which have been tried and found successful in inducing curriculum change. Our familiarity with research in learning and in supervision convinces us that each of the principles here is firmly rooted in careful research. Although we feel that the readability of this book would be diminished considerably were each of these principles to be documented fully, to state the principles as postulates will make for explicit understanding. The principles are arranged in three groups: philosophical, psychological, and operational. The philosophical principles (1–5) form a part of a philosophy of education, but they do not form a statement of philosophy. They deal with the concept of democracy essential for the participation of every professional educator. The psychological principles (6–9) offer a conceptual framework to suggest ways of thinking about some of the basic problems in curriculum change. A few principles in the change process relate closely to philosophical and psychological assumptions, but they have been separated to give emphasis to their operational importance (10–14). Without action all theory becomes largely academic.

The remaining portions of the book assume that the principles upon which we have arrived are valid bases for curriculum change. The subsequent chapters should serve to delineate particular activities in which the reader might very well engage to improve the instructional effort with which he might be concerned. Taken together, these concepts constitute a basis for action—a foundation for curriculum improvement.

Philosophical Principles

1. *Schools Exist to Help Children Learn.* Everything associated with the educational enterprise is designed to help children learn. How a school is organized, who teaches in the classrooms, what administrative policies are developed, how large the school site should be, what kind of lighting fixtures are utilized within the locker room, what kind of covering goes on the floor, how many mills should be levied, who is elected to the school board—these are problems which must be solved with one paramount objective in mind: helping children learn.

2. *The Purpose of Supervision Is to Improve Curriculum.* If schools exist to help children learn, the basic purpose of supervision is to facilitate this process. Supervisors owe their very existence in the education process to the fact that there is always room for improvement. A situation can almost always be improved and the purpose of supervisors and other instructional leaders is to improve curriculum. Some teachers and other educators may be threatened by the presence of supervisors because their existence implies that things should be changed. This poses a very real problem for those who work in supervision. It is a factor inherent in the

situation, and not one which can be ignored, although it most certainly can be overcome. Every activity a supervisor undertakes is aimed at one objective—helping children learn by improving instruction.

3. *Changing Curriculum Means Helping People Change.* Curriculum includes the ideas, experience, and knowledge we sometimes call *subject matter*. It also includes the way in which these things are organized; their sequence and their internal relationships to one another. Third, curriculum includes the way these ideas are made available within the learning situation or the method which is employed. A further factor is a person who directs the learning by virtue of the kind of person that he is. Each of these facets of curriculum involves certain decisions by certain people, and, if one wants to affect the curriculum with which he works, he must consider the nature of the persons involved at every point along the way.

Tinkering with the minutae in curriculum may cause some minor changes to occur in the educational process, but for anyone seriously interested in effecting significant change, the people who are involved must be themselves changed. Unless those who work with the curriculum —principals and teachers—are changed as a result of the supervisory experience, effective changes in curriculum cannot be made. Revising a textbook, preparing a new syllabus, or administering new and different examinations will make some significant changes, but only if the people who are concerned grasp and accept the changes. They must come to have greater understanding of the area in which they work, of the methods which are most appropriate for imparting information and inspiring participation. They must develop skills and techniques of communicating, evaluating, and understanding which they may not have had before.

4. *The Supervisor Must Be Willing to Change.* During the course of curriculum development educators gain new ideas, new insights, unique relationships, and changed perceptions that are the heart and substance of curriculum change. And, like the colleagues in whom he tries to promote change, the supervisor must be willing to abandon cherished notions and let go of archaic ideas. Because of his leadership position the supervisor must strive especially hard to admit new evidence and accept new facts into his way of being if he would grow. What this striving requires most is an attitude or state of mind that he will be willing to undergo personal

change. Each instructional leader must repeatedly assess *his own* status and his own educational convictions and look for change.

5. *Equalitarian Relationships Are Imperative.* Working with others to improve instruction demands an attitude and philosophy predicated upon the worth and dignity of all. Curriculum as an area of inquiry is so broad and so involved that no one person knows very much. In his position, the supervisor has a more comprehensive grasp of the total situation than anyone else, but that hardly means he really knows what goes on in every classroom. Yet, what goes on in every classroom is the real heart of curriculum. It becomes essential to conceive a way of working in which all participants in the total enterprise are recognized as important and worthwhile and good. Some will have more ideas than others, and some will have better suggestions. Others will be more supporting and encouraging to the group, while still others will have real skills in collecting the facts. The supervisor's responsibility is to work with many persons from many fields representing many groups on an equalitarian basis; to accept all persons as equal participants in an important task.

Telling people they are free to speak their mind is one thing; allowing and encouraging them to speak is still another. Listening to all ideas regardless of source, and weighing each contribution according to its merits, encourages others to do the same. As the status leader, the supervisor cannot shirk responsibility, but he also cannot stifle others' participation and involvement. In general, the best and most simple way to assure oneself of maximum communication and minimum domination is to function as if every other person knew as much about curriculum as he himself does.

Psychological Principles

6. *Behavior Is a Function of How Things Seem to Be.* One of the dilemmas of the educative process is that facts are important, but only to the extent to which they are so perceived by the people involved. What things really are is never as important as *how things seem to be*—people act according to the facts as they understand them.

It is one thing to deplore this situation and it is quite another to utilize this knowledge for more effective supervision. For example, even if all of the research evidence in the world indicated that heavy cigarette smokers will get lung cancer and die, this information will hardly influence behavior unless it has some personal significance for a given individual. People's behavior is a function of how they perceive, and perceptions involve attributing personal meaning to stimuli, regardless of the nature of the stimuli themselves. What this means for educators concerned with improving the educative process and with supervision is that they must strive to see things as others see them, and strive to help them change their perceptions.

Facts alone, however, are not enough. Perceptions are influenced by many things, not the least of which are the individual's value structure and his basic needs; these aspects of human personality are not easily modified or altered. How an individual views himself and the importance he attaches to any isolated bit of information are distinctly related. Only those ideas and those pieces of information perceived as close to the self and personally meaningful affect behavior. Whether or not experiences are recognized as near or far psychologically and are considered a part of or apart from the self determine in large measure the extent to which they influence the individual perceiver. It is more than a truism that people behave according to the way things seem to them. It is a demonstrated fact.

7. Values Affect Behavior. Values influence what people do, and how they see the world about them. Values also serve as an organizing force for generating human action. People work for, believe in, and seek those things to which they attribute most significance.

Each individual's psychological system organizes values in hierarchical form. At the present time in our society, education is seemingly valued, but what people say and how they act may be two different things. The values with which educators must be concerned are those which manifest themselves in action. To say that education is more important than entertainment, for instance, and to pay more for entertainment than education points out the problem. Although difficult, of course, the solution rests in part upon a modification of people's value structure. If this may seem to be hitting "too close to home," be assured that all efforts at value change and value development must be open and forthright and directly involve all parties concerned.

Teachers hold many values that represent that target for change. For example, the idea of equating telling with teaching, or that grades motivate students, are common notions. The idea that so much ground must "be covered" is another value many hold, despite the fact that experimental evidence demonstrates conclusively that ground covered or facts acquired are only significant to the degree students are able to attribute personal meaning to each bit of information.

Other values relating particularly to middle class culture also represent a formidable area for concern. Insisting that lower class youngsters abide by middle class values without helping them explore those values intimately, for example, is expecting more than will ever happen in an average classroom situation. Valuing *cooperation* and then denying children opportunities to cooperate except upon command is another instance. Likewise, valuing truth and honesty and then contriving situations in which children must literally cheat to maintain their parents' affection (to get good grades) seems highly inconsistent. Values represent an important area in which supervisors must work. Values are loaded with emotional overtones and prejudices, but for those people who are genuinely concerned about improving instruction and who recognize real curriculum change involves changes in people, values are a potent source for change.

8. *Start with People Where They Are.* Probably no principle in learning is more firmly established than the idea that you must start with people where they are, moving from the known to the unknown, from the specific to the general. People in any situation manifest feelings, sentiments, and ideas at some particular level of development. To help these people move to some higher level, one must start with the particular level on which the individual is. Persons who have never had instruction cannot be expected to function effectively in a situation in which they have never had many experiences. Working with persons in groups is a good example. All people have worked in groups, of course, but the extent to which their experiences were of the nature of producing the "right" answer for a superior provides no background to operate in a truly open atmosphere in which each individual's ideas are actually accorded significance. Many teachers who have worked with groups for many years lack skill in group process. They are not skilled in listening, or sharing, or saying things without arousing others' defenses. They may not be able to synthesize ideas, interpret norms, or pull out the issues.

They may not actually know how to be honest with ideas, since they may feel that behind the stated purposes of the discussion rests another "gimmick" to fulfill an administrator's whims. If teachers understandably lack some of the skills essential to true involvement, the skillful supervisor will accept this fact and work from there.

In actual practice, this means assessing the sentiments and feelings of the group and adopting these to some degree before exerting pull. Unless a leader is a part of the group, unless he thinks as they think and feels as they feel no significant changes will be forthcoming. People follow a man they trust, and people trust a man who shares at least some of their common concerns.

9. *Capitalize upon the Halo.* Ever since the famous industrial production studies at the Chicago Hawthorne plant, scientists observing human behavior have noted that involving people in experimental situations causes them to behave differently than they usually do. From a research standpoint, this poses a very difficult problem. From the standpoint of curriculum change, this is a force for improvement. To overstate the case, if you experiment in education, things are bound to get better whatever you do. Such a statement is not literally true, of course, but there is some truth in it. It can probably be explained by the fact that extra attention is devoted to the recipients of the experimental variable when experimental situations are devised in education. They are carefully studied, observed, questioned, and they may even participate in the actual design of the project. As a result, they acquire a kind of psychological investment in the total undertaking and apparently strive to make it go. This extra effort, this striving, this unusual concern is often just enough to demonstrate significant change in what is being studied. Capitalizing upon this "halo" effect by involving people in a study of some particular aspect of their situation and looking closely for the facts can very well lead to improvement in curricular development.

Operational Principles

10. *People Who Are Affected Must Be Involved.* Involvement is a principle fundamental to democracy and to learning theory. The very essence of democracy is predicated upon the assumption that those who

are affected by any change should have some say in determining just what that change shall be. This is guaranteed in our political-social system through citizen participation and through our efforts to persuade our elected representatives once they have been chosen. Devising ways of involving people in decision-making is a difficult and time-consuming chore, but *unless decisions are made democratically they will be less than the best.*

This idea presupposes a belief in the commitment to free exchange of ideas and the power of intelligence, and assumes that the "best" answer under any given structure is not possible except in an atmosphere of give and take and concern for the truth. It also presupposes that ideas can be considered apart from their source and that the real merit of any proposal depends upon its internal consistency and ultimate utility. Vigorous exchange of information and the "collision of ideas" assure us that the best change will be achieved. Unless the principle of involvement is used, people learn quickly to reflect superficial adherence.

Significant and lasting change in education can only come about by such involvement. All who are affected by curriculum development and change must have a genuine opportunity to participate in the process.

The second purpose of involvement finds its roots in learning theory. Studies clearly indicate that learning which is purposeful, meaningful, and significant occurs most often when the individual learner is psychologically committed to the situation, i.e., involved. Finding ways of helping people weave the process of curriculum development through the very fabric of their experience induces involvement.

Both research and experience have shown that the odds are much better for effecting curriculum change through involvement than through dictum. Telling people what to do simply does not work. Unless people who are affected by decisions have some opportunities to think these decisions through for themselves, to consider the alternatives and argue out the possibilities, they will assuredly find ways of circumventing any decision imposed upon them. Someone once wryly said that "the curriculum is that which happens when the teacher closes the door." Certainly, very few teachers are "checked on" enough to know whether or not they are abiding by the most recent regulations or not.

Giving teachers textbooks which emphasize phonics is no assurance that the books will be used. Providing standardized examinations which purport to assess particular skills and factual learnings so that teachers can use them for diagnostic purposes gives no assurance that the tests will be so employed. Unless teachers themselves and the persons who work directly with them come to believe in and be affected by curriculum decisions, the odds are they will probably continue in their same old ways. Teaching people to do things differently is the very spirit of supervision, and teaching people to do things differently demands involvement.

11. *Communication Is Two Way.* To say that ideas must flow in two directions is to oversimplify the problem in curriculum development. Those who work to improve instruction soon learn that they must skillfully convey ideas to and get ideas from other persons to be effective. They must communicate in the educational hierarchy both with their administrative superiors as well as with their subordinates.

Communication is probably the biggest single problem in education, especially in a large school system. Yet, in a modern school system curriculum changes occur so frequently and with such rapidity that helping everybody who is involved and affected to be aware of and participate in the developments is a serious undertaking. It is one which cannot possibly be left to chance. Working at the business of communication is a never-ending job, but it must be done.

12. *Change Starts with Issues.* Curriculum development begins with issues—issues are those areas in which the answers are not yet known. In education, we have generally two kinds of problems presently facing us. First, we have to do as well as we now know how. The great abundance of research now available delineates fairly clearly certain bases upon which curriculum development can build. The research in reading, for instance, has been quite exhaustive; likewise, we know a lot about the financial aspects of school organization and how to group our resources and facilities for optimum development.

Second, we hardly know what the problems are in many areas in the educational undertaking. What kind of impact do different kinds of teachers have upon students' personality development? Which ideas and in what kind of an organizational pattern should they be to help children comprehend and appreciate the full meaning of the concepts of democracy, capitalism, set theory, or capillary action? Teachers can throw these ideas out to children and require them to read books, but what are the best methods for insuring understanding? Which examples and illustrations presented in which order after which introductions and under which conditions will promise us success?

In many areas in curriculum, we are only beginning to see the problems clearly. It is in these unknown fields, these problem situations, that the issues lie. It is here then that curriculum workers must begin.

As the real challenges lie with the issues, so the real opportunities lie here, too. These are the genuine problems which baffle teachers daily—the problems which have "built in" attractiveness and enable those who labor in the curriculum field to seek psychological attachments so essential for evoking change in those involved. Those who dare to tackle the unresolved issues find curriculum development lively, challenging, and exciting.

13. *The Best Basis for Change Is the Facts.* Probably no other area in human activity is so value-laden as curriculum. Every educator has his own notions about what is wrong; what ought to be included and excluded, which methods are most effective and which are of less value. This is a natural situation, very widespread, and very difficult to cope with. To work with diverse groups representing heterogeneous philosophies, the person who wants to make sound, rapid progress in curriculum change must resort to the facts. Theories, speculations, hunches, and tradition are all places from which to start, but significant change demands the facts.

Facts in curriculum involve students' attitudes and teachers' personalities; knowledge learned and skills acquired; organizational structure and costs per pupil; dropout rate and dropout reasons. They involve teacher satisfaction and parental expectation; knowledge of who exerts influence within the community and what the local power structure is. How many children actually fail; why they do; and what their teachers think about retention are all facts bearing on curriculum development.

To get the facts means that someone must do research, and examine the accumulated data. Because facts are not always readily accessible, curriculum developers must find ways of securing factual data and help with their examination. To press a particular theory or evoke an established cliché is not getting the facts which is the only effective means to purposeful, rational curriculum change.

14. *Success Is Important.*   Supervisors who are effective accept the fact that "nothing succeeds like success." A cornerstone to effective change is involving people so that they move from the known to the unknown, and experience satisfaction and success along the way. Actions an instructional leader takes must culminate in some observable product—people need to *know* they are moving ahead. Writing a curriculum bulletin for the sake of writing a curriculum bulletin is not real change, but tangible proof that people's efforts are resulting in changes being publicly acknowledged as good is very important.

Although supervisors themselves must be able to live with the uncertainty of not immediately knowing how effective they have been, they must see to it that progress is recognized and achievement in others is acknowledged as it occurs. Significant undertakings can be especially recognized because all who participate in curriculum development respond to encouragement, praise, and reward.

Summary

Progress in education depends upon change. If the supervisor is to be responsible for exerting leadership in curriculum development, he must learn to act boldly but with intelligent decision. He must find ways of reducing the lag from research to practice so that it will be more comparable to that in the fields of medicine or missiles. These are exciting times, and this book is written to those people who want to go places and do things in the field of curriculum change. It is an action book, and though it presupposes that "Rome wasn't built in a day," it also implies that a lot of blocks were laid there every day.

Education can and must go forward. What people seek is a sensitive and literate instructional leader who can mobilize their energies. Fourteen principles have been described whose themes will run throughout this book:

1. Schools exist to help children learn.
2. The purpose of supervision is to improve instruction.
3. Changing curriculum means helping people change.
4. The supervisor must be willing to undergo change.
5. Equalitarian relationships are imperative.

6. Behavior is a function of how things seem to be.
7. Values must be changed.
8. Start with people where they are.
9. Capitalize upon the halo effect.
10. People who are affected must be involved.
11. Communication is two way.
12. Change starts with issues.
13. The best basis for curriculum change is the facts.
14. Success is important.

In the chapters which follow, specific suggestions about how to begin, how to organize for curriculum change, how to study the curriculum in action, how to communicate, and how to influence others about curricular matters will be approached in precise detail.

3 Establishing Relationships for Change

Seeking and accepting a responsibility in supervision is different from seeking and accepting a responsibility in teaching. Supervisors play an entirely different kind of role, and how one gets a position and how one begins are more important than for almost any other position in education.

Accepting a Position as Supervisor

People hear about jobs in supervision in many ways. There may be a vacancy in a particular school system. During a course at summer school, a student may hear about an opening in a nearby district. Some alert college professor may be impressed by a student's actions in an educational conference and tell some superintendent.

Because of the nature of the position, it is probably advisable that someone comes seeking a supervisor. Certainly, there are exceptions to this general rule, but the psychology of being asked is very important because it gives a good vantage point from which to bargain—not for salary or working conditions especially, but for a clarification of responsibilities and expectations. Once a potential supervisor is approached, whether he accepts or rejects the job, his major task is to probe the mind and philosophy of the men with whom he must work, and these explorations must be in considerable detail. A contract is a two-way obligation, and during the time he is being considered, he must recognize that he is considering the position. He will be giving his time and energy and his enthusiasm and skill. In return, he will be receiving certain considerations —a salary, retirement, prestige, and satisfaction.

Because supervision is a unique job, it is essential to explore in great depth the myriad details involved. What are present school board policies of promotion, retention, and grading? He will need to know the salary schedule, for the teachers involved are a direct reflection of this basic policy.

What is the nature of the job? What is expected of the person who holds it? Is he supposed to be at his desk four days a week and in the field one? Will he be responsible for the testing program or curriculum guides? Who will be responsible to him, and what will be the nature of this relationship? Is his a line or staff position? Does it carry authority or is he expected only to assist or advise? He will need to probe these points in great depth.

It is especially important for the prospective supervisor to discuss precisely the nature of whatever limitations will be imposed upon him. Exactly what is it that he cannot do? What areas are off-limits and what topics are excluded from his responsibility? Will he have an opportunity to reflect his views in any of these areas, or are they the complete responsibility and domain of some other individual? How much travel money will he be authorized? How many out-of-state conferences may he attend? What are the financial considerations?

To whom will he be responsible? Will the superintendent "go through" him on all matters pertaining to instruction or will the superintendent handle things as they arise? How does the supervisor's position relate to other central office staff positions? On what level will he be functioning and with whom? What are they like? Can he talk to them while he is there? How do they feel about an outsider moving into this position? Are any of them applying for the job themselves?

What will be the supervisor's relationship to the superintendent? The principal? Who is in charge when the superintendent is out of town? To what extent is there a total "system"? What is the philosophy of the school board and the superintendent about uniformity and similarities among schools? Should all schools use the same textbooks at the same grade level? Is there a system-wide testing program? How are the results utilized?

For what kinds of reports and forms will the supervisor be responsible? Will there be records to keep and requisitions to authorize? To what extent will his duties be unrelated to instruction? Will he ever serve as intermediary in an administrative dispute? Who works with teachers who have noninstructional problems? If, for example, a teacher strikes a child and the parent complains to the superintendent, who handles a case like this?

These questions are designed to give the potential supervisor an idea of some of the problems he should pose when he is thinking about accepting a position in supervision. Finally, of course, whether or not a given position "fits" his personality is a major factor. All things considered, however, it is probably to his advantage to clarify precisely and in writing (he can accept the position by stating these things in his letter of acceptance) exactly what he understands the position to be and the relationship involved. Generally, his responsibilities should be narrowly defined to include instructional and curriculum problems only. But curriculum is a very broad field, and although it is probably not to his advantage to deal with administrative details such as teacher allocation and materials distribution, he should exercise some influence over these factors, at least through persuasion at regular staff meetings. For the most part, he must seek a position in which the administrative chores are minimal. Because of the problems of their position, for many administrators a broken furnace pipe or an irate parent is more real and demanding than curriculum development. During the time of considering a position, then, it is essential for a supervisor to get an accurate estimate of the administrative support and backing that would be available. Once he accepts the job there will be problems if he does not have a good idea of how the professional land lies. A genuine concern for instructional improvement, a willingness to change, and according curriculum and instruction importance over all other things are requirements that are essential.

Unless curriculum comes first, a curriculum supervisor has little hope to accomplish much, even over a long period. Finding out exactly how the top echelon feels about curriculum change is fundamental because unless the superintendent and the board are at least willing to consider innovation and change, if not encourage it, the supervisor's efforts are useless. In getting the job, his responsibility will be to assess accurately the superintendent's willingness to delegate responsibility and his real concern for how children learn. His personal security will reflect some of these things, and one can look for cues, such as how much he talks and how much he listens. Does he sincerely strive to understand and comprehend others' attitudes and convictions? Is he relaxed and easy to communicate with? Does he call his subordinates by first name? One must try to estimate the kind of situation in which he will be working. Unless there is both support for change and room to move, the curriculum worker may find himself tied down, unable to act.

Initial Activities

Once the supervisor accepts the position, he must move methodically. He should issue no directives, make almost no requests; nor should he tell anybody what to do, for a while at least. He should look for signs of professional jealousy and dissatisfactions. His major responsibility for many weeks or even months will be to get the feel of the total situation in which he is working.

He must plan his activities so that he gets into every school and meets every principal within a matter of weeks, listening to their problems and asking minor detail questions. He should let them talk about the building, the cafeteria, and the new things they are doing, expecting them to be somewhat cautious and defensive, even unwilling to share. The curriculum worker should recognize that they also need to size him up, know what his beliefs and convictions are. He must try to understand their point of view.

Later he may initiate certain minor requests of changes in activities. The supervisor's first few weeks and months must be time spent in developing communication lines and working to assure that they will stay open.

There probably will be other supervisors, and if one serves in a leadership role with them, the problems are the same. Some of these persons without doubt already have special relationships with the superintendent, principals, or teachers and they may be threatened by the appearance of a head supervisor. They also may genuinely desire mature assistance and direction for the supervisory program, and welcome his presence. Whatever their personal skills, interests, and deficiencies, his job will be to move and to mold them into an effective supervisory team. For all practical purposes he has three approaches: individual, group, and total situation.

Relationships with Individuals

The new supervisor should invite individual supervisors to give job descriptions as a start. Listening to each person's view of his job would be a second step. The job of pulling out of each supervisor a complete, accurate description of what he does and why takes time, skill, and patience.

By anticipating reserve and expecting only partial cooperation, at least with some of the staff, the head supervisor must again be prepared to move into the area without passing judgment. He should expect to be asked for approval of present practice, and should respond by a genuine reception of the notions. However, his general approach should be one of suspended judgment because his first effort should be to comprehend and identify with his subordinates' expectations and aspirations, appreciating their feelings and understanding their problems. This base will be a better point of departure when the time comes for him to initiate change than one purely of his own making. He must satisfy the sentiments of the group before he can begin to lead. His own ideas and philosophy can deviate from the status quo; but, unless he is close enough to the local norms to see things from that view, he is likely to begin from a completely different point, which would be unfortunate.

Relationships with Groups

In general staff meetings with other supervisors, the new supervisor can begin to define his role more carefully and more completely. What is supervision? What does it mean? How do supervisors work most effectively? What does research have to say about instructional leaders? What is the difference between pull and push in curriculum development? Exploring questions with the supervisory staff enables one to observe them in actual operation, how they function in a group situation, what they believe, how they communicate, and where their values lie. How secure is each one personally? Where do personal animosities, if they exist, reside within the group? Who refuses to talk? Some persons may be very vociferous in a personal dialogue, but refuse to state their position or show their hand in the group. This may indicate that certain power-struggle relationships exist which lie beneath the surface. Others may talk all the time, but have little to say. Talking may be a cover-up for their inadequacies or an effort to achieve status in the eyes of a new man.

Whatever the case, group interactions are excellent opportunities to see the professional level at which the supervisory service is probably being performed. In these situations, a new supervisor's opportunities for involvement are somewhat more. That is, although he is a new member of the situation, the dynamics of the group in action permit him to inject a bit more of himself into the professional scene. However, his major effort at early participation should take the role of question asking and information seeking. What do you do when a particular problem comes up? Where is that school, and what is the principal like? The real importance of such questions is to place the new supervisor in a dependent position from the point of view of the older supervisors—he will be acknowledging that he needs their help. Asking for help is a direct admission that he is not all knowing and all powerful. For a new person in a new situation to behave otherwise is professional suicide. Letting others know from the beginning that he wants and needs their help is a foot in the door, and if the open door will help him later, so much the better. The fact is, he cannot function without their assistance and support, so getting it early is an important task.

Understanding the Total Situation

Getting the feel for the situation and getting to know it are related but dissimilar. The artistry of supervision demands that one act intuitively at times, and unless a supervisor has a full appreciation and accurate feel for the situation, he may go astray. Equally important is knowing everything he can about his total situation.

He must have accurate, current information about every aspect of the situation in which he works. This includes detailed lists of information about his school district and its locale—names and locations of every school, names of principals and teachers, streets, community leaders, news media, reporters' names and how to get in touch with them, community groups and their interests in education. He must know the expenditures per pupil, beginning and maximum teachers' salaries, number of children in the system, qualifications of the teachers, expenditures for instructional and noninstructional items, building program, sites for new schools, proposed board policies, and adopted policies.

Since molding and moving public opinion will be one of his major responsibilities, the supervisor should accept any task requested of him in community service and become acquainted with as many persons and situations as possible in the process. Purposely affiliating with civic organizations may be one approach. On the other hand, not being especially active in a particular one allows him to be active in all.

Schools represent the aspirations of their people, and the curriculum worker's job will be to help the people raise their levels of aspiration and see opportunities in education they never dreamed possible. He must show how education increases the earning power and extends the tax base; how it brings more money into the community and lets people lift themselves by their own bootstraps; how it increases voter participation and attracts new industry and raises everyone's standard of living. Unless he is able to "get at" the community to tell these benefits, his efforts at curriculum improvement will be sorely limited. One of the prime requisites of the supervisory function, therefore, is to get to know the community very well.

To work effectively in supervision, the curriculum worker will need factual, descriptive data about his situation. All of the pertinent details must be immediately available. For all practical purposes, they will have to be comparative. For example, knowing that it costs the tax payers in his community $3.37 per day to send each child to school is only meaningful if he knows what other communities of similar economic levels are spending. This means he will have to collect information. Annual reports of the superintendent may be one source. The state department of education may be another. The National Education Association publication, *Rankings of the States,* is a handy, comparative guide from which to work and *General Social and Economic Characteristics of the States* may be another. The supervisor must acquaint himself thoroughly and deeply with the administrative aspects of his school system so that he can participate intelligently in important discussions and influence opinion effectively.

Briefly, these facts may be important: total expenditures per pupil in average daily attendance and the proportion of these funds which go for teachers' salaries, administration, maintenance, transportation, capital outlay, and for bonded indebtedness. How do these figures compare to those in surrounding districts? To other districts comparable in size but located elsewhere throughout the state? To other similar districts throughout the nation? How do these figures compare for one's own school system according to the data ten years ago? Twenty years ago? Has there been a significant shift? How about a comparison of these same data to other school systems ten years ago or even twenty?

In dealing with these facts, a supervisor needs to seek a trend or pattern of operation that will give him some insight into the *instructional effort* his school system is making in comparison to what it might do. Numbers by themselves are seldom important, but when held up to other figures for previous years or nearby districts, they take on added significance.

Other facts are also important. What is the mill rate for the district? How has it changed? What limitations presently exist regarding the financial base for schools? How long has it been since the last bond issue? How successful was that last effort? What is the sentiment among the board and among the community for such a venture now? How successful have other school systems in similar circumstances been in their efforts to raise additional funds?

What do the projected enrollment figures look like? What has been the growth in the past ten years? How are projections made? What basic data go into their composition? How accurate have projections been in previous years? How many children are presently on double session? How does that figure compare with other districts? How many children have been on double session in the school district each year for the past ten years? Is the district making any progress or catching up? Is it always a year behind? What is its status?

How many new teachers were employed last year? What kind of a turnover does that represent? What is the average length of service for teachers in the system? Why did they go? How are new teachers attracted to the district? Is there an active recruitment program? Who is responsible for this recruiting? Does the district actually get new teachers this way, or do most of them come from some other sources? Is there a brochure describing the school district for prospective professional workers? Is it attractive and effective? Is there close liaison with nearby universities and college placement officers? Who is responsible for maintaining these relationships? Does he do the job satisfactorily?

Teachers are the lifeblood of the professional enterprise. Salary schedules, tenure policies, contractual arrangements, professional leave regulations, inservice training opportunities, extension courses, professional organizations—all matters that vitally affect teachers' welfare and their morale, must be of real and direct concern to the supervisor. Improving the lot of professional peers is his major responsibility, so that anything which he can do to make it more possible to attract and keep competent, capable personnel and eliminate undesirable, ineffective professionals will improve instruction. Since his efforts may be limited largely to persuasion rather than decision-making, he must have recourse to those who make the basic policy decisions regarding personnel if he is to upgrade the program.

Other data are also important. What is the retention rate within the district; how many children fail each year? What is the present policy and feeling about grading and retention? When was this policy determined, and who made the recommendation? What were their motivations? How do teachers feel about this policy? Parents? Children?

How many children drop out of school each year? What studies have been done about their reasons? How do teachers really feel about these dropouts? What do the young people do after they quit school? What proportion of the total community has finished the fourth grade? Eighth grade? Twelfth grade? How many are illiterate? How many went to college? How many go to college from each year's graduating class? What has been the pattern over the past ten years? How many of these who begin, stay and finish four years? How many do advanced study and graduate work?

These questions are all specific and all involved. Nevertheless, current, accurate data on questions such as these are important if the supervisor wants to be effective in improving instruction. He must have facts and figures, and know their sources. He must not talk "off the top of his head"; he must be able to document what he says. Getting to know his situation can be an exciting but laborious chore; it will give him an excellent base from which to operate because he will always have his feet planted firmly on the facts. As he accumulates these data, he will gain feeling and acquire poise which will reflect confidence for him to communicate convincingly to persons with whom he works.

The Image of the Supervisor

As the curriculum supervisor begins to know precisely and exactly what is going on in his situation, he will need to begin to create an image in the minds of those with whom he works. People must come to think of him in strong but positive terms. They must view him as someone who knows where he is going and how he intends to get there, but at the same time they need to conceive of him as a person who will achieve those goals in cooperation with other people, not at their expense. He must be recognized as an authority, but not as authoritarian; he must know about what he speaks, but his ideas must go beyond the limited experience of a particular situation. Insofar as possible, he must present and generate an image of a practical scholar in the field of instruction. He must talk in teachers' terms, but his view must be beyond their level of operation.

Everyone builds an image in the minds of other men; the supervisor's particular problem will be to build an image that will enable him to function and achieve his ends to improve educational opportunities for youth. As he acquires a knowledge of the people and the facts within his school system, he will slowly be building an image in the minds of all. Because it will probably be his responsibility to show a face to the broader public, through speaking engagements and other media, it is imperative that he recognize himself as slowly becoming an institution in his own right. He must realize that through his own efforts, he hopes to sway the tide of public sentiment and marshal opinion in favor of schools. To do this, he must acknowledge the fact that his own unique personality and the image it sets are powerful determiners of the success of his venture to improve instruction.

Creating an image is serious business, difficult to do, and time consuming. The supervisor's responsibility at present is to recognize that this will be a part of his professional repertoire. An image should, therefore, be created carefully and thoughtfully over a period of time; cultivated for an instructional end.

Communication

In relationship to all of these activities, a supervisor must concern himself with the problems and the processes of communication. For the practitioner in curriculum improvement, lack of communication skill is tantamount to failure, unless he can convince and persuade those with whom he works and the total community that the results of his endeavors and studies warrant consideration and implementation. As is true in any field, leaders in education find ready acceptance of their ideas if they are soundly based, sincerely advocated, forcefully projected, and beautifully stated. The supervisor must make every honest means of persuasion at his command. He must communicate often and well.

Communication is a never ending responsibility. It spans all of an educational leader's activities and encompasses all of his concerns. It involves not only reaching every segment of the community and every member of the professional staff, but also creating a means for ideas and information from every corner of the district to come to his attention.

While the output or information sending operations represent but half of the communication process, for present purposes we will assume a way of channeling information in from outside a supervisor's office. This will happen only if he develops a climate conducive to encouraging free expression and participation, and if he promotes an atmosphere and attitude of sharing and understanding. Through an organized effort such as the one which will be described in the next chapter, he should receive communication from every corner of his community, professional and lay alike. If he keeps these communication lines open he will know the thoughts and concerns of his district at large.

Getting information out is the problem of concern to this point. Publishing bulletins or making speeches should get the job done, theoretically. However, this is not a theoretical problem—it is a very real one involving thousands of persons and many means. The problem demands an understanding of the forces facilitating and impeding the flow of ideas from one source to another. In the sections which follow some of the communication vehicles available to the supervisor are identified, along with specific suggestions for their effective use. In every case, these suggestions are minimal and exploratory; it is his responsibility to know his own situation in detail and to tailor his operations to fit his needs.

Communicating to Lay Groups

Getting ideas to the general public involves working with television, radio, newspapers, civic groups, and curriculum councils. Each of these presents particular problems and special opportunities, so that the supervisor will need to assess the unique characteristics of all media in his situation. For example, in working with television stations it is essential that he know the program director at each station in his community personally. Program directors, more than producers or even station owners, have access to the time spots. Obviously, many persons would like to have access to television without charge. Since education has such a universal appeal, many program directors are very willing to provide regularly scheduled opportunities for schoolmen to communicate to the general public. If the supervisor seeks these times and uses them well, he will make a major stride toward public understanding and acceptance of his efforts for curriculum improvement.

Television is a powerful medium. It reaches more people than any other means of communication. It enables one to talk personally with thousands of people simultaneously. Television can do more good or more harm than almost any other single communication device. In using it, one needs to recognize the power of the medium and work with it to achieve significant ends. Plan programs for maximum impact. One must school oneself or others who will appear on the show for perfect performances. One must look at the camera; talk to one person, project one's personality; be honest and sincere; be dynamic; appear alive. One must generate interest by projecting his voice and personality like an actor on the stage. Television is an unusual medium, and persons watching will consciously or unconsciously compare an amateur with professionals on television.

Newspapers represent another powerful medium for sharing concerns. Editorial policies across the nation vary in support for educational undertakings. Some newspapers represent essentially conservative interests, and give an appearance of negative support for schoolmen in general. But whatever the actual content and style of a local publication, newspapers still print the news and schools are generally a major source of news in most communities.

The supervisor should feed a steady stream of news stories and pictures to the paper about curriculum change. Some will find their way into print. Many reporters will strive to help him get important information to the total public by straight news items day by day. If it becomes necessary to undertake a major disagreement with newspaper policies and positions, another medium of communication should be sought.

In general it is the supervisor's responsibility to find ways of using the newspaper to achieve his objective to improve instruction in his schools, sharing all information and making no effort to distort the facts or withhold information. The persons on a supervisor's staff who have the most frequent contact with newspaper sources must be persons who generate confidence and trust and present the school district to its greatest advantage.

Making speeches to civic groups will undoubtedly take a great deal of a curriculum worker's time. Community groups such as PTA's, business men's organizations, and religious assemblies are all interested in schools. A supervisor should never turn down an opportunity to talk to any group, large or small, about educational problems and curricular development in the school system. These groups are atypical in the sense that the participants are generally the more interested, more active members of a community, and these intelligent and dedicated people represent a major source of potential power.

A supervisor should approach each group as a genuine opportunity to win new friends and new supporters for education. He must be dynamic, use facts and concrete illustrations to demonstrate progress and outline the areas of need, neither skirting issues nor avoiding conflicts. He should expect attacks of straw men and extreme positions, but he can also expect majority support for the cause of learning and belief in schools. Since many newspapers have regular representatives at civic group meetings, preparing copies of speeches may lead to even a wider audience. Having a manuscript of the speech available guarantees accurate reporting, especially of controversial problems.

Communicating with School Groups

In school situations, a supervisor must work patiently and regularly to create relationships essential to curriculum change, assuming a peer relationship and purposely seeking to relate to others so that he overcomes any superficial image which may have resulted from television appearances or newspaper stories. He must share his convictions and his experiences; he must pull rather than push, and struggle with the personal problems and interpersonal tensions of his group. He must present his ideas along with the ideas of others in the group, and work together day by day for curriculum change. Placing trust and confidence in other members of the group will enable him to share his ideas.

Establishing a Role as Supervisor

The first year is a very important one for the supervisor and for those with whom he works. During this first year, he must get the feel and set the tone, and he must begin to create an image. But he was hired to improve instruction in some general or specific way, and unless he makes progress in this area, he is a failure.

A new supervisor must set some kind of time table for himself for the first academic year; at least two months should be spent on each of three major undertakings—getting to know his situation, setting the tone and creating an image, and finally, setting a pattern for continued operation. About the middle of the first year, he must carefully but cautiously conceptualize a way of working that will pervade his function for the years to come. Basically, what he has to do involves creating relationships and understandings that will enable him to work effectively to improve instruction with all persons concerned about curriculum. His efforts should grow naturally out of his understanding of the total needs of the school system, and it should reflect the wishes and aspirations of the people with whom he works.

The supervisor must set the pattern before the first year is out, however. He must clarify for himself exactly how he wants to function, and test his ideas out on his superintendent and associates. Unless he projects a new way of working on the basic problems in curriculum and instruction, subsequent efforts may well be lost. If he is to be effective in supervision for curriculum change, he must take the long view. He must recognize that his first year on the job is primarily job training regardless of previous experience.

4

Devising a Structure for Change

Organizing the Plan for Change

If the curriculum supervisor is to encourage innovation and departure from the routine, he must assure himself that he is both informed and informing in all that transpires. Setting the pattern is an important task. Briefly, the idea of a pattern means that he will ultimately develop an organizational scheme for coping with the complexities of curriculum change. Any plan for organizing a school system for curriculum change will necessarily have several parts. The plan which is described here represents a blend of ideas and operations; it is an organizational procedure which will and has worked. With minor innovations, it is appropriate for any school system with from ten to eighty thousand youngsters. For purposes of this discussion, the plan described presupposes a medium-sized school district covering fairly diverse kinds of local subcommunities.

Policies Affecting the Establishment and Function of Curriculum Councils in Riverside School District

The following policies relative to the establishment and function of a series of curriculum councils are hereby adopted by the district board of public instruction as

official policy. Included in these policies are statements of the assumptions underlying curriculum councils, their organization and structure, and their function.

I. Assumptions

1. Schools exist to help students learn.
2. The instructional program is the primary means to help young people learn.
   That is, the instructional program is the heart of the educational enterprise.
3. Educational purposes can most effectively be realized by the organizational instructional effort called curriculum.
4. The curriculum in our schools can be and must be continuously improved.
5. Curriculum consists primarily of what is commonly called subject matter and
   method. Both are important.
6. Many forces operate to affect curriculum (e.g., class size, availability of funds,
   number of books in the library, etc.), and though these are not curriculum, they
   must be considered in any major effort to improve instruction.
7. To improve instruction we must work to improve both the content of the various
   subject matter fields and the methods whereby these facts and ideas are handled
   in a classroom.
8. The most effective way to bring about desirable change in the instructional program is to involve those persons who are most concerned with the curriculum:
   teachers, principals, parents, and students, wherever possible.

II. Organization

There shall be established in Riverside a Curriculum Council and five different
area curriculum councils. In addition, each school shall have a group whose responsibilities shall be directly related to improving the instructional program of that school.
The major purpose of this organizational structure shall be to facilitate communication among the various persons concerned with the instructional program in the
Riverside district public schools.
1. The Riverside Curriculum Council shall consist of 25 members representing
   various geographical, professional, and interest areas. This council shall meet
   monthly (or as the occasion demands) on the third Thursday of every month at
   9:30 A.M. Further, this council shall elect a chairman and a vice chairman. The
   assistant superintendent of instruction shall serve as secretary. Minutes of each
   meeting shall be distributed to each school, the superintendent, each school board
   member, and such other persons as may be interested.
2. The membership of the Riverside Curriculum Council shall be determined as
   follows:
   (a) Five persons from each area curriculum council: one secondary school prin-
       cipal, one teacher, one elementary school principal, one lay person, and one
       senior high school student.

(b) The assistant superintendent in charge of instruction and such other members of his staff as he may feel should be included (ex officio).

3. Each curriculum area shall include, where practical, a senior high school and all of its associated junior high schools and their feeder elementary schools. From these schools and their associated groups shall be developed area curriculum councils. Each area curriculum council shall include the following persons:
(a) The principal of each school
(b) One teacher from each school
(c) One lay person from each school
(d) One student from each school where feasible. Further, each council shall elect a chairman and a secretary. Minutes of each meeting shall be distributed to each of the schools in that particular area and to the assistant superintendent in charge of instruction, who will maintain a continuing file of the proceedings of each area council.

4. Schools shall be assigned to the following area curriculum councils. Areas may be redefined and new schools assigned to appropriate areas at the discretion of the assistant superintendent in charge of instruction.

Area I	Area II	Area III
Smith H.S.	Central H.S.	North Side H.S.
Jackson J.H.S.	East J.H.S.	Wilson J.H.S.
Burton Elem.	Park J.H.S.	Creek J.H.S.
Black Elem.	Jones Elem.	Grant Elem.
Marion Elem.	Webster Elem.	Glen Elem.
Dill Elem.	Hill Elem.	River Elem.
Lake Elem.	Forker Elem.	Union Elem.
	Judd Elem.	

Area IV	Area V
Ridge H.S.	Lakeside H.S.
Vocational H.S.	Todd J.H.S.
Pine J.H.S.	Blue Elem.
Rodgers Elem.	Topper Elem.
Lincoln Elem.	Wilson Elem.
Oak Elem.	Marks Elem.
Parsons Elem.	Azalea Elem.
Willow Elem.	
Walnut Elem.	

5. Each school shall have a curriculum council which will work directly with the area curriculum council on matters of instruction. The size of these groups and their membership shall be left to the discretion of each school principal.

III. Function

The major purpose of each of the various curriculum councils shall be to improve instruction in the Riverside public schools. Further, their general method of operation shall be accomplished by means of research. That is, the various curriculum councils established here shall strive to cope with instructional problems either by systematically and comprehensively reviewing the pertinent published research reports, or by conducting experimental or other type research projects themselves, or both.

1. The Riverside Curriculum Council shall function in the following manner:
   (a) Isolate problems related to the curriculum in Riverside schools.
   (b) Study these problems carefully through research.
   (c) Make recommendations based upon these studies to the school board and such other groups as may be directly concerned.
2. The various area curriculum councils shall function in the following manner:
   (a) Assist the district curriculum council in identifying curriculum problems pertinent to the entire district. Further, each area curriculum council may also identify problems in instruction which are peculiar to that particular area for further study.
   (b) Assist the district council in carrying out its studies of the problems isolated for research. Further, each area curriculum council may also do research on the problems of instruction which are peculiar to that particular area.
   (c) Assist the district curriculum council in implementing those recommendations which are adopted.
3. Each school curriculum council shall function in the following manner:
   (a) Assist the area curriculum councils in their efforts to help the district councils identify instructional problems. Further, each school council may also identify problems in instruction which are peculiar to that particular school.
   (b) Assist the area curriculum councils in their efforts to help the district council study instructional problems. Further, each school council may also do research on the problems of instruction which are peculiar to that school.
   (c) Assist the area councils and the district council implement those recommendations which are adopted.

The policies described here in detail constitute a plan for curriculum improvement. While in this case the plan aims at improving instruction in one school district through research, the basic idea is that this organization is designed to give strength and power to the efforts to improve instruction of those concerned with supervision. With this point in mind, we will look at some of the specific aspects of this policy statement and note what fundamental ideas underly its concepts.

First, the introduction states that these policies are *official*—this is an extremely important step. As official policy they carry board approval and board support. This means that the board is committed to examining recommendations and data which the curriculum council produces.

Second, the statements of assumptions clarify the basic purpose of the educational effort, and, at the same time, define in general terms the area involved. The definition is narrow enough to limit responsibility to those properties which are uniquely curriculum, but it is broad enough to acknowledge that curriculum itself is subject to many other factors, not all so narrowly defined, permitting the curriculum councils to go beyond subject matter and method, which are generally conceived to be the extent of the concern of instructional persons. For example rewriting curriculum guides and helping teachers with their methods will make some difference, but if inadequate salaries destroy teacher morale, classroom techniques are relatively unimportant anyway.

The purpose of the eighth assumption is to make explicit the notion that changing the curriculum means changing people's ideas, and it is designed to give substance to the idea that many people must be involved in curriculum change. It assures those who are concerned of an opportunity to participate in the shaping and fixing of the instructional program.

An analysis of the second part, the organizational structure of this scheme, reveals several fundamental principles inherent in this part of the plan. First, there are three levels of operation: the district council, which includes representative members from all over the district to give the curriculum effort direction and form; the area councils, which bring together persons within a given feeder system; and each school, which by this policy is encouraged to study its own program as well as to help the other councils. Second, these councils are organized so that teachers, parents, and principals can tackle problems in grades K through 12, which is important. Education is a total process for the child. All twelve years must be considered as an entity of related parts, and improving instruction must proceed from this idea of total process.

The area councils are the spirit and soul of this whole idea; the backbone for instructional change. Wedding elementary and secondary people establishes a real basis for curriculum improvement not possible in systems which try to function with elementary and secondary levels apart. Combining responsibilities at the central office level is not adequate. Only if persons who work with curriculum every day in classrooms and school buildings think of K through 12 as a unit will total program development be possible.

Various subsections of almost any school district have unique problems of a curricular nature that demand solution. Identifying with special local problems enables all participants to "see" accomplishment and change that might be lost on a larger scale.

In examining the third part of this organizational plan, two important ideas are apparent. First, the district itself is committed to improving instruction through research. Second, the purposes are simple. Making curriculum decisions grounded in systematic study and careful research enables a district to proceed with assurance in curriculum change. With a simple format to guide their actions—identify problems, study them, and make recommendations—it is possible for all segments and levels of the curriculum enterprise to focus clearly upon the goal.

In actual practice, the district council functions in an overviewing, coordinating, policy-making capacity. The area councils carry the burden of curriculum improvement, and with these groups, the supervisor makes the greatest contribution and achieves the greatest growth. In other situations, efforts and activities of individual schools assume special significance, and the supervisor works with particular segments of a given staff.

Having a plan for change must precede any major effort at curriculum change. The plan described here is simply a vehicle, a device, but if used properly, it can facilitate instructional change and professional growth. As a medium for communication about an important concern—curriculum improvement—such a curriculum council can give a supervisor a springboard to systematic change.

A workable plan is only half of the problem. It is imperative that the superintendent be committed psychologically to what the supervisor is doing. Then, from the beginning his responsibility will be to work directly and frequently with the superintendent during the time a pattern is emerging and before it is completely set. The superintendent's thinking and his convictions must also be included. The curriculum worker and the superintendent should exchange ideas as the plan evolves.

A supervisor has a professional responsibility to relate to the superintendent as his administrative superior, while working with him as an intellectual peer. The superintendent knows more about the total system, but the supervisor knows more about the curriculum. The supervisor must relate to his superiors in the same way he relates to his subordinates, on an equal plane. From this position he must teach the superintendent things about curriculum and organizing for program change. The superintendent is his best professional friend and strongest ally, whom he must help to know his plans to help children learn.

Working with other supervisors is a matter of equal concern. Staff meetings and informal discussions are probably the best place to thrash out the details of a curricular change proposition. The curriculum supervisor should present things in writing and encourage reaction and suggestion from all, and should take the proposal item by item, word by word to see how others react, interpret, and feel. His efforts in these sessions should be to understand their feelings, and not defend his own point of view. He must listen to their comments and collect their detailed responses.

One of the purposes in seeking help from colleagues is to profit from their suggestions. However, to share one's hopes and plans for curriculum change is equally important. The give and take should be mutually beneficial, but it must be give and take. In all of his efforts to solicit professional reaction, the curriculum worker must deal openly and honestly and without commitment to the ideas involved. He must help the plan emerge from an intensive study of the local situation and his broader goals.

How do principals feel? If the supervisor's plan is to be successful, the entire idea must be supported by almost every man. Each principal must understand, appreciate, and literally agree that what the curriculum worker has in mind is a very sound thing, or it will not be successful.

Principals are people who hold the key to dramatic change. One must conceptualize a plan for curriculum improvement that will guarantee these people an important role. From the very beginning the supervisor assures their participation and active role. Getting their reactions on particular ideas as he visits their schools is one approach. Exploring the problems at principals' meetings is yet another. In general, each and every principal must have a genuine opportunity to think these ideas through and react with the supervisor to their implications, potential, and ultimate worth.

Will this cause them to lose control of their own particular school? Will they have to make their teachers change their ways? How can they explain the whole idea to the PTA? How much time will it take from their schedule and when and where will meetings be? These questions, most of them defensive, will be the kind that the supervisor hears. His job will be to explain to the principals what he presently knows and at the same time to demonstrate a willingness to weave their ideas into the plan as it evolves.

If he is working in a school system the size of Riverside or larger, he may have some difficulty getting to know very many teachers as the first year goes by. Acknowledging that his efforts will fall short of satisfactory attainment, during the course of the first few months meeting with teachers' groups and faculty meetings will be a key role. To chat informally with every teacher that he can, to try to relate names and faces and schools, and to discuss where he stands and why are very important. The supervisor must seek especially those dominant individuals who are respected by staff and children alike, and must ask their help for testing his feelings and trying his notions on them for size.

The plan outlined here calls for all principals to participate in curriculum councils at the area level. Some teachers, some parents, and perhaps some students will be involved at the district, area, and school level of operation. Organizing for curriculum improvement will be successful only to the degree that competent, diverse groups of people are brought together on common concerns. From that point on plans will take shape, but if, and only if, the composition of school and lay groups is acknowledged from the beginning as important and playing an integral role. Ultimately, of course, all persons function on an equal basis, all have one voice, and every person's vote the same as any other's. This fundamental premise, then, suggests that the curriculum supervisor begin first with the principals, then teachers, and finally parents, in that very order. If students join, they should be added last.

Unless the supervisor moves slowly, step by step, some principals, who may not fully comprehend the entire plan for curriculum change, can feel threatened in the presence of teachers or parents. For curriculum councils to be effective, "yes men" should not knowingly be involved. If principals only select those parents or teachers over whom they feel they have control, the basic idea of generating power for curriculum development may be seriously hampered at the outset. Certain precedents should be established with caution and care. Frequency and length of meetings are important details. Who presides and who defines the agenda are also significant factors. Getting the plan into operation involves a lot of skill—keeping it going and making it function is still another role.

How Curriculum Councils Work

In conceiving of a curriculum plan, the supervisor must envision efforts over an extended period of time. In taking the long view, one imperative will be to have a detailed plan. He must map out curriculum council meetings a year in advance, checking holidays and conflicts and avoiding meetings during the months of September and May. He must set a simple set of rules: meetings start on time and end on time, without exception, and never run longer than 90 minutes. Whenever possible, coffee and cookies or other light refreshments should be served.

District council should probably meet once a month at a convenient, comfortable location, free from distraction and readily available to all. The curriculum worker should expect to have to do a lot of explaining as the meetings get under way and as more new persons join the first few sessions. Immediately, however, the group must move into serious consideration of instructional problems so that they can see progress. For about the first year, it will be necessary for the supervisor to preside, since no one else shares the conception of the potential for change.

Area council meetings should also conform to certain expectations. Although the supervisor meets with them, he does not insist that area meetings be held in or near his office. Area councils should always meet on the same day of the week so that a habit of participation can develop easily and naturally. From the very beginning, this supervisor must insist that each area council develop its own leadership; his role is to act as consultant and friend. He should encourage members to select a chairman and secretary, suggest rotating from school to school.

A brainstorming session might be an appropriate beginning. It should take about 30 minutes. The supervisor should begin to identify without comment or other noticeable sign every problem in instruction which the various members of the district council can name. As he moves around from area council to area council meeting, he should explore each of these suggested problems in more detail and carry the list of problems to each area council meeting and suggest these items for possible study. For buzz groups of persons from the same school to go over the list carefully, to talk about each item, and to identify those of major importance to them and their particular school is a good starting point. After 30 or 40 minutes in small group sessions, the entire area council might gather and talk about their ideas in a more general way. Ultimately, it might be helpful to take the list of problems back to individual schools to seek further faculty opinion on the problems that are most pressing.

Between district council meetings, it should be possible to make the rounds twice with every area council and have a good consideration of the important ideas in need of improvement and study. After a summary tally, the ten most frequently mentioned problems can be presented before the district council for an exhaustive discussion of each. The list should then be narrowed to three or four significant areas. If this process has been thorough and careful, these final problem areas will be of genuine concern to most people involved.

How does one study these problems through research? Where does one begin? It might be very legitimate at this point for the supervisor to ask for a small group to give some specific assistance. He might suggest to the district council that they appoint a steering committee composed of an elementary principal, secondary principal, teacher, parent, and student to meet with him at some future date to outline a way to approach these problems in more detail. He has his own personal work to do in addition to this. How does he get started?

Needless to say, the supervisor must have at least some understanding of research design and an interest in research himself or the plan outlined thus far will not function at all. This plan presupposes that research is the best base from which to make curriculum decisions, and it also presupposes that the curriculum worker or some person readily available to him has at least a minimal interest and reasonable design skills.

Accepting these inherent limitations, at this point it would be wise for the supervisor to ask himself some questions. What kinds of specific problems were posed during the discussion before the final ones were chosen? What recurring themes kept running through the total plan? What administrative problems have principals posed most often? What solutions do they suggest? The supervisor must review all of the things that have happened since he has been on the job to relate them to the specific problem areas, to think through three or four different researchable questions and tentative design, and to make a note of them. He must outline specific procedures and possible outcomes in each case, including particular difficulties that might occur along the way. He must weave certain problem areas together into broader concepts, and pose problems in terms of questions to be answered, such as the following list.

1. What course content should be placed at each grade level in each subject field?
2. What is the impact of different teachers upon students' motivational levels?
3. How does departmentalization in the elementary school affect youngsters' motivation and achievement levels?
4. What is the effect of class size upon reading achievement at the first grade level?
5. How many students in Riverside schools are in classes of more than 30? 35? 40?
6. How many students fail at each grade level in Riverside schools?
7. Does class size have any appreciable effect upon teachers' morale or their physical well being?
8. What is the best method of teaching reading?
9. Why do students try to do good work in school?
10. What factors are related with students' failure in reading?
11. What is the effectiveness of a remedial reading program in junior high school compared to a situation in which every teacher teaches reading every day?
12. What effect will team teaching in large groups have upon students' attitudes toward school?
13. What is motivation? How can we measure it? Can it be taught or learned?
14. What effect does learning a foreign language in the elementary school have upon students' achievement in reading?
15. Should music be required beyond the lower grades?
16. Will individual and group counseling improve failing students' achievement?
17. How do parents feel about the present grading policy?
18. Why do students drop out of school?

While these represent more precise delineations, they are still too vague to investigate carefully or effectively. With such a list of topics, however, the supervisor can now proceed to develop a general description of how each one might be studied, outlining on about one page the exact nature of the problem as he sees it, how it might be studied, which schools might be involved, what kind of data could be collected, what results he might expect, and so on. All of the problem topics should be gone through and a list of possible approaches to the study of each developed.

When the supervisor first meets with his steering committee, he must see what they have to say. Do they have any specific suggestions about how to approach the problems? Although the members of the steering committee will be sincerely interested in helping in any way they can, they will probably lack experience with research design or methodological procedures. The supervisor will probably need to review some of his own suggestions for action, and should go through each problem in detail and suggest other possible approaches as they arise. Studying the reactions of the committee is important. Do they seem to feel that the problems are more than they can handle—do they shy away from actual studies and prefer to talk? Do they think that with his help the other members of the various area councils would be willing to try? He should follow up on the reservations expressed by his small group and consider them in serious detail. Are his proposals really off base? Is the committee fearful of trying to do research on its own when the members never have before? Are the questions which he has suggested really those which interest them and which reflect the total council's views?

If these representative persons feel the supervisor's proposals have no possibilities, the odds are no one else will either. If their concerns are primarily due to apprehension and lack of experience, they can be surmounted with the curriculum worker's assistance and other aid. If the problems are not significant or pertinent to their particular interest, he probably should start again. If the general ideas are acceptable, he should propose a very specific course of action for their consideration. For instance, he could suggest that each area council assume responsibility for developing one curriculum guide, grades one through 12 according to a preconceived plan, and also undertake one experimental project especially to their liking from among those suggested. There would be nothing compulsory about these ideas, but they would provide a basis for proceeding and for giving cohesion and unity to the total effort. If the steering committee feels such a suggestion would be reasonable and in fact effective, the supervisor can move into area council meetings and proceed from there.

Curriculum Improvement in Practice

Chapters 5 through 9 describe a series of curriculum improvement efforts which are based upon the theoretical and practical framework outlined in Part I. In effect, each chapter sets forth one or more examples in quasi case study form. Several propositions are implicit in these illustrations.

Using research and evaluation of curriculum as a basis for improvement is more of a "way of thinking" than a "set of rules" or procedures to be followed. Asking questions is central to this "way." Throughout all of these illustrations the nature and the range of questions are described. Learning to ask questions about curriculum is a very difficult but necessary skill. Getting valid and useful answers to curriculum questions is important, too, and each case illustration describes efforts to select or devise observational tools or procedures by which answers can be generated to the questions which have been posed. But learning to examine the assumptions which underlie questions, to sequence events and observations so that the logic of the approach will produce worthwhile data, and to search for interrelationships by means of divergent questioning or creative observational tools are all part of this "way of thinking" which is described. The empirical approach, in other words, proceeds from an experiential and an experimental mode, but is grounded also in the principles and philosophical thought of man.

The cases selected for inclusion in these chapters are meant to be illustrative rather than definitive; thus, they reflect a range of concerns and a breadth of sophistication and skill. Like teachers, curriculum workers have to start with people at their level of understanding and activity. What is intended in these illustrations is a variety of approaches and topics and results. Each case study also illustrates what every experienced researcher knows, which is that "one always gets less than he hopes for, but he always gets more than nothing." In other words, curriculum improvement through careful evaluation and research is no panacea, but it will produce significant curriculum change.

For the reader's convenience, each of the case illustrations included in the next five chapters has been set in special type to set it apart from the remaining portions of the chapter. One can read each case separately or read it as a part of the whole chapter. In addition, the tests and other materials referred to in each case illustration are included in the appendices at the end of the chapters for the reader's use. Each represents a tool which was selected or designed to procure pertinent information relative to the particular curriculum questions which were posed.

Part II, therefore, is meant to "put flesh on the bones" of the principles which were outlined in Part I. It is hoped that the reader will view these case illustrations as examples of curriculum improvement efforts in local schools. They are not meant to be prototypes, but rather incentives and specific elaborations of the practical and theoretical principles which constitute the framework of this book.

5 Curriculum Studies Involving the Community

The school becomes an institute that actively influences the community when it accepts the challenge to unite with community leaders to meet community problems. Any school district has many community related problems. Two such problems are described here as they might be studied by area curriculum councils. The first study is an examination of community vocational opportunities. The second study outlines an effort to identify and describe a particular kind of educationally deprived population which characterizes an area of most communities.

An Area Council Studies Vocational Opportunities

Any honest effort to examine the concepts of motivation and course content in education ultimately leads to a consideration of the purposes of education and why schools teach what they do. Why do we have schools? What purposes are served by having children memorize the parts of

speech and memorize the binomial theorem? Will demonstrating competence and skill with true-false examinations make young people better
citizens who are more law abiding and interested in their community?
What kind of work opportunities are available? How many persons are
employed in each of the various kinds of jobs? How much do young
people entering the world of work expect to earn? What expectations do
employers hold for prospective employees? Can high school graduates
add and subtract or write a satisfactory letter? How interested are employers in what the schools teach? Do they really care, or are they only
interested in keeping taxes down? What proportion of recent graduates
have remained within the community, and how many others have left for
other areas? Why did these people go? What kind of post high school
educational opportunities exist for those who finish school in an area but
want additional training?

A survey of the community's needs in term of employment opportunities, employers' values, and salary possibilities may give guidance counselors data with which to work directly and effectively with youngsters. It
may also give principals and teachers clues about the effectiveness and
desirability of their present instructional program. Knowing employers'
feelings is no assurance that schools will be able to adopt curricular
content or organization in response, but knowing how one major segment of the public feels about the products of the educational stream can
provide insights for curriculum change.

What kind of vocational opportunities are available in Riverside? How
many students are involved in these programs? Why are there so few
students participating? Should these programs be housed in a special
school, or should they be part of a larger comprehensive program? What
advantages are involved in having students attend a special school? A
comprehensive school? Is there a stigma attached to attending a special
vocational school? Does seeking to avoid this stigma by staying in a regular academic program insure many youngsters' failure and possible dropout? How do academic teachers feel about vocational programs? How do
guidance counselors feel about them? Is there hidden tendency to encourage all youngsters to participate in general academic courses and avoid
vocational preparation? Are guidance counselors really only concerned
with the college bound? Do scheduling provisions permit changes in program without punishing a student for such changes by denying credit?

These questions provide many approaches to problems in vocational studies. Undertaking any or all of them would depend in part upon the intensity of feeling and immediacy of need. Studying the responses of the area council and helping them select some phases of the total problem area for intensive investigation could be a very important role for the curriculum supervisor. Depending upon the previous experiences of the group members—whether or not they have experienced success in curriculum research on a problem they've had before—may dictate the course of action the supervisor takes. Let us assume for a moment that these problems have been discussed for years with the superintendent and with other supervisors, but no action has ever been taken. If the supervisor undertakes a study that might take several months to complete, the members of this area council may lose interest and sight of their goal. It may be more appropriate to help them undertake some short term operation they can get in motion and complete in a shorter length of time. Helping them have success experience may place the supervisor in a position to move with them later into the deeper, more fundamental problems. A survey, or some descriptive type investigation, could serve not only to lay the ground work by providing important data for subsequent studies, but also to enable these people to gain confidence in themselves and their ability to conduct curriculum study. The curriculum supervisor's job must include helping people move from where they are to new and higher levels of operation. The following study describes the kind of report which might result from such an approach.

A Study of the Vocational Opportunities and Related Problems in Riverside School District

The Problem

One of the major functions of public schools is to help young people prepare themselves for life in the adult world, including the "world of work." Most persons believe that schools should provide both information and experiences that will enable young people to become responsible, contributing members of our society. Vocational guidance and training are considered as essentials in any modern educational undertaking for adolescents.

The purposes of this study are to find out what kinds of job-opportunities are available in Riverside and to determine what kind of people employers seek.

The Procedures

During the month of February, a survey was made of the yellow pages of the telephone directories of all communities within Riverside. The names and addresses of four business concerns were selected from each page of these directories, and the employers were mailed a two-page questionnaire (see Appendix A) requesting five kinds of information: the number of persons employed in different kinds of positions; the number of persons hired during the school year; the number deliberately discharged (fired) during the school year; the monthly salary; and a brief description of each position involved. Finally, employers were asked to indicate the relative importance of various personal qualities in a prospective employee. Specifically, each employer was asked to rank eight human attributes in order of their importance to him in employing new people for his business. For purposes of this study, the relative values accorded each attribute were arranged together for all respondents so that a mean value was obtained. Finally, these eight attributes were ranked according to their average for all employers' responses.

Job Data. Questionnaires were sent to 726 employers, and returns were received from 159. This represents a 22 per cent response. Table 1 outlines the basic data obtained from 143 of these returns; not all questionnaires were usable.

The Results

From these figures one can see that more than 40 per cent of the persons, employed as of December, had been hired during the previous twelve-month period. Further, for every three people hired during that length of time, one was deliberately discharged by his employer. Turnover was especially great in certain areas.

A detailed examination of the various data indicates that persons working in managerial-supervisory and technical-skilled categories were relatively stable; fewer persons were hired and fewer fired in these areas, proportionally, than any others. Persons working in the unskilled areas were hired and fired more frequently, reflecting considerable turnover among the employees. It is also obvious from these figures that the greatest number of opportunities are in the technical-skilled job category. Almost 30 per cent of all jobs were so described.

Table 1

Pertinent Data about Vocational Opportunities in Riverside Obtained from 143 Employers

Job Category	Average Monthly Salary	Total Employees as of December	Total Hired During School Year	Total Fired During School Year
Managerial-Supervisory	$570.12	640	44	16
Sales	495.27	568	127	36
Secretarial-Clerical	284.68	849	452	76
Technical-Skilled	404.88	1327	96	37
Craftsmen-Semiskilled	315.50	450	279	160
Laborers-Unskilled	231.40	674	894	359
TOTAL		4508	1892	684

Table 2 describes the relative ranking of eight human qualities according to employers' desire for these attributes in prospective employees. These qualities are listed in the order in which they were desired by the employers in this sample, "Mean Value" indicating the arithmetical average which resulted from all responses.

Conclusions and Recommendations

The purposes of this study were to find out what kinds of job opportunities are available in Riverside, and what kinds of people employers seek. Descriptive data were obtained from 143 employers representing 4508 employees throughout the country, and valuations of employees' qualities were also collected.

Several interesting observations are apparent in these data. Three will be discussed in some detail. The reader is urged to recognize that these observations go beyond the data and represent one person's interpretation of the

Table 2

Qualities Desired in Employees in Order of
Their Importance as Ranked by 136 Employers

Rank Order	Quality	Definition	Mean Value
1	Dependable	Punctual, honest, hard working, can be counted on, conscientious, persevering.	3.00
2	Competent	Skillful, performs his duties well, has real ability for his job, accomplished worker.	3.07
3	Intelligent	Clear thinker, resourceful, sensible, thoughtful, uses good "common sense," creative.	3.55
4	Cooperative	Helpful, understanding, harmonious, works well with others, "pitches in" and does his part.	4.38
5	Agreeable	Friendly, pleasant, congenial, able to "get along" with other people, tactful, tolerant.	4.67
6	Educated	Can read, write, spell, and compute well, has a good academic background, knowledgeable, made good grades in school.	4.78
7	Trained	Experienced, well prepared, understands and possesses the "know how" and special skills for his job.	5.63
8	Flexible	Open minded, adaptable, willing to try new ways of doing things, able to adjust to different situations.	5.83

significance and implications of these findings. Other readers might reach other conclusions.

Apathetic Community? More than 700 simple, two-page questionnaires were mailed to employers in Riverside, each accompanied by a letter of explanation urging assistance with this study. The significance of the survey to each employer and to the schools was emphasized, and return envelopes were provided for the respondent's use. Further, an offer to share the results of the study was included. That only about one-fifth of the employers contacted provided the necessary information may be an indication of public apathy. It may also mean that the data requested was not readily available, that the employers identified did not perceive the significance of the project, or that the questionnaire itself was confusing and not readily understandable. Certainly the instrument was not particularly appropriate for some of the larger industries contacted, since it called for oversimplification of information from their point of view. The exact reason for this poor response is not clear, but such an apparent indication of poor relationships with local employers warrants further careful study.

Job Opportunities.   These data clearly indicate that most of the rewarding jobs for prospective employees, financially and in terms of stability, generally require post high school education. There are apparently many more positions demanding technical skills and advanced training than any other single kind of opportunity. Students should probably be encouraged to make preparations for schooling after high school graduation; counselors should collect and disseminate pertinent vocational data about Riverside; and the school board and the entire community should marshal support for additional educational facilities and programs beyond the high school level. A public junior college which would specialize as a technical institute seems imperative. Positions in medical technology, nursing, auditing, accounting, electrical equipment repair, telemetry, data processing, electronics, mechanics, and photography and layout, for example, constitute the major types of technical positions available for which advanced training would be essential, according to this survey.

Employee Qualities.   Asking employers to rank the qualities they desired in prospective employees resulted in certain observations. The two qualities ranking highest—dependability and competence—were apparently fairly well agreed upon as being especially important. Likewise, those two qualities ranked lowest—trained and flexible—were also listed by most employers as less important more frequently than any others. Evidence about the remaining qualities was less decisive, and though the latter may be significant, the authors feel that only the extremes may be reliable.

Asking employers to rank the qualities they desired in prospective employees might be interpreted as one way of asking them what they consider to be the major purposes of school. In other words, if employers want certain kinds of people to work for them in their particular place of business, it may also be reasonable to assume these same employers feel that developing these kinds of people is a major responsibility of the schools.

Following this logic, it would appear that the 143 employers in Riverside who participated in this study really feel that teaching youngsters to be dependable and competent is much more important than teaching them to be trained or flexible; or incidentally, to read and write and spell precisely. If this is so, certain fundamental questions arise.

How can schools teach children to be dependable? What is the difference between competence (ranked high) and trained (ranked low)? Further, can

young people develop competence without being trained? What kind of educational programs are most effective to achieve these ends? What is the
proper relationship of vocational education and general education, and how
can curricula be conceived to best meet the needs of each youngster and
the needs of society?

These questions must be thoughtfully explored. It is the opinion of the authors that allocating units for particular courses or writing syllabi for others
is no solution. A systematic and comprehensive examination of the basic purposes of education is the first step, and then finding ways and means of translating those objectives into teaching materials and methods could directly
follow. If the hunches about apathy in the community prove to be correct, a
general program of community education and public involvement may be the
only effective solution. In short, nothing less than total community involvement seems to be required if we expect to make significant progress.

An Area Council Studies Educationally Deprived Children

In nearly all communities, some schools will be faced with the problems
of transient workers' children or itinerant students. In almost every case,
these youngsters represent real challenges to the school system in which
they attend school. They may not begin their schooling until November,
and by April their families may move on to other states. This brief period
may be the only schooling they ever get. Because of the very nature of
these families, attendance, even during that time the child is enrolled, can
be a major problem. These children may be retarded educationally by
several years. Records about their other school experiences may be inadequate, and their desire to do good work in school may represent a low
level. Many of them will not know how to read at all, and others may
be several years behind the average pupil of a similar age. If a supervisor
has students like this in his school system, what can he do?

Are they able? How many are actually involved? How long do they
really stay in the schools? What kinds of physical disabilities do they
have, if any? Are they undernourished? How effective are the schools'
efforts to help them learn? Where do they come from? Where do they
go? Do the usual teaching methods "reach" these students? Would
special procedures be more effective? Should they be grouped with all of
the other students, or should they be separated in special "opportunity

classes"? What happens to their social and intellectual development when they are in class with other children? What happens to such development when they are separated in a room by themselves? What effect does the continuous in and out traffic of short term students have on the regular students? Do teachers tend either to ignore these transient students or give them undue amounts of attention and time?

Talking about these problems is one thing; getting accurate data is another. First of all, it involves defining "educationally deprived." It means reviewing current records to see how many youngsters presently meet this definition, reviewing all available information on these pupils and studying their needs, hypothesizing that a particular educational situation can help them learn more than some other kind, then trying it out to see. It means trying one method and then another so that each of these children has every opportunity to profit from the school district's offerings. At the same time, no child in regular attendance should be deprived of any comparable opportunity in a supervisor's eagerness to help the underprivileged. Where does one begin? The report outlined below could be a beginning effort.

A Study of the Number and Characteristics of Educationally Deprived Children in the Riverside School District

During the past several years the elementary schools in the North Side area of Riverside School District have been faced with a great number of children who are educationally deprived. Many of these children enroll in schools for limited periods of time. Further, the majority of them come from what has sometimes been called "culturally deprived" areas or from socioeconomic situations in which many of the advantages commonly afforded most children today are not present.

The Problem

In an effort to ascertain whether or not this problem was sufficiently extensive to warrant special attention, Area Three Curriculum Council undertook a study to answer the following questions: Do we have children in our schools whose experiences are so unique and so limited that a conventional class-room program fails to meet their educational needs? How many are there? What are they like? What kind of educational opportunity can we provide to best meet their own particular needs?

The Procedures

To answer these questions a three phase project was undertaken. First, the principals from four of the elementary schools involved developed criteria to identify such children. Second, each principal searched the student's cumulative records with his teachers and identified all of the children who were currently enrolled in that school or who had been enrolled during the present school year who met these criteria. Third, extensive data on each child were accumulated for further study.

Criteria. It was decided that children who met all or most of the following critera would be considered so unique and so deprived educationally that a conventional classroom situation probably did not meet their educational needs:

(a) Live in short-term rental areas
(b) Live in very low socioeconomic sections of the community
(c) Have very irregular attendance
(d) Are rejected by their peers and by the community
(e) Parents are unskilled laborers
 (f) Have not been in any other school this year before enrolling
(g) Need free lunch
(h) Are mentally retarded
 (i) Stay in school only for a short time
 (j) Do not announce departure
(k) Be known to school authorities (may return year after year)

Identification. The principals and teachers from Grant Elementary School, Glen Elementary School, River Elementary School, and Union Elementary School each made a careful search of their school records for children who met most of the criteria listed above. The names of these children were isolated, and their records set aside for further study.

Collection of Data. Information was collected for each child identified. Because of the nature of these particular children, there were many instances in which only partial data were available. Wherever possible, however, these facts were assembled: age at last birthday, recorded as of April 1; sex; intelligence quotient; name of I.Q. test used; deviation in reading level from expected level; attendance record; number of years of schooling completed

by the father; number of years of schooling completed by the mother; number of different residences within the last 12 months; date of arrival at local
school; date of departure from local school; number of school days registered
at local school; destination, if known; and father's occupation.

The Results

Two hundred sixty-nine children were identified in the four schools who met
the definition of "educationally deprived" child as described above. Of this
number, 201 were or had been at Grant Elementary School, 20 at Glen Elementary School, 34 at River Elementary School, and 4 at Union Elementary
School. These 269 children represented approximately 16 per cent of the total
school enrollment in these four schools. Because of the very nature of the
problem under study, there was a definite possibility that some of these
children were counted twice, since approximately 30 students were known
to have departed from one to another of the four schools participating in this
study. However, the total number is not considered large enough to be significant.

Age. The average age of these 269 children was 9.61 years. Table 3 shows
the precise breakdown according to age:

Table 3

Number of Educationally Deprived Children
According to Age

Years of Age	No. of Children
6	32
7	26
8	36
9	35
10	39
11	41
12	31
13	18
14	5
15	5
16	1

Many of these children were also overage in grade. For example, at Grant Elementary School, which had the largest portion of the students, 8 were overage in the first grade, 9 in the second, 17 in the third, 12 in the fourth, 12 in the fifth, and 11 in the sixth. In other words, almost a third of the children were retarded educationally one or more years.

Sex.   Out of the total of 269 students, 152 were boys and 117 girls.

Intelligence Quotient.   From the available data, the mean I.Q. score for these children was computed and found to be 78.96 points, which is well below average. It should be pointed out, however, that scores were not available for many children, and since this represents only partial information, it is suggestive only.

Reading Level.   Standardized test data were not available on many of these children, but from that which was available, it would appear that most of these students are reading considerably below expected achievement level. Expected achievement level was defined grossly as that reading level at which a child should have been reading if he had been placed in the proper grade according to chronological age when the test was administered. The mean reading level was 1.02 years below expected level, as defined above.

Health.   Using very general definitions, Table 4 shows the health status of 256 students: more than a third have some health problem.

Table 4

Health Status of Educationally Deprived Students

General Health Condition	No. of Students
Good health. No observable defects.	151
Malnutrition	61
Poor eyesight	19
Deaf or hard of hearing	8
Ringworm or hookworm	9
Speech defect (cleft palate, stutterer, etc.)	5
Other	3
Unknown	13

Arrival and Departure. Because of the many special problems it creates for school personnel, the dates of arrival and departure and length of stay for these students is especially important. Table 5 describes the number which arrived and left each month, beginning with school registration in August.

Table 5

Arrival and Departure Dates of Educationally Deprived Children

Month	No. Arriving	No. Departing
August	61	0
September	36	8
October	34	20
November	38	26
December	10	8
January	47	46
February	18	46
March	15	17
April	10	24
Total	269	195

From these figures it appears that the maximum number of educationally deprived students actually present at any one time in all the four schools combined was approximately 120. Further, about 74 students were still enrolled in the four schools as of May 1.

Attendance. One of the most significant statistics concerning these children is average length of stay and their attendance record. For these 269 students, the mean length of stay was approximately 56 days, and the mean attendance record during that period of enrollment was 79.25 per cent. In other words, the average child spent about 45 days in one of these schools.

Family. Of the 269 children involved in this study, 173 were living with both parents, 22 with one parent, 9 with neither parent but with other relatives, and 9 with persons other than their own relation. Thirty-three students' home situation was unaccounted for. The mean number of siblings for this group was 3.26, indicating that these children generally came from fairly large families. The mean number of years of education for the fathers of these children was approximately 6.4 years and for the mothers was approximately 8.9 years.

Conclusions and Recommendations

Two major conclusions seem warranted. First, there are many educationally deprived children in the elementary schools of the North Side Area. Second, these children probably need a special educational program. Considering the fact that there are more than 250 educationally deprived youngsters in the elementary schools of the North Side area, and considering the fact that these youngsters are both culturally and educationally retarded, the members of the Area Three Curriculum Council hereby recommend the following:

(1) Establishment of two nongraded elementary classrooms in Grant Elementary School for children who are educationally deprived. Every effort should be made to keep these classes below 30, but the principal should assign students to these classrooms at his discretion. However, he should always endeavor to include only those children who would be considered "educationally deprived" as the term has been discussed in this study.

(2) Employment of a teacher's aide assigned to teach in these classrooms in addition to regular teachers.

Inasmuch as the total number of children involved varies from month to month and from school to school, it is felt that two classrooms at Grant Elementary School would serve as an effective pilot study to determine whether or not making special provisions for these children would be especially beneficial.

Nongraded classrooms are suggested for two reasons. First, the educational and cultural levels of these children vary extensively. When they are placed in a regular classroom, an undue burden is placed on the teacher. Differences in abilities and achievements are magnified. Further, the "traffic" in and out of a regular classroom during the year makes it difficult for the regular children to profit most effectively from their teacher's efforts. The nongraded classrooms should be maximally beneficial to all of the children who are involved—those who are educationally deprived and those who are not.

Since the turnover in the nongraded classrooms will be great, and since the ability levels, age levels, and achievement levels will vary greatly, a special teacher's aide should be assigned to work half time with each of the regular teachers in these nongraded classrooms. The problems of providing special materials, working with small groups, and maintaining classroom control will be much more apparent in these special classrooms because of the very nature of the learners involved. Therefore, the professional teacher must be assisted in his efforts to provide maximal educational opportunity and stimulation for children whose cultural background and experience leaves them "intellectually starved."

It is recognized that these nongraded classrooms will present a tremendous challenge to the school personnel concerned. Therefore, it is suggested that only outstanding teachers be selected for these positions and that they be given every bit of encouragement, assistance, material, special teaching aids, and personal consideration possible. Their chore will be exceedingly difficult, but their task very important. Through this special situation it may be possible, perhaps for the first time, to create a learning situation in which these children will have a genuine opportunity to experience an educational program directed especially at their needs and abilities.

If these recommendations are accepted, Grant Elementary School should be encouraged to make a special effort to evaluate the effectiveness of this program next year. In addition, both the faculty and administration should also be encouraged to make a concerted effort to acquaint the parents and the community both with the problem, and also with their efforts to resolve it.

Finally, because it hardly seems likely that these children exist by themselves without older brothers and sisters, those parents who are charged with the responsibility of providing for the education of children beyond the elementary level in the greater North Side area are hereby urged to consider the possibility of examining their own situations with care.

Summary

These two examples pose different ways to study community problems. Every supervisor has unique problems in his own community for which particular research methods would be a logical approach. This is the way progress is made. The schools are a dynamic force in the growth of the community.

Even more special than his work with the community is the supervisor's relationship to the growth and development of the boys and girls in the schools. The next chapter describes several ways in which curriculum research can look at students.

Appendix A
Employer Questionnaire

Please Read *Very* Carefully

Part I—Directions:

Listed below are several different categories of occupations. Would you *please provide the following information about your employees* by job classification?

A. Brief description of duties performed
B. Approximate average monthly salary
C. Total number of persons *employed* as of December
D. Number of persons *hired* during the school year
E. Number of persons *fired* during the school year
  (Note: this should include only those persons you deliberately let go or encouraged to resign because you were dissatisfied with their work for one reason or another).

Job Category	Job Description	Average Monthly Salary	Total Emp. as of Dec.	Number Hired in School Year	Number Fired in School Year
Managerial-Supervisory					
Sales					
Secretarial-Clerical					
Technical-Skilled					
Craftsmen-Semiskilled					
Laborers-Unskilled					

Please Read *Very* Carefully

Part II—Directions

Listed below are several human qualities which some authorities feel are important in various types of work. When *you* interview a person for a job, which qualities do you consider most important? *Please rank these in the order of their importance to you* as an employer. That is, place a "1" beside that quality which you consider most desirable in a prospective employee. Place a "2" beside that one which you consider next most important, then a "3," and so on, until you place an "8" beside that quality which you consider less important than all of the others. All of these characteristics are probably important, but *which ones are more important to you as an employer and which ones are less important?* Since you may have many different kinds of positions in your business, please complete this form according to the way you feel about *most* of the persons working in the various positions in your establishment.

Your Ranking	Quality	Definition of Quality
_____	Agreeable:	Friendly, pleasant, congenial, able to "get along" with other people, tactful, tolerant.
_____	Competent:	Skillful, performs his duties well, has real ability for his job, accomplished worker.
_____	Cooperative:	Helpful, understanding, harmonious, works well with others, "pitches in" and does his part.
_____	Dependable:	Punctual, honest, hard working, can be "counted on," conscientious, persevering.
_____	Educated:	Can read, write, spell, and compute well, has a good academic background, knowledgeable, made good grades in school.
_____	Flexible:	Openminded, adaptable, willing to try new ways of doing things, able to adust to different situations.
_____	Intelligent:	Clear thinker, resourceful, sensible, thoughtful, uses good "common sense," creative.
_____	Trained:	Experienced, well prepared, understands and possesses the "know how" and special skills for his job.

6 Curriculum Studies Involving Students

To find better ways to help children learn and more effective ways for schools to teach is the curriculum supervisor's most challenging responsibility. The most direct way of attacking this problem is by studying the child. Riverside has undertaken several studies involving the child. How ready was he for school experiences when he entered? Later, as he became better known in the school, how motivated was he? Was there a connection between his motivation and his achievement? Did his grades reflect an adequate measure of how well he was learning? What is known about failing students in Riverside? Studies involving children are the most rewarding in education because one gets direct results. By studying children directly, one gets to know them better, and by knowing students better the schools will be able to provide a better instructional program.

A School Council Studies Readiness and Academic Achievement

First grade teachers typically give readiness tests to their new students during the first few days of school. Are these tests any good? Do they predict accurately youngsters' achievements in first grade work? Can school people have any faith and confidence that grouping children according to readiness scores will be helpful and not harmful to any during those first few weeks?

The questions can be answered at least three ways. First, the manual for the readiness test can be checked to see what kinds of correlation coefficients were obtained in the developmental studies for the instrument available in varying degrees of detail with different readiness tests: These data indicate the utility and validity of the instrument. If a teacher understands statistical concepts, correlation, and statistical significance, the data might make sense and be of real value. Otherwise, the teacher can only accept the test on the face value of the reputation of the publisher or how adequate the manual "sounds." Second, any first grade teacher who has used readiness tests for any length of time has some definite opinions about their use and value, and could probably offer suggestions. Studies of teachers' opinions are very appropriate, but they should not be taken as direct evidence. There is considerable evidence in existing research to indicate that in some areas teachers' judgments are extremely reliable and accurate, but in others they are inconsistent and inaccurate.

A third way teachers might obtain pertinent information would be to administer the test, measure the children's achievement later, then actually determine the relationship between these measures for their children. They would be involving the first two approaches, but there would be much more accuracy in the result.

The supervisor encourages teachers to enter into a simple study of their own situation by explaining correlation to them so it has real meaning. He should review the assumptions underlying readiness tests, achievement tests, and grading, and help teachers devise a way of collecting data and organizing it so it has practical and educational significance. He must study the results of statistical analyses and help teachers interpret meaning from the various data involved. With them he should draw conclusions from the data and compare these conclusions with those reported elsewhere in the manual and other studies, reviewing again the purposes of readiness testing and achievement testing to see if present practices are compatible with stated goals and measurable outcomes.

The curriculum supervisor works with small groups of teachers and the principal of a school and helps them understand the tools with which they work and the meaning these things hold for them. At the same time, he helps them clarify the purposes of education and their own role in relationship to these purposes—all through an exhaustive examination of a simple but very important problem for them.

The Relationship of Readiness Scores to Academic Achievement

The Problem

Helping six-year-olds learn to read and to compute are generally considered the major responsibilities of first grade teachers. To help them know more about their students and to make their instructional efforts more effective, many teachers in grade one use readiness tests. Theoretically, those children who score higher on readiness tests should be able to make greater progress in reading and arithmetic than those who score lower.

Several first grade teachers were concerned about this theoretical assumption. Are readiness test scores really accurate predictors of academic achievement for first grade students?

The Procedures

During September, five first grade teachers at Burton Elementary School administered the Metropolitan Readiness Test to each of the students in their classes. In May, each teacher administered the Metropolitan Achievement Test to these same students. Rank order correlation coefficients (rho) between readiness scores and achievement scores in word knowledge, word discrimination, reading, and arithmetic were computed for each of the five groups participating in the study. Complete data were available for 114 youngsters.

The Results

Table 6 shows the relationship between readiness scores and achievement scores in each of the four areas for all five first grade groups. These coefficients of correlation, all positive and all moderately high, suggest that there is some definite relationship *between* readiness scores obtained early in first grade and achievement scores obtained later on standardized tests in reading and arithmetic. Interestingly enough, readiness and achievement in arithmetic seem more closely related than readiness and the various achievement scores in reading. In effect, these data imply that readiness scores are fair predictors of first year academic achievement.

Table 6

Correlation Coefficients (rho) between
Readiness Scores and Achievement Scores
for Five First Grade Groups

Group	Readiness and Word Knowledge	Readiness and Word Discrimination	Readiness and Reading	Readiness and Arithmetic
A	.80	.79	.82	.74
B	.61	.68	.69	.75
C	.48	.56	.73	.59
D	.80	.52	.79	.91
E	.48	.48	.44	.58

An Area Council Studies the Grading System

Evaluating pupil progress and determining achievement and growth through grades represent a serious problem for almost all teachers. What is the effect of grades upon students' attitudes toward school? Will students work harder if they get good grades or if they get poor grades? What do grades mean? Do all teachers grade the same? Is the present grading policy clear and understandable? Do all teachers adhere to the policy as it is now? What constitutes a grade of "A" and "B" and so on? Are there established minimum standards which all students must achieve in order to be promoted? Who determines these standards? Who decides whether or not any given child has achieved or not achieved? What is grade level? How many children presently achieve below grade level? How many children should reasonably be expected to achieve grade level? Is grade level a satisfactory standard of expectation?

A school system may have a fairly carefully defined policy regarding grading that may either simplify or confound the problems involved. For example, a rigid policy may restrict teachers from their point of view. Because evaluating pupil progress and reporting to parents is such a far reaching activity, it may very well represent a fertile source of data for study by an area council. If teachers are dissatisfied with the grading policy, encouraging a study of marking practices may release tensions as well as produce significant data.

Let us assume that some teachers have complained severely about grade policy and feel that it is quite unfair. Suppose that after extensive studies, a majority or even a sizeable minority of teachers indicate dissatisfaction with current marking practice. Then there may be real reason for reconsideration of the policy as presently adopted.

Grading in Riverside Schools

The Problem

Grading and reporting to parents is a perennial difficulty for teachers. Disagreements and misunderstandings are common, and the search for a common philosophy and uniform procedures is a typical problem in many school systems today. What kind of grading system do teachers prefer? How do students feel about grades? What reactions do parents have to the present Riverside grading system? This case is a study of these problems.

The Procedures

During the fall every elementary teacher in the Riverside Public Schools was furnished a questionnaire and asked to indicate his feelings about the precise statement which had been adopted by the elementary principals two years before and which was considered "grading policy." Also included were five brief questions about this policy and related matters. Completed questionnaires were returned unsigned to the principal's office and then forwarded to a central location. Out of 1314 questionnaires made available to teachers, 796 were returned. This represents a 60 per cent response. These responses were analyzed by grade level and for the entire group as a whole.

A modification of this questionnaire was also sent to 45 parents in one school in an effort to determine whether or not parental attitudes corresponded with teachers' feelings. These parents represented a random sample from this school, but this school could not be considered typical for Riverside.

Finally, 193 seventh, eighth, ninth, and eleventh graders in one school also responded to a modified version of the same questionnaire. Their reactions and their comments were studied carefully for some indication of students' feelings about grades and grading. Again, these students might be considered representative of this one school, but this school did not represent Riverside.

The Results

Teachers' Responses. During the course of this study it became apparent that there was much confusion about what actually was "policy" for grading in the Riverside schools. A thorough search of the *Administrators' Handbook* revealed some directives about "A-Excellent, 94–100," etc., but most elementary teachers felt certain there was more. It was finally concluded that the Elementary Principals Association had agreed that this "policy" is, to all intents and purposes, apparently agreed upon by many persons, but not actually approved as "school board policy." Most of the confusion centered around interpreting the phrase, "grade level," which is not defined at any point in any way.

1. Each subject must carry a letter grade for each reporting period.
2. Letter grades will be interpreted as:

A-Excellent	94–100
B-Good	87–93
C-Average	77–86
D-Poor	70–76
E-Failing	Below 70

3. Children who are attaining a minimum standard for the grade will be given "C." "A" and "B" grades will be given to those children who do above minimum work for the grade level. A child below grade level will be given a "D." According to teacher and principal judgment, those

children who are working sufficiently below grade level and who, in their opinion, would profit by being retained in grade, will be given an "E."

The general pattern evident from the responses described in Table 7 would imply that most teachers felt this policy is good, although there is more disagreement apparent among teachers of the lower grades. More than one fourth of all teachers responding, however, think this is not a good policy, which represents a sizeable negative opinion on a matter of this type.

Table 7

Responses of Different Groups of Teachers
to the Question "Do you personally think the
current grading policy is a good one?"

Group	N	Per Cent YES	Per Cent NO	Per Cent NO RESPONSE
Grade 1	155	63	34	3
Grade 2	132	69	26	5
Grade 3	126	69	26	5
Grade 4	123	76	19	5
Grade 5	115	77	19	4
Grade 6	105	70	27	3
Grades 7–12	12	92	8	0
Special Areas	28	46	43	11
TOTAL	796	70	26	4

Table 8 indicates the proportion of teachers who state that they do or do not personally follow this policy in all of their grading; whereas the first question endeavored to establish the extent to which the policy was actually approved.

Again, most of the teachers who responded to this questionnaire indicated that they did follow "grading policy" as described. The fact that almost one-seventh of the teachers polled deliberately and knowingly indicated that they did not follow this policy, however, seems to indicate some strong minority sentiment in the profession. The fact that this many teachers probably work with and grade more than 3500 Riverside youngsters in their classrooms indicates the extent to which this feeling may be significant. Again, the pattern

Table 8

Responses of Different Groups of Teachers
to the Question "Do you personally follow
the current policy in all of your grading and
reporting practices?"

Group	N	Per Cent YES	Per Cent NO	Per Cent NO RESPONSE
Grade 1	155	79	15	6
Grade 2	132	89	10	1
Grade 3	126	86	12	2
Grade 4	123	82	15	3
Grade 5	115	86	11	3
Grade 6	105	73	22	5
Grades 7–12	12	92	8	0
Special Areas	28	64	29	7
TOTAL	796	82	15	3

apparently seems to reflect some shift in sentiment among sixth grade teachers toward less rigid adherence to the present policy.

Table 9 shows the extent to which teachers felt satisfied with the present policy. This question directly complemented question number one, and was designed to give additional data about teachers' feelings.

Obviously there is widespread dissatisfaction with the present system of grading and reporting to parents, if these data are correct. Whether this represents typical professional dissatisfaction as the result of inability to do a difficult job perfectly, or whether it indicates general disapproval with the present way of doing things is not readily apparent. Since more than a quarter of all teachers responding expressed themselves negatively to question one, "Do you personally think the current grading policy is a good one?" it may be that there is a reservoir of negative feeling existing among the elementary teachers in Riverside toward the present grading policy.

In analyzing questions about comments received by teachers from parents or specific suggestions which teachers had, two major generalizations appeared. First, many teachers felt that the present grading policy is both discouraging and unfair to low ability students. Further, in these teachers' estimation, many parents think that "C" is a poor grade, which causes problems.

Second, teachers also indicate that they realize "an A in one class is not the same as in the next," and so on. The great variation among teachers' interpretations is indicative of the fact that the present grading system is not realistic. In other words, some teachers seem to feel that a child's grade in school is probably more a function of *who he gets* rather than *what he does,* however desirable the latter might actually be.

Table 9

Responses of Different Groups of Teachers
to the Question "Are you satisfied with our
present system of grading and reporting
to parents?"

Group	N	Per Cent YES	Per Cent NO	Per Cent NO RESPONSE
Grade 1	155	48	50	2
Grade 2	132	52	45	3
Grade 3	126	54	41	5
Grade 4	123	59	33	8
Grade 5	115	54	38	8
Grade 6	105	54	43	3
Grades 7–12	12	83	17	0
Special Areas	28	54	42	4
TOTAL	796	54	42	4

In making specific suggestions for improving the grading system, 75 teachers felt that conferences would be helpful while 53 teachers indicated a desire for some kind of check list for attitudes, effort, and work habits. Fifty-two teachers specifically suggested that children should be graded according to their ability, while 42 said they would prefer a satisfactory-unsatisfactory S-U system. Others made comments about using plus and minus signs, making written progress reports, and using a numerical marking system.

Students' Responses. One hundred ninety-three secondary students in one high school completed questionnaires and returned them unsigned to their teachers. The same policy which had been quoted to teachers was written out for these students, and their feelings about this policy solicited.

In response to the first question, "Do you understand this grading policy?"

94 per cent said "yes" and 6 per cent said "no." Apparently most of these young men and women felt they knew what the stated policy meant.

When asked, "Do you personally think this is a good grading policy?" 73 per cent agreed, 22 per cent disagreed, and 5 per cent did not respond.

The third question asked of these students was more involved. "Do grades mean the same thing in different courses? That is, is an 'A' in one course equal to an 'A' in every other course? Is a 'C' in one course equal to a 'C' in every other course?" Only 19 per cent marked their questionnaires "yes," 69 per cent marked "no," and 12 per cent did not respond. Obviously most of these secondary school students feel that there are definite variations in grading procedures among teachers.

The fourth question was especially interesting. "Do you think teachers sometimes use grades as threats or clubs to try to make students work harder?" Almost three quarters, 73 per cent, said "yes," and 24 per cent said "no." The others were undecided. Apparently most of these young people feel teachers sometimes use grades in negative ways, if "threats" or "clubs" might be interpreted that way.

Following up this question, those students who answered "yes" to whether or not they thought teachers sometimes used grades as threats or clubs were asked: "If your answer to number 4 is 'yes,' do you personally think this is a good idea?" Here 50 per cent said "yes" and 50 per cent said "no." Apparently about as many feel that teachers should use grades as threats or clubs as are opposed to such a practice.

Some specific student reactions are described below in quotations from their questionnaires. These comments are probably not representative, but may serve to indicate some of the flavor of these students' sentiments.

"I don't think a teacher should ever threaten a student. He should encourage the student to do better, but should not use the grade he will give him as a threat."

"I feel it's different in different cases. With some students it *will* make them work harder, but with others it brings rebellion."

"A grade for its sake alone is not adequate. The important fact is the knowledge acquired. Too much emphasis is placed on grades."

"Yes I do. Sometimes we have to be shocked into studying. Sometimes they are used as encouragements."

"I don't believe any student likes to sit and hear a teacher bawl him out for bad grades."

"No, because the grades you make do not actually show what you have learned. Some people get so nervous during a test that they forget things. Even though some people make bad grades they are really doing the best they can."

"I do not think grades should be used as threats to a student. When a student makes a grade, it is his grade. The teacher has no right to threaten to flunk him or change his grades in order to make the student try harder.

Many times it does not make the student try harder, but rather make him rebel."

"Some students who make poor grades are doing the best they can, and using grades as threats or clubs to get them to work harder won't help them, and sometimes it makes them give up."

"The more pressure you put on someone the harder he has to work, and the more he will get out of the course than just working without this pressure."

"If a student must be bribed by grades, it is too bad. Grades and grades alone should not be what a student aims for. He should reach out for knowledge. If he doesn't have this desire for knowledge, a bribe of a good grade won't help him at all."

"I think teachers sometimes use grades as threats or sort of warning. This sometimes makes the student resent the teacher, and not care what kind of grades he makes from then on."

"Threats discourage me rather than encourage me, and I think they discourage other people also."

"The grades you have made are yours, and I don't think a teacher has the right to take off points for a discipline problem. I think it makes the student mad and harder to get along with."

"I believe if a student is threatened by a teacher with a lower grade than he really deserves, the student usually gets a 'chip' on his shoulder and does even poorer work during the next grading period."

"This would tend to make the student stubborn, or at least it would me."

"The teacher sometimes says your grade out front of the class just to make you mad. The grade should be between you and the teacher, not everyone in the class."

"If a student cannot make the grade, he is usually not putting enough effort into his subjects."

"I think teachers should understand their students more so that the student feels entirely sure, and free to ask him anything."

"I think a student should be given at least a little credit for trying since not everyone is real smart."

"Make grade system lower so more people can pass."

"I think that your effort should enter into the system. Some of us work as hard as we can and still make bad grades."

"I don't know of a way, but some of the teachers could participate more in the classes. A class is not interesting if the teacher doesn't seem interested."

"Stop putting so much stress on the grades and bring out the learning point of view."

In general, most students seem to understand the present Riverside grading policy, but apparently hold rather strong feelings about some of the negative ways in which they see this policy being implemented. Further, these young people also seem to think that grades are more a result of *who* a student has for his teacher than *what* he achieves.

Parental Reaction. Forty-five parents from one elementary school responded to six questions. When asked if they understood the grading policy, 97 per cent said "yes" and three per cent said "no." Further, 91 per cent said they personally thought this was a good policy, while 9 per cent disagreed. When asked about their satisfaction with the present system of grading, 86 per cent said they were satisfied, 14 per cent were not.

"Do you think that all teachers grade about the same? That is, do you think an 'A' with one teacher means the same thing as an 'A' with most teachers, and so on?" To this question, 55 per cent of the parents said "yes," 45 per cent said "no." More than three-fourths, 77 per cent, felt that children should be given grades in everything listed on the report card; 23 per cent felt otherwise. Finally, 71 per cent indicated that they knew all they wanted to know about their child's progress in school after seeing his report card every six weeks; 29 per cent felt a need for additional explanation, parent-teacher conferences, and requests for consideration of "effort" in the grading process.

Conclusions and Recommendations

The general pattern of these data seem to indicate three things: there is dissatisfaction, misunderstanding, and misuse of the grading system in Riverside schools today. A thread of discontent runs throughout the study, and although in certain cases this discontent represents a minority, in some instances this feeling is quite widespread.

Several recommendations seem in order. These are directed to particular groups.

Recommendations to School Board. There is evidently a paradox at the present time about "grading policy" in the Riverside Public Schools. This paradox has two facets. First, most teachers feel the "policy" is more inclusive than it actually is as defined in the *Administrators' Handbook,* and what actually *is* policy is neither clear nor widely understood. Second, the apparent "policy" (statement adopted by Elementary Principals Association but not included in the *Administrators' Handbook*) is precise in a vague way. That is, the statements about "above grade level" and "below grade level" give an air of logic and precision to an indefinite thing: what is grade level?

Is grade level that point at which most children should achieve? Is it reading level as reflected in a given set of publisher's textbooks? Is it grade placement on a standardized examination? Because this is a very complex phenomenon, a few illustrations may be in order. Technically, grade level is that point on some achievement measure at which *most* children fall: the modal value. With any large number of youngsters this modal value is also the mid point or median, just as with any sizeable group grade level also represents the average or arithmetical mean achievement level for the particular students involved.

Speaking precisely, then, grade level represents that point above which 50 per cent of any average group of youngsters achieve and below which 50 per cent achieve. In other words, grade level represents a mid point *by definition,* and by definition half the children are at that point or below. For any teacher or parent to expect *most* youngsters or all youngsters to achieve at grade level or above is to expect an arithmetical impossibility. To relegate any child who achieves "below grade level" to a "D" or "E" grade is to guarantee failure for extended periods of time to large segments of any average student body. There are some who feel that it is something less than moral to compel children by law to attend a school and then devise a system of evaluation which assures their continuing failure. This policy, if it is policy, must be reexamined and redefined.

Because of the existing paradox, this committee recommends that the Riverside Board of Public Instruction adopt an experimental attitude toward grading and reporting to parents, and encourage those schools which so desire to develop new and different ways of reporting pupil progress, if they agree to study these new procedures carefully and systematically.

Recommendations to Teachers.   The most significant observation about students' achievements is its variability. The range in achievement at the first grade level is between three and four years; at the fourth grade level between five and six years; and at the sixth grade level between seven and eight years in reading comprehension, vocabulary, the mechanics of English composition, literary knowledge, science, geography, and history. To assume that all children either *do* or *should* achieve at *grade level* is to be professionally naive. Sophisticated teachers recognize that variations in achievement exist in first grade and increase consistently from that point on. Further, they devise means of evaluation which are predicated upon this basic notion; they recognize that the only real basis for and best measure of what a child should achieve in a given area is past achievement in that area.

Suppose, for example, that at the beginning of sixth grade one youngster was reading at third grade level. Suppose that through diligent effort and good instruction he was able to achieve at fifth grade level by the end of that school year. According to present policy that student should receive a "D" or "E" grade, even though he made two years growth in one academic year. Teachers must work to encourage changes in the basic assumptions inherent in the present "policy."

Probably no area of professional activity reflects a greater lack of professional competence than the area of teacher-made tests. One illustration may suffice. A teacher prepares a list of 20 questions and "gives a test." Each question counts 5 points; the number of correct answers is multiplied by 5, and a percentage score determined. This percentage score is then interpreted in a table, A-94 to 100, etc. and "grades" assigned. Several questionable assumptions make this a very dubious practice.

First, assuming that each problem is of equal difficulty and equal importance is usually without basis. Further, unless teachers are very careful, the 20 items selected will seldom be representative of what was supposed to be measured. Also, 70 per cent is probably far too low to represent satisfactory achievement. Who would want to fly in an airplane with a pilot who made 71 per cent on his flight exam? Examinations and tests should be teaching devices primarily and grading devices secondarily. Students whose achievement levels are below satisfactory should be retaught until they have learned, not told to "do better next time."

Averaging all grades together represents another stifling procedure. Suppose, for example, that the basic objective of a fifth grade spelling teacher was to have each child spell every one of 1000 selected words correctly by the end of that school year. If, on a final examination any youngster spelled every word correctly in the entire list but had only spelled half of them properly each week as he went along, the teacher who averages all grades together would incorrectly evaluate that child, who could and did spell every word without error. Averaging marks over a period of time makes sense logically but not psychologically. It seems plausible and reasonable to teachers and even students, but it punishes the slow starter and rewards the fast starter even though both may get to the same goal.

Finally, there is considerable evidence that teachers profess to evaluate achievement, but in actuality grade on neatness, politeness, and obedience. Teachers must clarify their expectations precisely and frequently, both to themselves and to their students. *Assuming* that all children know exactly what the purposes of a particular lesson are or what will count for a grade is a serious error, and it is one which all teachers must constantly strive to avoid. Likewise, teachers must constantly be aware of the limitations of their assumptions about grading. They dare not let a systematic, logical, mathematical approach to grading deter them from their basic purpose—helping children to learn. Learning is more important than grading.

Recommendations to Principals. Because there is some confusion and misunderstanding about grades and grading, each principal is encouraged to exert leadership with his faculty to explore the hidden assumptions and subtle meanings involved in everything to do with grades. A thorough understanding of the variations in grade level between publishers, for instance, or between test makers is important, and a knowledge of how to use test data, teacher-made or standardized, for instructional purposes is a major responsibility of instructional leaders. To ignore these problems is to abdicate professional responsibility.

An Area Council Studies
Academic Failure

How many students failed last year in Riverside and were retained? At which grade levels did these retentions occur most frequently? Is there any significance to the variations in proportion of retention from school to school or from grade level to grade level? Which schools fail the most students and why? Do students who fail do significantly better the following year? What are the policies about retention? When were these policies devised? How do teachers feel about these policies? Are they uniformly applied? Are there any children in one school who are retained who would not have been had they attended another school within Riverside district? What is the effect of failure upon students' motivation to do good work in school? How many students fail because of excessive absences? What is Riverside's policy about attendance workers and their efforts? Are there visiting teachers? Are there provisions for the home-bound when they are ill?

Getting simple figures on a district basis about the number of persons promoted and retained by school and by grade level may open up new vistas for study. Let us suppose that the average retention rate in grade seven is more than five times as high as the average retention rate in grade six over the past ten years. What does this mean? Why the sudden change? Are that many more students really less able in grade seven than they were in grade six? What are the attitudes of junior high school teachers toward assisting youngsters in the transition from elementary-self-contained classrooms to the complex departmentalized set-ups of junior high school? Are there opportunities to preserve some of the stability of the elementary situation to help youngsters "bridge the gap" more easily and more adequately? Would a block of time in seventh grade reduce the failures in junior high? Will special guidance and counseling services for adolescents help them achieve?

Questions like these enable one to move into the problem of why students fail. Studying the effect of failure upon student development may give indications of areas in which curriculum change can most readily occur. Does the fault lie with the student himself or with the teacher or the curriculum materials themselves? How can the school help each youngster to release his personal potential? Do some teachers actually drive students out of school? What is it that these teachers say and do which makes work difficult for these low achievers? Is this behavior verifiable, or does it represent, instead, students' fears and apprehensions? How can supervisors work with such teachers? Are tests available or can they be devised which would enable principals to make more accurate estimates of teachers' own basic drives? What is good teaching? Who are the good teachers? Can principals rank their teachers in terms of general effectiveness? Would it be possible from a group of more than one thousand teachers to identify the 100 most able and the 100 least able? Could these teachers be asked to participate in an intensive study designed to identify observational techniques or test items which would discriminate among teachers according to ability? If such a test instrument could be devised, would it have utility in selecting prospective teachers? Could universities and colleges be encouraged to be more selective in their teacher education programs using these studies as a basis? What behaviors characterize good teachers and what behaviors characterize poor teachers?

Any consideration of problems such as these poses other problems. Studying what motivates youngsters to do good work in school is a legitimate area for curriculum study up to the point that precise looks at teachers are involved. Problems involving teachers are tough to skirt and tough to handle because some of the most significant aspects of the learning situation are being touched upon—the nature of the teacher's impact upon student development. Raising the issue may be a worthwhile professional experience.

Academic Failure:
A Study of Unsuccessful Students in
Riverside Schools

The Problem

Last year, 2512 students failed in Riverside Public Schools and were retained at the same grade level for the next school year. The rate of failure was particularly high at the first, seventh, and tenth grade levels. The purpose of this study was to uncover some of the factors involved in the failure of students in the seventh and tenth grades of Riverside Public Schools so that parents, teachers, and principals would be better able to help these students have more worthwhile educational experiences. Research in education clearly indicates that successful experiences facilitate learning. Although a non-promotional experience may be appropriate for a given child, it is not in the best interest of children in most cases of failure in our schools today.

The Procedures

There were 379 seventh grade and 223 tenth grade students in Riverside Public Schools who received failing grades in two or more subjects for last year and who were recommended to be retained in the same grades this year. Questionnaires were sent to all schools in which these students were in attendance last year. One hundred twenty-three or 32 per cent of the seventh grade and ninety or 40 per cent of the tenth grade questionnaires were returned. The cumulative records of these boys and girls were examined carefully to determine reasons for failure and retention.

A select group of lay people conducted depth interviews with a representative group of tenth grade students who were retained last year. These interviews were recorded on a tape recorder and the tapes have been studied by qualified professional educators.

The findings from the questionnaires and tape recorded interviews have been used in the preparation of this report, which is intended as an exploratory study aimed at opening up new possibilities rather than resulting in convenient solutions.

The Results

This study identified several characteristics of these students who have been retained in the seventh and tenth grades throughout this school year.

Personal Characteristics.   In the seventh grade, this student was a boy in 63 per cent of the cases, who had an average age of thirteen years, eight months as of June 1. His health was generally good, but was considered poor enough to have affected his academic achievement in 19 per cent of the cases. The socioeconomic level of his home was often average but was considered low in 48 percent of the homes represented. In the tenth grade, this failing student was a boy in 70 per cent of the cases who had an average age of sixteen years, one month as of June 1. His health also was generally good, being poor enough to affect his school work and attendance in only 10 per cent of the cases. The socioeconomic level was considered low in 56 per cent of the cases.

Educational Characteristics.   Intelligence tests have been recorded for 76 per cent of the seventh grade students and indicate an intelligence quotient of over 100 in 26 per cent, between 90–100 in 24 per cent, and below 90 in 50 per cent of the cases. One third of these students had been retained once previously and one tenth had been retained more than once. He received failing grades in most of the academic subjects but slightly more often in mathematics and slightly less often in science. His attendance was generally poor with a record of more than ten days absence during the year.

In the tenth grade, intelligence tests were on record for 79 per cent of the students who were retained and indicate an intelligence quotient of over 100 in 48 per cent of the cases, between 90–100 in 32 per cent, and below 90 in 20 per cent of the cases. One fourth of these students have been retained once previously and 3 per cent have been retained more than once. He received failing grades much more often in science and much less often in social studies than in other academic subjects. His attendance record showed that he generally had less than ten days absence during the school year.

General Observations.   Throughout this study an effort was made to find general characteristics of these students that might not have been readily apparent from specific statistical data. These observations were made after studying all questionnaires and tape recordings.

The number of children who have left school since the seventh grade have shown in the statistical data appearing in the tenth grade. The average age was seven months younger relative to his grade than was the average age of the failing seventh grade student. This would indicate that the older children have generally dropped out of school. The better school attendance at the tenth grade level seemed to indicate that those with poor attendance may have left school. There were fewer instances of students with a previous record of retention in the tenth grade than in the seventh grade, and most of those who had been retained were retained since the seventh grade. This too would indicate that a large number of students retained in elementary grades might have dropped out of school before reaching the tenth grade. There were many subtle indications throughout this study that non-promotion and dropouts are closely related.

There was an attitude that seemed to characterize all the parties concerned in non-promotion. The student did not seem to care that he had failed. It was not determined whether this lack of concern resulted in failure or from failure. Many of these students apparently had no clearly defined aspirations or goals for themselves. They were vague and uncertain in their answers to questions about what they wanted to do or where they wanted to go. There was even a strong indication that a large number of those who were interviewed had lost contact with reality. In many cases they seemed unable to acknowledge, even to themselves, that they were not doing well in school.

The school also seemed to lack real concern for a failure. This study showed that the school had devoted more time to rationalizing a failure than to studying the reasons for failure and remedying them. This same lack of concern was sensed in the homes of these children. These homes were not often very involved in the problems of education of these children. Throughout this study there were apparent home factors affecting the education of failing boys and girls, which too often reflected a lack of sincere concern for education.

Conclusions and Recommendations

Specific recommendations were directed to particular groups who have certain responsibilities in the development of education in Riverside Public Schools.

Riverside Board of Public Instruction. There were a few cases in which the health of the child prohibited his physical presence in school but would not have prevented his having been taught at home. A survey should be made to determine the need for a teacher to teach homebound students since this present study indicates that the number of children who failed because they were sick at home was much more a problem in the seventh grade than in the tenth grade.

A need for a much broader guidance program in the elementary schools was indicated. Many potential dropouts can be identified while they are in elementary school. The immediate goal should be the securing of one guidance resource person for every 1000 students in elementary schools and one full-time counselor for each 500 students in junior and senior high school.

Emphasis and development of the visiting teacher program is very important since the unsuccessful student generally is having attendance problems. Because many of these problems are the result of home and community situations, the present visiting teacher program should be expanded by the addition of personnel with training and experience in school social work. The ultimate goal should be one school social worker for each 3000 students.

There is a need to expand the present psychological services to five trained, full-time school psychologists. Since many of these children who have been retained need psychological services beyond those possible in the local school, the school psychologists must be able to work not only with the students on identifying their problems, but also with the teachers and parents, and must follow through cooperatively with community agencies in an effort to assist the students in solving their problems.

The students involved in non-promotion need the individual attention of professional teachers, which is not possible in an overcrowded classroom. The pupil-teacher ratio should be such that these students may receive more understanding guidance with the problems that caused their failure in school. The basic assumption of the Riverside policy relative to grading should be carefully reviewed. This study indicated a wide difference of standards between schools and even between teachers within a single school. The evaluation of students' progress also varied from school to school. Every effort should be made to develop a policy that will more clearly define standards and communicate more effectively the evaluation of every student's progress.

Curriculum Director, Riverside Public Schools. There is an urgent need to continue studies underway and to develop further action research projects. These have served to bring many problems in sharper focus and have opened up many new possibilities. Study must be continued by the area and district curriculum councils to make possible a real impact on school problems. Many of these projects and studies relate directly to the problem of non-promotion in our schools. Specifically, the curriculum director should strive to synthesize all of the research findings pertinent to these various problems and present possible courses of action before the superintendent and the school board.

The curriculum director should also become involved in the development of a curriculum planned to meet the specific needs of these pupils who are not experiencing success in school. This is a general problem that can best be improved by someone in a position to exercise general influence on the curriculum. There needs to be study on pre-vocational courses and experiences, vocational courses and experiences, and basic education to meet the needs of the low ability student.

School Principals. Principals of both elementary and secondary schools throughout the district should exercise aggressive leadership in attacking this problem of non-promotion. Because each case is an individual problem that relates only to each individual pupil, the problem becomes more complex as we view it from a district-wide vantage point. Profound effectiveness of our schools will be possible only if this problem is met at the local school level where the individual child is experiencing his educational problem.

Principals of elementary schools are encouraged by this study to consider the applications of competent male teachers for appointment as elementary school teachers. Previous research has indicated that male students who are underachievers respond more positively to strong, supporting male teachers than to women instructors.

Individual Teacher. The classroom teacher remains the most effective force to bring about successful experiences for all children. It is recommended that he utilize every possible school or community service to increase his effectiveness with this student who is experiencing failure, has experienced failure, and will continue to experience failure as long as his individual problem continues unsolved.

Finally, and perhaps most important of all, each teacher must examine his own philosophy regarding the purposes of education. The fact that fewer than 50 per cent of the adults over twenty-five years of age in Riverside have completed high school seems to indicate that something is happening in school which causes many of the young people to drop out from every segment of society. It seems evident that many teachers set standards and contrive a logic to their testing and grading systems which guarantee unsuccessful educational experiences for many boys and girls.

What can teachers do?

Be Positive. Nearly all evidence in learning theory supports the thesis that praise is better than reproof and that success facilitates learning more than failure. "Nothing succeeds like success."

Set Realistic Standards. Compelling children by law to go to school and then establishing achievement standards that are too high probably causes more problems for youngsters than it solves.

Clarify Objectives. After having set realistic standards, it is still not reasonable to expect children to "do better" or "try harder" without providing them with the incentive or the opportunity to reach appropriate goals. If neatness and politeness are desired objectives they should be worked toward in their own right. To profess one purpose and evaluate another confuses both parents and students.

Emphasize Teaching Rather Than Testing. Arrange teaching procedures so that students have an opportunity to learn from mistakes revealed in testing rather than having testing only for the purpose of determining grades. Averaging grades without allowing students to profit and learn from their mistakes assumes that what was *not* learned in one situation may be transferred as a learning experience to a new situation. This cannot be possible.

Be Human. Imagine what it would be like to have to go to school day after day experiencing frustration and failure. Strive to assure that every child has as many successful experiences as possible. Promote positive attitudes toward school by being positive toward students, liking them, accepting them, and nurturing their uniqueness and their individuality.

This problem of non-promotion cost the schools of Riverside District $800,000 this school year to repeat an educational experience that research has shown to be unsuccessful in a vast majority of the cases. It seems imperative to continue study of this problem and to give wide dissemination of those techniques which we as educators find to be effective for our own situations.

A Study of Students' Motivation to Do Good Work in School

The Problem

Creating a learning situation in which students learn involves at least some understanding of what it is that motivates young people to do good work in school. Some persons believe that motivation is essentially inherent; students come to school with their energies and enthusiasms for learning already a built-in part of their psychological framework. Others think that teachers must attempt to do something to learners "to motivate them" so they will want to learn.

Faced with the problem of trying to get a sharper picture of students' motivations, a group of interested principals, teachers, and parents from Area Five Curriculum Council posed the following question: "What motivates young people to try to do good work in school?"

The Procedures

To answer this question, a very simple Sentence Completion Test was administered to approximately 1065 students in six elementary, six junior high, and six senior high schools in Riverside during the month of April. Approximately 400 fifth graders, 325 eighth graders, and 335 eleventh graders were asked to complete the following incomplete sentence two times: "I try to do good work in school when . . . ."

This procedure obviously represents a relatively gross attempt to assess students' motivation. However, previous studies have reported success with the device. Further, since the SCT is essentially a projective-type instrument, it was felt that this oblique way of probing youngsters' motivational structures might actually be more productive than a more direct approach.

Students were selected from the fifth, eighth, and eleventh grade levels in an effort to determine whether there were important differences in student motivation according to grade in school. The schools selected represented various geographical and socioeconomic sections in the district. In each case the sentences were completed under the guidance of a parent especially instructed for the purpose. Students were directed not to sign their names.

Following the data gathering sessions, responses from all students were put together and sorted into several broad categories. These categories were selected and defined after an initial inspection of several hundred responses. The complete sorting process involved four distinct stages.

First, five persons went through all of the responses together and sorted them into these major groupings: those which revolved around the teacher as a person or were related to something which the teacher did; those which clearly pertained to the individual student himself; those which involved recognition of some sort or other; and a miscellaneous group which included responses pertaining to the physical conditions of the room, an interest in the subject matter itself, etc.

Following this initial sorting, the responses in each category were sorted a second time for verification and then further divided into subcategories. Third, one person then sorted through all of the responses a final time, verifying placement in the broad categories and in the subcategories. Following completion of this final sorting process, a final breakdown was made according to grade level.

The Results

There were 2128 usable responses from approximately 1065 students. Of these responses, approximately 26 per cent related to the teacher, 38 per cent related to the student, and 36 per cent related to external factors of various types. Table 10 describes the proportion of these responses by grade level.

Table 10

Proportion of Responses in General
Categories According to Grade Level

Category	5th Grade	8th Grade	11th Grade
Teacher	20%	30%	31%
Student	45%	33%	36%
External factors	35%	37%	33%
TOTAL	100%	100%	100%

Several important observations are apparent from these data. First, no single category accounts for most of the responses. Second, there seems to be a definite indication of focal point of responses from student to teacher between the fifth and eleventh grades. In other words, students in the secondary school apparently placed greater dependence upon the teacher to get them to try to do good work in school than students in the elementary school. This fact is probably exactly opposite from that which might have been expected. This point will be explored in more detail later.

Table 11 describes in more detail the responses in each of the subcategories included in the general grouping under "teacher." For example, the following responses were included in these subgroupings: "I try to do good work in school when . . . ."

"I am not angry at the teacher or when I feel good. Sometimes the teacher makes me angry by saying I did something when I did not do it."

"I am not tired and the teachers aren't mad and when we discuss the subject."

"the teacher is not in a bad mood. And when a teacher *does not* tear you friendly."

"the teacher is not in a bad mood. And when a teacher *does not* tear you down in the class and make you feel like you're stupid. And when they give you a little encouragement in class, also."

"the teachers aren't crabby."

"the teacher gives me more freedom and doesn't gripe about every little thing."

"I enjoy class, the teacher, and the atmosphere I am in, also the people I am around. Some teachers in this school and many others are very BORING!"

"I can. That is most all the time. Sometimes when I am reading the teacher keeps on talking and it bothers me, then she asks questions and I cannot answer her because when I was reading she was talking. Sometimes I cannot read the board so it is hard for me to do my work."

"I am not bothered by anyone and when I have the material to work by. I try to do good work in school when I know how to do the problems, etc. When I cannot get much help on something and get real discouraged I do worse work or sometimes when I do it by myself it comes out better."

"I have a good teacher. When I say good teacher I mean one who makes it clear what she's trying to explain. One who doesn't give you a lot of questions to answer from the book then take it up."

"I have the cooperation of the teacher and can see that he wants to teach us as well as he can about that particular subject. If, however, the teacher is short on patience and easily gets mad, then I have very little desire to do my best for that teacher even though this action will hurt my grade."

"I know the teacher is helping you all he can, and it will help me in later life."

"I like the teachers that are teaching me, and when I am in a friendly class. When I get an urge to do good work."

"my teachers, principals, and school mates are interested in me. In other words, when my environment is fairly good."

"my teacher appreciates it and gives it the due credit, and when I respect the teacher."

"I'm asked to or if the teacher tells me to do my school work. I will obey school rules. Whenever I am asked to do something I shall do it and not say anything."

"the teacher knows how to keep order. But there are discussions, and when the subject is interesting. But more than anything else I like a teacher who is not boring. (And when the class is not overcrowded.)"

"conditions around me are pleasant. Some teachers bring about a kid not liking one subject—they really put a scare into them where they don't want to come to school. The teacher's personality and humor have a lot to do with a kid doing good work in school."

"The teacher likes me and when I like my teacher very, very much, and when I am happy and gay, and when my school friends like me I do my work as best I can in school."

"I understand the work real well and feel good. Sometimes I just can't get interested in the work enough to do it. I like to do school work if the teacher doesn't give me too much or make me mad or anything. Right now I'm not interested."

"I am encouraged by the teacher and feel that they like me. It is much harder to do good work when I feel uneasy around the teacher."

Table 12 describes those responses which related directly to the student himself. For example, the responses were typical of statements included in this category: "I try to do good work in school when . . . ."

"I study, practice, and study some more. Also when I keep my mind on my work. I go to bed early each night so I may do good work—but I don't. I'm a natural born oaf."

"I think it will help in future plans. I also try to do good work so that I can make my parents proud of my work. I also try to get good grades so I can get ahead in the business world."

"I am good, when I am not scared or excited, when I am paying attention and not talking and not being fussed at."

"I feel confident that I may be able to do the work I am given."

"I set myself a goal and am encouraged to reach it."

"I want to, or when I am too lazy. Sometimes I try to do good work, and I can do good work if I try, but I never try. I can get my class work and tests OK, but my homework I never do because I am too lazy."

"I am in a good mood. I really try to do good work any time in the year, because I want my grades to come up this year even if it is just a little bit. Thank you."

"I understand the work, feel like doing it, and have the ambition, which is seldom, because I'm usually worried about other things, and school work has no special appeal to me."

"I can. With the pull that is on students to participate in outside activities, this can prove to be very difficult at times. Church work, school work, club work—which is most important? I try to divide my time to include all three."

Table 11

Proportion of Responses Related
to Teacher

Sub-Category	5th Grade	8th Grade	11th Grade
Material is pre- sented clearly	2%	3%	2%
Student likes teacher and subject	8	9	8
Teacher makes the subject interesting	1	2	8
Teacher is not grouchy	1	3	2
Teacher is in a good mood	0	2	1
Teacher is fair and understanding	1	2	2
Discipline is main- tained	0	2	1
Teacher assigns work to be done	6	4	2
Teacher shows interest in student	1	3	5
TOTAL	20%	30%	31%

"I think of the importance of doing good school work. Making all 'A's' is not so important to me. The most important thing to me is doing my best in my school work."

"I think about it. I try to do good work but Dad and Mom say all I think about is boys. And I always sit in the back of the room and I hardly hear and I always have the urge to talk and I always do."

"I want to. When I want to do good work in school I can do good work. That is, if I have girls off my mind. Most of the time I have girls on my mind, and when I do I can't do good work."

"I am not nervous and my eyes do not hurt and when I feel good. I love school, but when I do not feel good I hate it."

"I am not tired and I don't feel sick and I understand my work. And I try to do my best work when I don't have much work to do."

"I think of how our nation is advancing in knowledge. I believe that every student should do the best he can today in school because most jobs in life today require more education than before. We must try to better ourselves more than our parents, who didn't have as much of an opportunity as we do today in our schools."

"I am not overloaded with extra school activities such as magazine drives, selling tickets to plays, etc."

"I see that my work is finished and checked over before it is turned in."

"I feel good. Mostly I try to do good work all the time. When the teachers feel good and when I don't have a lot of pressure upon me."

"I get a good breakfast and get enough sleep, and when I am feeling well."

Table 12

Proportion of Various Responses Related to the Student

Sub-Category	5th Grade	8th Grade	11th Grade
Use certain study habits	6%	4%	1%
Enough time to study	2	1	1
Will be useful to me someday	1	4	13
When I feel good	16	12	11
When I am not afraid or worrying	1	1	0
When it is necessary	0	1	1
When I try	3	4	4
Whenever I can; all the time	16	6	5
TOTAL	45%	33%	36%

From these figures, it would appear that students' feelings are important in understanding their motivation to do good work in school. Further, it would also seem that older students are much more concerned about the relationship of school experiences to their future lives than younger students.

In Table 13 the proportion of students' responses which have been included in this category related to external factors are described. This category included statements which youngsters made about working for better grades, about what their parents might say, etc. For instance, the following quotations were included in this category: "I try to do good work in school when . . . ."

"I need the money my dad pays me for good grades."

"there is an especially big test, when something I particularly like is being studied, when there is a chance to get ahead or make some money by doing well on a certain test, and when I just feel like working."

"ever my mother says she will give one dollar for every 'C.'

"I think about my car being taken away, when I think about college, and when I think about the $5 I will collect for each 'A.' "

"I don't have many things to do. I also do it for my parents, because I don't like to be called dumb."

"People don't come and boss me around and call me dumb, for that just doesn't go with me."

"Betsy tells me to and when Betsy makes 'A's' I make 'A's.' Betsy is a smart and intelligent girl, but she is unfaithful."

"my parents say I get some money for bringing home a good report card."

"I need to make up for previous low grades in order to have a high 'B' or 'A' for the six weeks grade. Also, I am pressured by my parents to maintain high grades."

"I am playing sports so that I won't be dropped from the team. I also try to do good work in school when I know I'm going to need my father's car."

"I know that if I don't I will be restricted. As an example, I was restricted this six weeks because I made bad grades in three of my subjects. Therefore, to get off restriction I must work harder to get a better grade."

"I enjoy a subject and I am not forced into any kind of embarrassment."

"I am required to do so to protect my pride and pass the year and watch my teachers smile at me for making a good grade."

"I am doing S.R.A."

"It is something I like to do and when the work is for my education."

"I can take the subject I want."

"I know that it is very important to my grades. If there is an important test, I will study harder and do my best, but when I know it does not matter, I don't bother to do anything."

"ever I'm not bothered or distracted by other people, although some of my teachers just bore me with stuff I already know."

"I especially want my parents to be proud of me and want them to know that I'm capable of their belief in me that I can do good work."

"Mother brags to others about my achievements, so that I will not disappoint her or myself and therefore I can maintain my record."

"I am trying to please my mother. She is so pleased when I make good grades, so I try to make good grades for her."

"I'm not pressured. Last year my grades were 'B' and because of this my parents neither restricted me nor tried to force me to make good grades. This year my grades are not too good and right away I am restricted and am being pressured by my parents and teachers. I have lost the desire to work hard toward a college education."

Table 13

Proportion of Responses Related to
Various External Factors

Sub-Category	5th Grade	8th Grade	11th Grade
When I get good grades or for a test	13%	13%	15%
When I have the approval of others	1	3	3
When people don't push me around	0	1	1
Teacher is out of the room	1	1	0
The room is quiet and cool	11	10	3
The subject is interesting	6	8	10
Miscellaneous	3	1	1
TOTAL	35%	37%	33%

Conclusions and Recommendations

After a careful study of the data, two conclusions seem warranted. First, no single factor accounts for a significant proportion of the total number of responses, although five factors do account for approximately half of the responses. Second, there appears to be a definite shift in the sense of responsibility for doing good work in school from the student to the teacher over a period of time.

No Single Factor Important. Throughout this study it was apparent that students try to do good work in school for many reasons. Significantly, no single kind of response accounts for a large portion of the total responses. This would seem to imply that students' motivational patterns are both diverse and complex.

A careful examination of the data indicated that five types of responses did account for about half of the total number: interest in the subject matter, liking the teacher and the subject, grades and other forms of recognition, the students' physical and emotional status, and the physical factors in the classroom situation (light, temperature, distractions, etc.).

Responsibility for Learning. Perhaps the most remarkable generalization drawn from this study relates to the fact that there seemed to be an unmistakable shift in the sense of responsibility from student to teacher over a period of time. In other words, younger students seemed to evidence greater personal initiative and inherent motivation while older students apparently assumed that teachers ought to do something to make them want to learn. In effect, older students seemed to place greater dependence upon the teacher than younger students for their own learning. Increased independence and personal initiative would be expected, theoretically, at least, and hoped for among more mature students.

Considering all of the data and the major conclusions described thus far, these recommendations seem to be in order.

Recommendations to Teachers. Since youngsters apparently are motivated by a whole host of factors and since no single factor seems to be especially important to a sizeable segment of any group, teachers are urged to select and devise a variety of instructional techniques in their efforts both to tap and to create students' motivations to do good work in school. Simultaneously, teachers should also strive to cultivate an intense awareness of each student's total way of behaving. That is, since some students seem to respond positively to approval, others to marks in school, others to direct instructions, others to optimum room conditions, and others to a variety of additional factors, teachers must continuously study their own students carefully for clues as to what it is that motivates them to do good work in school. In the opinion of the persons conducting this study, *the most effective teacher will be that one who is most able to "fit" his instructional techniques to each child's unique needs.* In effect, the art of teaching may very well lie within this realm of "fitting" methods to each learner.

Teachers must also demonstrate an obvious concern for students and their personal feelings. The data in this study repeatedly showed a concern among students about their own physical and emotional health, and about others' feelings toward them. Students are, first of all, people, and they must be treated as human beings first and learners second. Physical and emotional needs are more basic than the desire to know.

Finally, one of the "hidden" facts which persistently recurred throughout this study was the effect of the impact of a teacher's personality upon a learner. This is an especially important point, because a teacher's actions and behaviors are manipulable, they are factors which he can vary and control. It is strongly recommended that teachers consciously strive to *use* their personality as a major tool to implement their education purposes. The vigorous impact of a dynamic personality upon a learner may do more to promote motivation toward school than any amount of exhortation.

Recommendations to Administrators. This study demonstrates the complex task facing teachers attempting to evoke or capture students' motivations. "Individualizing instruction" has to be more than a byword; it must be achieved. The gradual but persistent tendency to increase the number of youngsters with whom a teacher must work each day, however, is in direct contradiction to this essential objective.

If administrators are really concerned about devising circumstances in which a teacher can teach and a child can learn, they must provide innumerable opportunities for students and teachers to have close, intimate learning experiences. In effect, creative administrators will seek to contrive organizational patterns which maximize personal contacts between teachers and students. Large classes and large group instruction appear to facilitate those purposes of education which are directly related to the dissemination of information, but they also appear directly antithetical to increasing or tapping students' motivation. Providing information is not enough. Students must be helped to make this information an integral part of their lives. This task, which is difficult under the most favorable circumstances, is probably impossible when teachers have large classes every day.

Questions for Further Study. During the course of this research, several questions arose which seemed to warrant further study. They are listed below.

1. What do teachers think motivates students to do good work in school? How do their ideas compare with the results actually obtained from students in this study?
2. What do students really learn when their parents give them money for getting good grades in school? Are all of these learnings desirable?
3. What type of home situation is most conducive to fostering desirable attitudes toward school in general and learning in particular?
4. What type of organizational pattern in a school will best enable teachers to utilize and to promote students' motivation?

An Area Council Studies Motivation and Achievement

Most of the studies described so far have been simple in design, but some area councils may demonstrate an almost academic interest in certain topics. Their immediate problems may not be as pressing as their desire for a deeper, longer look at the basic phases of the learning process. In such a case different kinds of questions are asked that result in a different type of curriculum study.

What is motivation? Who are the motivated students? What are they like? How do they see themselves and others? What kinds of personality patterns do they reflect? Is there any relationship between their personal and social adjustment and their success in school? How do these youngsters respond to stress? What kind of deep-seated needs do these students evidence? How do their teachers see them? Do certain teachers "bring more out of" highly motivated pupils than other teachers? Is there such a thing as institutional press or school climate that reflects itself in the motivation or achievement patterns of young people? What is an underachiever? What causes underachievement? Is there such a thing as overachievement? Will a comparative study of over- and underachievers indicate any directions for teachers or administrators? What is the relationship of socioeconomic factors to underachievement? How do these socioeconomic factors manifest themselves in affecting achievement?

Questions such as these indicate concern with a major aspect of education. During the course of planning sessions, the curriculum supervisor should single out attitudes and examine them with care. For instance, what is expected achievement? How do teachers define or determine in their own mind how much any given child "ought" to achieve? Are these standards reasonable? What assumptions underlie their use? Are there any major disagreements in the council itself concerning the utility of definitions and assumptions? For example, what kind of achievement record should one expect from a youngster with an IQ of 110? 85? 140? Is there a direct relationship between ability as measured by a conventional IQ scale and achievement in school? Is this relationship tenable? If a child with an IQ of 90 makes straight A's in junior high school, does this mean the IQ test is not valid, that the child is doing more than should be expected, that the teacher's grading system is unrealistic, that standards are too low? On the other hand, if a pupil has an IQ of 125 and he makes straight C's, how does one answer these very same questions? Do emotional factors enter into the picture at all? How do we measure these emotional overtones? Are they really basic determinants of achievement, or annoying side issues basically irrelevant to the problem at hand?

Some people maintain that what an individual thinks of himself and others has considerable influence on his motivational structure and his achievement level. Is this correct? What is self concept? How do we measure it? What things exist within the educational situation which make any appreciable impact upon a youngster's concept of himself? Is this something which changes readily or persists more or less in the same form from year to year? Are people born with certain kinds of conceptions about their self or are these learned?

Many studies have been made on these problems, but many teachers have not had an opportunity to study these research reports themselves. However, self concept considered in the abstract is one thing, and self concept as a factor affecting learning in "my very own" classroom is another.

In the discussions which must inevitably precede commitment to any given problem area, questions such as these reflect a deep and abiding interest in the fundamental problems of human learning and with understanding what it is that helps children learn. They provide a good basis for entering into intensive studies of the problems involved.

Given an opportunity of this scope will mean, however, that several steps will be necessary before an area council begins work. Considering the complexities involved, it would be appropriate for the supervisor to meet with a smaller group of the area council, perhaps some of those principals who seem especially interested, and plan details with them. Because the problem is of greater proportions than others described, the principals may need a special opportunity to work carefully with the supervisor so that they will not demonstrate lack of knowledge before the entire group.

This calls for an exceptional sensitivity; it will be necessary for the curriculum worker to sift out the genuine reluctance and dissatisfaction from the hesitance based on inexperience and lack of skill. Keeping communication channels open and maintaining free and easy relationships will be important; inviting criticisms and reactions as progress is made will be valuable.

A Study of Several Factors Related to Motivation and Achievement of Fifth Grade Students

This study represents the concerted efforts of school administrators, teachers, and parents to examine in detail a complex phenomenon—student behavior. Early in the study certain dissatisfactions arose with the basic design, but hoping that some worthwhile information might evolve despite these limitations, the members of Area Four Curriculum Council pressed their activities to completion. All of the data and every possible conclusion were examined with great care by each member of the council, and though the writing was accomplished by one person, the thinking of many is reflected in this case study.

The reader is cautioned that the limitations of this study place an extra burden upon him to use these data with genuine reserve. For instance, since the completion of the project one critic has pointed out that some of the statistical procedures may actually have been inappropriate. The report is presented here primarily as an illustration of the kind of research that public school people can tackle if they desire, and further, in the hope that some of the data may provoke additional interest in a very important but "slippery" educational problem.

The Problem

American schools today are faced with the problem of helping young people learn vast amounts of information in short periods of time. In effect, schools are confronted with the task of maximizing student achievement. In an effort to explore some of the factors affecting achievement, the members of Area Four Curriculum Council posed the following general questions. Who are the high motivated students? Who are the low motivated students? Who are the overachievers? Who are the underachievers? What are they like? How do these students compare and how do they differ?

Specifically, these particular questions were examined in some detail. First, what is the precise relationship of various personality characteristics to academic achievement and motivation? Second, is it possible to determine the kind of impact different teachers have upon students' development? Third, does the "climate" of a total school or the size of a given class have any appreciable effect upon youngsters' growth?

The Procedures

To answer these questions, a five-phase study was initiated. First, all of the fifth grade students in several elementary schools in Riverside School District were measured with the motivation index. Second, students who scored in the upper and lower 20 per cent on the motivation scale were identified for further study. Third, the achievement records of these high motivated and low motivated students were examined for variations from the expected achievement levels. Fourth, the over- and underachieving students who had previously been identified as high motivated were separated from the over- and underachieving students who had been identified as low motivated. Fifth, these students were studied intensively.

Measuring Motivation. All of the fifth graders in 15 elementary schools in Riverside were administered a modified Junior Index of Motivation. In all, 1216 students were involved. The Junior Index of Motivation (JIM Scale) (1) as modified is a 40-item "Yes-No"-type questionnaire read aloud to elementary students by their teacher. The JIM Scale measures students' motivational levels. The validity of the instrument has not been established with elementary students, since it was originally developed for use with junior high school pupils. It was expected that the present study might actually provide certain data relative to this question, however.

Selecting Upper and Lower Groups. From the total sample of 1216 students, the upper and lower 20 per cent, as measured by the motivation index, were isolated for further study. Specifically, this included those students who scored 31 or above on the JIM Scale and those who scored 22 or below. The mean JIM Scale score for all 1216 children was 24.46, with a standard deviation of 4.62.

Identification of Over- and Underachievers. The next step involved identifying overachievers and underachievers from the high motivated and low motivated groups. For purposes of this study, it was assumed that students' achievement could be expected to vary according to their ability to learn, as measured by the Kuhlmann-Anderson IQ test. In other words, achievement level, as measured by grade placement in reading and arithmetic on the California Achievement Battery, was expected to vary one tenth of a grade level for each point of IQ either way from 100. For example, if a student had an IQ of 100 and was tested in October of the fifth grade, (fifth year, second month) his expected achievement as measured by a standardized test would have been at 5.2 grade level. If he actually achieved at 6.2 grade level or higher, however, this child was assumed to be an overachiever. On the other hand, if a child's IQ was 107, his expected achievement level should be 5.9 (i.e., 5.2 plus .7). If his achievement as measured by a standardized test was actually at 4.9 grade level or lower, this pupil was assumed to be an underachiever.

For the purposes of this study, only those students who were achieving at least one or more full grade levels *above* expected in either reading or arithmetic, but who were also overachieving to some degree in the other area, were considered to be overachievers. Further, only those students who were achieving at least one or more full grade levels *below* expected in either reading or arithmetic, but who were also underachieving to some degree in the other area, were considered to be underachievers.

Comparison of Groups.   Those students who were identified as high motivated overachievers, high motivated underachievers, low motivated overachievers, and low motivated underachievers were isolated for further study (2). Specifically, they were subjected to a series of controlled observations, including measurement with the California Test of Personality, Bills' Index of Adjustment Values, Sarason's General Anxiety Scale and Test Anxiety Scale, and a 12-item Sentence Completion Test instrument. In every case students were segregated from their regular classes and tested by specially trained persons who were unknown to them. Sometime after this testing session certain other data were also collected from students' cumulative record folders, including the names of their fourth and fifth grade teachers and the size of the class they were in during grade four.

The Results

Out of the total sample of 1216 fifth graders initially measured with the Junior Index of Motivation, 249 high motivated and 235 low motivated students were selected for further study. From these two groups, 23 high motivated overachievers (HMOA), 68 high motivated underachievers (HMUA), 39 low motivated overachievers (LMOA), and 33 low motivated underachievers (LMUA) were isolated for intensive study. Table 14 summarizes certain pertinent data about these 163 youngsters, including the results of analysis of variance and chi square tests of significance, where appropriate.

Several observations are immediately apparent from these data. First, more boys were overachievers and more girls underachievers. Second, overachievers tended to have lower IQ's than underachievers, regardless of their motivational level. (This may be due to the regression factor, and this point will be explored in more detail later.) Third, high motivated students tended to have higher personality scores, regardless of their IQ level. Fourth, high motivated students tended to make slightly higher achievement scores both

Table 14

Comparison of Various Groups of Fifth
Graders on Different Measures

Test	N Total	HMOA 23	HMUA 68	LMOA 39	LMUA 33	Statistical Significance
N Boys	15	29	28	16	9.67*
N Girls	8	39	11	17	
Motivation Index	31.78	32.85	19.85	19.24	634.44**
Kuhlmann-Anderson IQ	93.61	119.09	87.33	114.27	105.01**
California Personality (total)	113.13	115.55	89.84	98.37	18.23**
Grade Placement Reading	5.62	5.99	4.91	5.56	6.10**
Grade Placement Arithmetic	5.65	5.79	5.31	5.47	5.50**
General Anxiety	11.30	8.68	15.33	14.00	7.51**
Test Anxiety	14.22	13.15	13.23	12.85	.11

* Chi Square significant at .05 level with 3 df.
** F-ratio significant at .01 level with 3 and 159 df.

in reading and arithmetic than low motivated students, regardless of IQ. Fifth, high motivated students, tended to evidence less general anxiety than low motivated students, regardless of IQ level, though overachievers seemed to be slightly more anxious than underachievers. Sixth, there seemed to be no significant differences in test anxiety scores, as measured in this study.

Students' Personality. Table 15 shows a comparison of the mean subscores on the California Test of Personality for the various groups involved in this study. These data seem to indicate that high motivated students consistently made higher adjustment scores than low motivated students. Further, with a few important exceptions, underachievers tended to make consistently higher adjustment scores than overachievers when the motivation factor was held constant.

Finally, in the high motivated groups, both over- and underachievers made similar scores in the personal adjustment portion of the test, but with one exception (family relations), high motivated overachievers consistently made lower social adjustment scores than high motivated underachievers. In the low motivated group, overachievers consistently made lower scores on both the personal and social adjustment portions of the tests.

Table 16 shows the number of students from each of the four groups who scored in the different categories of the Index of Adjustment Values. It is apparent from these data that no statistically significant differences existed among the various members of these groups according to the way they saw themselves and others, as measured by the IAV.

Table 15

Comparison of Mean Scores of Various Groups of Fifth Graders on Sub Sections of California Test of Personality

Sub Area of Test	N	HMOA 23	HMUA 68	LMOA 39	LMUA 33	F-ratio
Self Reliance		7.52	7.59	6.44	7.15	2.76
Sense of Personal Worth		8.91	9.22	7.62	7.88	5.10
Sense of Personal Freedom		10.17	10.07	8.49	9.45	5.81*
Feeling of Belonging		10.35	10.57	8.33	9.85	13.79*
Withdrawing Tendencies		8.61	8.43	5.31	5.94	12.86*
Nervous Symptoms		9.13	8.94	6.69	6.70	9.65*
(Personal Adjustment)		54.69	54.82	42.88	46.97	14.01*
Social Standards		10.13	10.92	9.46	9.82	14.06*
Social Skills		9.22	9.97	7.87	8.91	10.33*
Anti-Social Tendencies		9.52	9.71	6.82	7.64	17.24*
Family Relations		10.26	10.03	7.69	8.24	9.19*
School Relations		9.70	9.69	6.97	7.27	12.85*
Community Relations		9.61	10.41	8.15	9.52	12.48*
(Social Adjustment)		58.44	60.73	46.96	51.40	18.42*

* F-ratio significant at .01 level with 3 and 159 df.

Table 16

Comparison of Number of Students from Various Groups Who Scored in Different Categories of the Index of Adjustment Values

Group	N	Categories				CHI SQUARE
		$++$	$-+$	$+-$	$--$	
HMOA	23	10	4	9	0	
HMUA	68	28	16	20	4	
						2.20
LMOA	39	15	6	16	2	
LMUA	33	14	5	12	2	

Chi Square not significant with 6 df. Categories $+ -$ and $- -$ combined so that expected frequencies would exceed five cases, as required for computational purposes.)

Following are responses of students in each of the four groups to the Sentence Completion Test-type statements. All of these responses were sorted into categories one time and then resorted for verification. Because these data are relatively involved, only the more obvious interpretations will be discussed.

In completing the sentence, "I have the most fun when . . ." more low motivated underachievers' responses fit the "free play" category than high motivated overachievers', and more low motivated overachievers prefer organized, planned sports and games than students from the other three groups. Also, more high motivated overachievers said they had fun "with people" than youngsters in the other groups.

Few important differences seem apparent in responses to "most of the other students in this class . . ." However, in completing the item, "The best teachers are those who . . ." several important discrepancies are obvious. First, twice as many high motivated overachievers responded in terms related to good instruction than did high motivated underachievers; they preferred those teachers who "teach best." Second, more low motivated underachievers preferred teachers who were "nice," while high motivated underachievers preferred teachers who were "strict" and who "have control." Noticeably, several low motivated underachievers liked teachers who "aren't strict."

In finishing the sentence, "I try to do good work in school when . . ." high motivated overachievers wrote responses related to personal effort and initiative more frequently than students in the other groups. Being "happy" was more important to low motivated students and to high motivated overachievers than to the high motivated underachievers. The high motivated overachievers also try harder than the others when "there's a test."

"My mother is the kind of person . . ." evoked fewer "is kind and good" responses from low motivated overachievers, but more "likes children" from this same group than any other. Likewise, none of the high motivated over- achievers saw their mother as a person who "has fun," though they did see her as one who "likes to do things."

Another statement which brought forth several interesting variations was "I like a teacher . . . ." Here many more overachievers prefered a teacher who "is nice," while more of the high motivated underachievers again men- tioned their preferences for "strict" teachers. Likewise, the low motivated underachievers again said that they preferred a teacher who was "not strict."

In examining the responses to "Good grades make me want to . . . ," more low motivated underachievers said "be happy," while more high moti- vated underachievers wanted to "show joy" and "keep them up." More high motivated overachievers resolved to "try harder," although all respondents showed this reaction to a noticeable degree.

"I think what I am doing right now will show *that I am a good worker"* the overachievers said more frequently than the underachievers. On the other hand, low motivated students tended to feel that what they were doing would show that they were "smart," whereas high motivated students were more likely to complete the sentence in terms which said that they felt it would show that they could "think." The high motivated underachiever seemed more certain that the response would indicate "how I feel."

"School is the kind of place where we *work,"* was more common among both groups of underachievers, while a greater proportion of high motivated overachievers stated that it was a place where they "like to go." More over- achievers than underachievers indicated that they "learned" at school, al- though the majority of *all* respondents said school was a place "where we learn."

More of the low motivated youngsters "feel sad" while high motivated over- achievers tended to "feel discouraged" in completing, "When I get poor marks in school I usually . . ." A sizeable minority of each group, however, indicated that poor marks generally caused them to "try harder."

Finally, in finishing the item, "My father is the kind of person who . . ." more high motivated students described their father as one who "is kind and good," while more low motivated overachievers said he was "mean."

Impact of the Teacher and the School. After collecting and examining these data, it was questioned whether or not individual teachers had a greater or lesser influence on students' motivation or achievement. The idea of class size also came up, so that it was decided to go back to each youngster's cumulative record and determine the name of his fourth and fifth grade teacher, and the size of class he had been in during his fourth grade experience. Although the students involved in this study were fifth graders, the various achievement and intelligence tests had been administered early in their fifth grade. It was assumed, therefore, that their fourth grade experience had exerted more influence upon their achievement than their brief experience in the fifth grade. Since the motivation scale was administered in the late part of the fifth grade, however, this same assumption was probably not correct, so that for purposes of assessing the effect of a teacher upon a student's motivation fifth grade teachers were identified.

Table 17 shows the mean size of class in which students in the various groups were enrolled during their fourth grade. Since the necessary information was not available for all students, the number in each of the four groups is less than the total number reported before.

Table 17

Comparison of Fourth Grade Class Size for
Students in Various Groups

Group	Number of students for whom data was available	Mean Class Size Fourth Grade	F-ratio
HMOA	16	30.94	
HMUA	53	31.17	
LMOA	21	27.14	7.68*
LMUA	19	36.26	

* F-ratio significant at .01 level with 3 and 105 df.

It seems obvious from these data that larger classes apparently had an adverse effect on low motivated students' achievement. However, both groups of overachievers, high motivated and low motivated, had fourth grade experience in smaller classes than either group of underachievers. The statistical significance of the variations in class size is reflected in an F-ratio of 7.68, which is significant beyond the .01 level of confidence.

In studying the relationship of teachers to students' motivation, a listing was made of each student in the various groups and the name of his fifth grade teacher. In addition, a tally was then prepared for each teacher which indicated the number of students he had taught who were in the high motivated and low motivated groups. By studying these figures, it was possible to get some idea of the kind of impact a teacher made upon his students' motivation. Several patterns were evident.

First, some teachers seemed to be especially successful in motivating students, others were not as successful. Many other teachers made no consistent impact. Table 18 shows the actual data on three different teachers, portraying these patterns which have been described.

Table 18

Number of Students in High and Low
Motivated Groups Who Had the Same Fifth
Grade Teacher

Teacher-School	Number of High Motivated	Number of Low Motivated
A – 10	12	0
B – 5	0	9
C – 4	2	2

Teacher A from School 10 apparently did something in his class which caused students to be highly motivated, while Teacher B from School 5 seemed to get exactly the opposite result. Teacher C from School 4 evidently had no consistent impact upon his students' motivational levels.

In studying the relationship of teachers to students' achievement, a listing was made of each student in the various groups and the name of his fourth grade teacher. In addition, a tally was then prepared for each teacher which indicated the number of students he had taught who were in the overachieving or underachieving groups. Studying these figures made it possible to get some picture of the influence of a given teacher upon the achievement of his students over a period of one year's time (fourth grade). Table 19 shows data from four different teachers. Teachers A and B apparently functioned in such a manner that several of their fourth grade youngsters failed to achieve up to expected levels. Teacher C, on the other hand, seemed especially successful in helping students achieve. Teacher D got no consistent result.

Table 20 shows the breakdown of students in each group, by school. Schools 4, 6, 12, 13, and 15 apparently made no uniform impression upon their pupils. School 2, on the other hand, seems to have more high motivated underachievers, School 5 has mainly low motivated students, while School 10 seems to have more students who are highly motivated.

Table 19

Number of Students in Over- and Under-achieving Groups Who Had the Same Fourth Grade Teacher

Teacher-School	Number of Over-achievers	Number of Under-achievers
A – 4	0	7
B – 2	1	8
C – 5	4	0
D – 10	2	4

Table 20

Number of Students in Various Groups According to School

School	HMOA	HMUA	LMOA	LMUA	Total
1	0	0	2	0	2
2	1	17	0	1	19
3	0	0	1	3	4
4	2	7	3	3	15
5	1	0	8	4	13
6	1	12	3	3	19
7	2	0	0	1	3
8	0	1	3	1	5
9	0	1	3	4	8
10	6	10	0	0	16
11	0	1	1	1	3
12	3	3	2	3	11
13	4	7	6	5	22
14	0	3	2	2	7
15	3	6	5	2	16
TOTAL	23	68	39	33	163

Conclusions and Recommendations

The purpose of this project has been to study the relationship of personality characteristics, class size, school "climate," and teacher impact upon fifth grade students' academic achievement and their motivational levels. Because the study was essentially exploratory, no specific hypotheses were projected. Two different sets of conclusions seem apparent. One pertains to the original questions asked, while the other relates to the methodological aspects of the study itself.

Factors Affecting Achievement.   Given all of the various data included in this report, what interpretations are possible? The most obvious generalization seems to be that achievement in school apparently is a function of a series of subtle relationships, none of which are readily discernible, and all of which may exist in differing degrees and varying patterns. Learning in school is a complicated process, and there are no educational panaceas. Some clues are evident, however.

First, students' personality patterns apparently exerted some kind of influence upon the kinds and ways of their learnings. That is, throughout all of these data there seemed to be the suggestion that some personal and social adjustment facilitated achievement, but that either too much or too little impeded it. Likewise, too much anxiety evidently had adverse effects upon student learning, but some anxiety appeared to be desirable and perhaps even necessary for maximum academic achievement. In this same vein, there seemed to be some trace of dependence behavior evident among underachievers. For example, highly motivated underachievers consistently scored slightly higher than highly motivated overachievers on social adjustment sections of the personality scale, and repeatedly expressed their desire for "strict" teachers on the sentence completion instrument. Ability as measured by a conventional pencil and paper IQ test did not seem to be a major factor affecting students' achievement, at least as these variables were measured in this study. In all, there was some evidence that a curvilinear relationship may exist between certain personality characteristics and academic achievement, and that this problem definitely needs further study.

Second, class size apparently had a significant effect upon achievement; those students who experienced smaller classes were most likely to be overachievers while those who were in larger classes were more apt to be underachievers.

Third, some schools seemed to develop a "climate" that resulted in a persisting influence upon their students' achievement and motivation. In some cases these climates had positive results (i.e., high motivation and/or overachievement); in other cases, less desirable effects (i.e., low motivation and/or underachievement). Schools obviously exist within a larger social setting and whether this climate was a function of the leadership within the school was not evident from this study. The effect of social class and other societal influences upon achievement and motivation should be examined carefully.

Fourth, certain teachers evidently exerted a profound impact upon their students' academic achievement and motivational levels. Some of these effects were positive and some negative. Likewise, many other teachers apparently made no consistent impact upon the young people with whom they worked. Does this reflect a kind of "educational inefficiency" due to these teachers' inability to relate differently to different kinds of youngsters? This problem of teacher impact upon student development needs very extensive study.

Methodological Observations.   The original intent of this study was to conceive a design which would be both comprehensive and rigorous. This purpose has only been partially achieved; the concern for rigor seems, in fact, to have caused about as many problems as it has solved. The definition of expected achievement is a major case in point.

Most studies of underachievement select students from the upper third of the population group in terms of ability, for instance, and lower third in terms of achievement, or some such pattern. Such a definition is obviously workable, but just as obviously, it precludes any sampling of low abiilty underachievers by definition. Using the same logic it would be impossible to identify a very able overachiever. In this particular study, the mathematical model devised aimed, therefore, at identifying individuals of all ability levels who were either underachieving or overachieving; the margin of one or more grade levels above or below *expected* achievement level was supposed to insure a valid sample.

However, the repression phenomenon was apparently at work, and this resulted in a distorted sample in terms of ability. That is, evidently because of the regression factor, underachievers tended to have higher IQ scores while overachievers tended to have lower IQ scores (3). The problem of defining expected achievement precisely, however, has not been solved, and this is an area which must be explored in other research.

The second methodological observation relates to the validity of the Junior Index of Motivation (JIM Scale). Because the design of this study was such that upper and lower groups of students were identified initially on the basis of their JIM Scale scores, unless the instrument is valid, definite distortions were bound to occur. Throughout the data there ran the persisting notion that the JIM Scale apparently measured subservience and dependence phases of conformity. For example, the Pearson product moment correlation coefficient between JIM Scale scores and total California Personality Test scores was fairly high ($r + .50$), and some of the manual's descriptions of social adjustment imply acquiescence and submissiveness, though this was probably not intended. Likewise, a similar relationship was observed between JIM Scale scores and Sarason's General Anxiety Scale scores ($r - .34$). It must be remembered, of course, that these 163 youngsters represented extreme degrees of motivation and achievement, and this factor undoubtedly had some effect upon these correlations. There was, to be sure, certain evidence that the JIM Scale did measure a student's desire to do good work in school (see sentence completion data), but in reviewing the original assumptions inherent in the development of the instrument (teacher ratings of students' motivational levels), the question still exists. There was also some evidence that what the JIM Scale actually measured was social class, since more high JIM Scale scorers came from schools located in upper middle class sections of the community than did low scorers, who more frequently came from lower class groups. Future studies must explore the relationship of scores on the motivation index to actual student accomplishment, with such variables as sex, ability, and social class carefully controlled. Further, such studies must examine the extent to which achievement in school is a function of "doing as you are told," while parceling out the effect of individual initiative and "stick-to-it-iveness."

It should be pointed out in these limitations, too, that some of the conclusions obviously go beyond the data. This is especially evident in those sections pertaining to the impact of the teacher and the school upon students' motivation and achievement. This study demonstrates that some relationship exists between these factors; there is actually no evidence that this correlation is causative. This problem certainly warrants careful study.

No effort has been made to relate these findings to those of other researchers, although the reader may note certain relationships to some of the work of Thistlethwaite, Liddle, Bowman, Thelen, Getzels, and Jackson, to mention just a few. The conclusions reached here must be tenuously held because of the limitations of the design. Within the restricting framework described above, however, the following recommendations may be appropriate.

Recommendations to Administrators.   School administrators probably "set the tone" for their entire school and how students may be expected to achieve. Accordingly, principals should examine their every word and action with the purpose of ascertaining the exact nature of the impact they make upon their school. Second, the practice of grouping children according to ability as reflected in pencil and paper tests of intelligence may make sense logically, but it does not seem to withstand experimental scrutiny. *Grouping children according to motivation or personality or achievement with particular kinds of teachers* would probably be much more effective. Third, if class size does affect youngsters' achievement, every effort must be made to provide opportunities for children to have at least some intimate experiences in small groups with a teacher, though large group teaching may be very appropriate for certain purposes, too.

Recommendations to Teachers. Since different children apparently respond to different types of pressure, *the effective teacher must match his efforts with students' individual needs.* This demands great sensitivity. That is, some youngsters evidently need more group structure and individual direction from the teacher; others probably need less. Some pupils may need to have their anxiety level reduced, while others seemingly ought to have their anxieties increased somewhat. Since the impact of a teacher's personality appears to have a lasting and profound effect upon young peoples' motivation and achievement, teachers must study their own value system and their own behavioral repertoires with the idea of cultivating those action patterns which will assure high motivation and achievement levels among students without destroying individual creativity or personal responsibility.

Summary

Studies in this chapter have ranged from simple to sophisticated and somewhat more scholarly. The complexity of the research design is dependent on the members of the group who plan and execute it, and in many ways the supervisor must determine the level of difficulty at which they can experience success. He must use his knowledge of all the members and how they function as a team. Whether the design is simple or complex, there is value to be gained from every study. Implications can clearly be drawn for school people. First, schools effect changes in the behavior of students through the curriculum in many different ways. Second, it is in behavioral change that learning takes place. Third, school and community involvement in curriculum as it relates directly to students can be a powerful force in making the learning process more effective. In the next chapter Riverside's studies about school organization are examined. Many research studies have been done about school organization, but too often they cannot be applied to the problems in a particular system. We must be able to design ways to approach these problems.

Appendix B
JIM Scale
Student Questionnaire

Directions:

We are trying to find out how students think and feel about a number of important topics. In order to do this, we would like to ask you to answer some questions. This is not an intelligence test nor an information test. There are no "right" or "wrong" answers. The best and only correct answer is YOUR PERSONAL OPINION. Whatever your answer is, there will be many who agree and many who disagree. What we really want to know is HOW YOU FEEL about each statement.

Read each statement very carefully, and then indicate your agreement or disagreement by marking it, according to the following scale, in the appropriate space beside each statement.

+ 1 slight support, agreement   − 1 slight opposition, disagreement
+ 2 strong support, agreement   − 2 strong opposition, disagreement

You may have as much time as you need, so read each statement very carefully and answer it the best way you can.

1. Late afternoon is the best time of day.
2. Many children have often been punished without cause.
3. Students should be made to go to school until they are 18 years old.
4. Being right is more important than being kind.
5. School is more fun when teachers let students do things they want to.
6. Pupils who try should get good grades even if they make mistakes.
7. Successful people are those who make the most money.
8. The best way to spend a free evening is with a good book.
9. Most young people do not want to go to school.
10. Some new ideas are interesting, but most of them are not.
11. Practical people are usually highly respected.
12. Knowing the answer is more important than knowing where to get the answer.
13. Many young people feel grouchy.
14. The best people refuse to depend on other persons.
15. Some teachers make school more interesting than others.
16. A person's feelings on a topic are not as important as the facts.
17. There are more important things in the world than making money.
18. It does not really help much to study about people from other lands.
19. Life is mostly sorrow with just a little joy.

20. Some students have to study more than others.
21. Many youngsters often want to run away from home.
22. Being a good speaker is just as important as being a good speller.
23. Some teachers seem to enjoy making students suffer.
24. Our whole trouble is that we won't let God help us.
25. Most people worry more before they take a test than during the test.
26. No one seems to understand young people.
27. Learning to cooperate is more important than learning to compete.
28. Most people would like school better if teachers did not give grades.
29. The world we live in is a pretty lonesome place.
30. Social progress can only be achieved by returning to our glorious past.
31. It is very foolish to advocate government support of education.
32. Most people's hardest battles are with themselves.
33. There is nothing new under the sun.
34. Helping other people is the key to happiness.
35. Life seems to be one big struggle after another.
36. Most people just don't give a "darn" for others.
37. The best way to achieve security is for the government to guarantee jobs.
38. Some people do not appreciate the value of education.
39. Most young people feel uncomfortable around someone of the opposite sex.
40. Many new ideas are not worth the paper they are printed on.
41. Many teachers are not considerate of student's feelings.
42. Teachers are generally underpaid.
43. Being unhealthy is worse than being unhappy.
44. It is better to forget than to forgive.
45. Pupils who copy during an examination should fail the test.
46. Young people should be free to follow their own desires.
47. Listening to a good speaker is the best way to learn.
48. The present is all too often full of unhappiness.
49. Most people just don't know what is good for them.
50. Understanding yourself helps one understand others.
51. People who dream a lot at night are apt to be crazy.
52. Familiarity breeds contempt, so one should never be too friendly.
53. There is a real limit to man's intelligence.
54. People who are insulted generally deserve to be.
55. Experience may be a good teacher, but schools are better.
56. Wasting time is even worse than wasting money.
57. People who are quick thinkers usually jump to conclusions.
58. Most people do not have good ideas until they grow up.
59. When people are unhappy they should talk to someone about it.
60. Looking good is just as important as being good.
61. The best part of education is that which people teach themselves.
62. Famous people usually have a lot of money.

63. Most people cannot learn from the experience of others.
64. The dreamer is a danger to society.
65. Most teachers like to drive students if they have a chance.
66. God helps those who help themselves.
67. One can never desire too much of a good thing.
68. Being a liar is better than being a gossip.
69. Asking questions usually gets you into trouble.
70. Not many people in the world are really kind.
71. The biggest part of being successful is determination.
72. Teachers know more and do less than most other people.
73. Hope is really no better than worry.
74. School is not all that it's cracked up to be.
75. Everything that people do is either right or wrong.
76. Quick thinking is always better than being polite.
77. The gentle person often treats himself severely.
78. Everybody ought to do something worthwhile everyday.
79. We are never really as happy as we think we are.
80. All those who fail have worked in vain.

Notes

1. Jack R. Frymier, *The Nature of Educational Method* (Columbus, Ohio: Charles E. Merrill Publishing Company, 1965), pp. 107–155. See also Appendix B.

2. It was recognized at the outset that underachievement was possible, semantically, while overachievement seemed to represent a semantic impossibility. What was sought for in this study were variations from the typical to the degree that they were significant. In this sense, overachievement is a statistical possibility, even though the term implies a verbal paradox. Likewise, high motivated under-achievement seems to be a contradictory phrase. It was assumed, however, that many students really "try" in school, but some forces may operate to counteract their effort and thus reduce their achievement levels. If so, this study might identify some of these restricting factors.

3. This occurred, despite the fact that the theoretical expected achievement was 5.2, while the actual achievement median was 5.7 for both reading and arithmetic for the 484 youngsters initially identified as extremes according to motivation scores. This difference should have operated to enable high ability pupils to have a more definite opportunity to be overachievers. Further, if one chose to ignore the regression, it would appear that teachers may teach in such a way that low ability youngsters tend to overachieve and high ability youngsters to underachieve. It is tempting to say that regression accounts for this obvious conclusion; careful studies should be conducted to filter out this statistical idiosyncrasy, however, and determine whether or not teachers actually do "aim" their teaching at the average students.

7 Curriculum Studies Involving Organizational Factors

The organizational components of curriculum are often the focal point of concern in improving programs. Time, space, staff, and resources are all variables in the educational situation which can be manipulated. If we change the relationships between these variables, what will happen? If we organize the school day or the staff in a particular way, will children learn more? These are important questions.

Many educational innovations in recent years are primarily changes in organizational factors. For example, the non-graded school, team teaching, the core program, and modular scheduling are all efforts to improve education by modifying organizational relationships.

This chapter describes three studies aimed at curriculum improvement by varying organizational factors in the curriculum. The first describes an investigation of the relationship between class size and achievement in reading. The second involves a study of departmentalization and large group instruction in an elementary school. The third concerns the kinds and degree of problems faced by students moving from elementary to junior high school in terms of the nature of the organizational pattern of the elementary school they left.

A Study of Class Size and Reading Achievements

If reading achievement and overloaded classes were problem areas identified by the district curriculum council, combining these two concerns into one problem might prove especially meaningful. If the curriculum worker begins with a review of the related literature, he might be disappointed. The findings to date about the influence of class size upon academic achievement do not support those who believe in smaller classes. Likewise, neither do they support advocates of larger classes. Given the "no significant difference" data, superintendents and school boards may, however, interpret this as a green light for increasing class size. Studying class size means that one must step outside the definition of curriculum. Forces outside the curriculum may have profound effects upon the curriculum, and explorations ought to be continued. If more teachers will help children learn better and more quickly, then more teachers are needed. If the investigation shows that children in smaller classes actually do not make significantly more progress or growth than children in larger classes, then the problem will have to be examined in new perspective.

Where does one begin? What is a large class? What is a small class? How many large classes are there in the district? Where are they located? Are the teachers working in these situations comparable to those working with small class groups? How shall we measure achievements? Will there be any other factors involved of which we ought to be aware? How about the children's ability to hear effectively? Is their vision adequate? Were the students in large classes and small classes comparable in terms of ability when they began the year? How shall we determine ability for first grade students? Is a readiness test an adequate measure? Can we ask the psychologists to perform individual psychological evaluations on every child involved?

In all probability, a survey to determine variations in class size throughout the district might be a good beginning. Asking every principal to list the teachers by name and the number of students in every class would be a simple request. This would also present a base for comparison of the class sizes throughout the district if other studies were considered. For example, how many youngsters in the district attend school in classes of more than 40 students? How many in classes with fewer than 25? Is location of these schools of significance? Are there any conscious or unconscious forces operating which may have disturbed the usual procedures for allocating personnel to such an extent that certain schools or certain groups get an unfair "shake"?

An adequate and accurate picture of the class sizes across the district could provide insights beyond immediate expectations. In any event, it would serve as a benchmark for subsequent studies, as well as a good source of data now about which teachers were working with larger groups of children and which with smaller groups.

Let us suppose, that while looking at the data, it became evident that most of the groups with more than 36 students came from the section of a district where most of the underprivileged youngsters lived, and groups with 26 or less were in sections where most of the overprivileged students lived. Would this have any special significance in the supervisor's role? Suppose that the area council doing this analysis happens to be in one of the poorer sections of town—this represents their schools and their students—what then? Situations like this sometimes occur for many unknown reasons, but they do occur. This is the kind of situation a supervisor may run into when he begins to do curriculum research. It is an explosive problem, and how it is handled carries with it added obligations but also added opportunities. The supervisor is in a unique position of being able to right what apparently is a wrong, and to have the facts to support his recommendations all the way.

It is important that he recognize that when he begins to study his educational program carefully and completely, things will happen that he had not anticipated, but these events can be positive. The fascinating part about curriculum research is that one can improve instruction by digging out information helpful to all and, because it is factual, people can accept change easier than if they were told that "so and so is wrong and ought to be changed." Curriculum decisions have to be based squarely on the facts, and collecting facts and data is the supervisor's role.

The Effect of Class Size upon Reading Achievement in First Grade

The Problem

Schools exist to help children learn. The basic purpose of the elementary school is to help children learn to read. Reading is considered so important, most people assume that if children do not learn to read during these early years, the school has failed.

Many forces operate which affect a child while he is attempting to learn to read. Background experience, the availability of reading material, the value parents place upon the importance of learning to read, the skill and activity, hearing ability, eye dominance, and emotional stability are other factors which research has repeatedly demonstrated are also important.

Class size is still another factor which may affect a youngster in his efforts to develop skill in reading. Since reading is such a personal, individual activity, it seems logical that if a teacher has fewer students, he should be able to give each child more individual attention and personalized instruction than if he has more. Further, it would seem reasonable to suppose that in leaving the security of their own homes, children would probably also not become "lost" in an exceptionally large group.

Most of the previous research on the effect of class size upon academic achievement indicated other factors are more important than the number of students in each class. However, most of these studies have typically concerned themselves with the academic achievement of older students; many, in fact, are studies of college groups. Increasing the size of a secondary school or college class may not materially influence the achievement of these students. This does not mean, though, that six year olds would necessarily be affected the same way. Neither does it mean that they might not learn as much as they would in larger classes. Stated simply, the effect of class size upon first grade students' achievement in reading is not known. The purpose of this case study is to describe this very problem.

The Procedures

During March, the elementary principals in Riverside Public Schools were requested to submit a list of their teachers by name and the number of students each teacher had. Every principal complied. A study of the enrollments in various classrooms has been reported elsewhere. For the purpose of this study, all of those first grade teachers in certain schools who had more than

36 students enrolled in their classes were identified, and all of those who had less than 30 were also identified. This included six teachers who were teaching more than 36 first graders and nine who were teaching less than 30. The students enrolled in these teachers' classes were considered to be in "large" and "small" classes, respectively.

In May, each of these 15 teachers administered the Williams Primary Reading Achievement Test-Form D to her group. In addition, certain other basic data included reading readiness scores, age, hearing, vision, health condition, attendance, and whether or not the youngster was promoted or retained at the end of the year were also assembled. A complete analysis was made of all of these data.

The Results

Comparison of Teachers.   Tables 21 and 22 show certain information about each teacher. These figures indicate that though there were some incidental differences among the various teachers involved in this particular study, they were probably not significant. That intangible, "teaching skill," was probably much more important than these data, but because such skill is difficult to assess, it was simply assumed that variations in ability between the two groups would probably counterbalance each other. This is undoubtedly a questionable assumption, but one which had to be made for obvious reasons.

Table 21

Qualifications of Small Group Teachers

Teacher	Size of Class	Certificate	Experience
A	29	3	4
B	29	2	16
C	29	3	10
D	24	3	8
E	28	3	4
F	29	3	6
G	29	3	7
H	28	3	0
I	24	3	3
TOTAL	249		

Table 22

Qualifications of Large Group Teachers

Teacher	Size of Class	Certificate	Experience
A	40	3	5
B	40	3	32
C	39	3	8
D	38	3	8
E	37	3	9
F	44	3	15
TOTAL	238		

Comparison of Students. There were 249 students enrolled in nine small classes and 238 students enrolled in six large classes. Complete achievement data was available on 201 youngsters in the large class group and 219 in the small classes; thus 420 students constituted the samples included in this study.

The students enrolled in large classes were evenly divided according to sex: 100 boys and 101 girls. In the small classes there were 111 boys and 108 girls. The average age of students in large classes was 79.1 months as of January and in the small classes the average was 81.0 months as of the same date.

There were four students attending large classes whose hearing was below normal (i.e., lower limit above 20 decibels within frequencies of 500 to 4000), whereas eight students enrolled in small classes had a similar difficulty. Seventeen pupils in the large class group had some type of visual difficulty and 18 in the small class group had similar problems. Finally, seven youngsters in the large class group appeared undernourished to their teachers, while six in the small class group were similarly perceived by their teachers.

Previous studies have indicated the relationship between scores on readiness tests administered during the first month of first grade and achievement in reading as measured by standardized achievement tests at the end of grade one is sufficiently high to assume that readiness is a fair predictor of success in reading. In an effort to determine whether or not the two groups were similar in terms of potential success, scores on the Metropolitan Readiness Test were compared. These tests had been routinely administered to all first grade students in September. Because of absences and transfers, all students did not participate. The figures which follow, therefore, represent readiness data on 84 per cent of those students enrolled in large classes and 86 per cent of those enrolled in small classes. Table 23 shows the breakdown of both groups according to readiness scores.

It is obvious from these figures that the two groups were not comparable at the beginning of their first grade experience. In fact those students enrolled in the large classes had a distinct advantage in actually being more "ready." A Chi Square value of 15.48 computed according to the actual frequencies in each category indicates that this difference was statistically significant at the .01 level of confidence with four degrees of freedom. In other words, in terms of potential ability as measured by the Metropolitan Readiness Test, the students in the large classes appear to have had a distinct advantage at the beginning of grade one over those students in small classes. In other respects the two groups seem remarkably similar, with the exception that the average age of students in small classes was slightly higher.

Table 24 describes the mean achievement in terms of raw scores obtained on the Williams Primary Reading Achievement Test for students enrolled in small classes and large classes. This testing was completed at the end of May, following the administration of the readiness tests the previous fall.

According to these figures, the mean achievement of those students enrolled in small classes was greater than the mean achievement of those students in large classes. The t statistic of 3.40 computed to compare the difference between means indicates that this difference was statistically significant at the .001 level of confidence. In other words, the probability that this difference would have occurred by chance is less than one in a thousand. These data would seem to imply that there was cause for this difference.

Table 23

Proportion of Students in Large Classes and Small Classes at Various Readiness Levels*

Readiness Level	Proportion in Small Classes	Proportion in Large Classes
Superior	0%	2%
High Normal	2	5
Average	15	18
Low Normal	39	47
Poor Risk	44	28
TOTAL	100%	100%

* Chi Square of 15.48 significant at .01 level with 4 df.

Table 24

Comparison of Reading Achievement of
First Grade Students in Small Classes and
Large Classes

Group	N	Mean Raw Scores	S.D.	t
Large Classes	201	19.21	9.57	
				3.40*
Small Classes	219	22.58	10.79	

* Significant at the .001 level.

In terms of grade placement, those students enrolled in large classes had a mean grade placement of approximately 1.62 years, whereas those pupils enrolled in small classes had a mean grade placement of approximately 1.75 years. Because these figures were interpolated, they are difficult to interpret, but a reasonable estimate would probably indicate an average difference of a little more than one month's progress between the two groups in a nine month period.

This difference between mean achievement is especially important in light of the fact that readiness scores for students in small classes were significantly lower at the beginning of first grade. In effect, those youngsters in small classes overcame a distinct disadvantage and actually overachieved their fellow students who were enrolled in larger classes.

Another indication of academic achievement is reflected in retention and promotion figures. Theoretically, at least, teachers promote these youngsters to the second grade who have achieved first grade objectives and retain those who have failed to achieve those objectives. Of the 201 students enrolled in large classes, 46 were retained at the end of the school year. This represents 23 per cent of the total enrollment. Of the 219 pupils enrolled in small classes, 37 were retained. This represents 17 per cent of the total enrollment. The Chi Square value of 2.37 between actual frequencies indicates that this difference is not significantly large to assume that it might have occurred by anything other than chance. Even so, it is obvious that more youngsters in large classes were retained; the tendency itself may be significant.

Finally, students' attendance records indicate that pupils in the large class group had a mean of 91.20 per cent days in actual attendance, while those in small classes had a mean of 87.62 per cent days in attendance.

Conclusions and Recommendations

The purpose of this study was to assess the effect of class size upon first grade reading achievement. There were 201 first graders enrolled in six classes exceeding 36 pupils and 219 first graders enrolled in nine classes of less than 30 pupils involved in this investigation.

For all practical purposes, the two groups were similar in terms of physical health, visual and auditory acuity, and sex. Those youngsters enrolled in small classes were slightly older than those in large classes, but pupils in large classes had readiness scores significantly above those of students in small classes.

In terms of achievement, however, students in small classes achieved at a significantly higher level than students in larger classes. Further, there were fewer retentions among the students in smaller classes despite the fact that their attendance record was somewhat less than for those enrolled in larger groups.

In effect, then, there seems to be clear and unmistakable evidence here that class size profoundly influences achievement in reading for first grade students. Those students who are enrolled in smaller classes achieved at levels which were significantly higher than those attained by pupils enrolled in larger classes. This difference, which was evident on standardized achievement test results and, to a lesser degree, in the proportion of youngsters retained at the end of the year clearly indicates the need for maintaining reasonable class sizes for first grade students.

It seems apparent from this study that increasing the size of first grade classes has a direct, detrimental effect on children's learning. To permit the creation or existence of such classes would appear to ignore the findings of this report. The following recommendations, therefore, are made to principals and the Riverside Board of Public Instruction.

Recommendations to Elementary Principals. Every effort should be made to keep classes small in grade one. There are many times when this is extremely difficult, but ingenious administrators must constantly strive to assure first grade youngsters of a genuine opportunity to learn in a class which is not too large.

Recommendations to the School Board. Principals and teachers cannot keep class size down, however, unless sufficient teachers are assigned. It is recognized that allocating teachers is a difficult and expensive responsibility. However, in a school system which has an overall teacher-pupil ratio in excess of that of most other districts in the state, any effort on the part of a principal to keep first grade classes to a reasonable size automatically means that other grade levels in the elementary school will have larger classes, *unless he gets some special help.*

The Riverside District Curriculum Council, therefore, recommends that a thorough study of the teacher allocation procedure be made by the school board, with the end in view of adopting a clear-cut policy to insure first grade youngsters a maximum opportunity to learn in small classes without jeopardizing the class size through other areas of the elementary school.

Suggestions for Further Study. Considering the nature and importance of this study, the following problems may deserve further attention:

(1) What is the effect of class size upon reading achievement in first grade for students in classes of less than 25 and more than 30?
(2) What is the cost of reteaching youngsters who are retained one year in school for lack of academic achievement?

A Study of Departmentalization in an Elementary School

Let us suppose that one school within a system is confronted with a demand to vary organizational pattern because of new building developments. There are instances when school boards build new buildings and incorporate architectural concepts that enable building principals to employ notions of organization and instructional techniques beyond the conventional. For example, suppose the school system just completed construction on a new elementary school building, which includes one wing with folding doors between two rooms which open up to form one large classroom. The school board is eager to "try new things," and has directed the principal of this building to "experiment" with large group instruction during the coming year to see how it will work.

The principal of this particular school in this example does not appreciate being "directed" to "experiment" with large group instruction; he resents this kind of intrusion into his professional role, but he also feels it is probably worth a careful try. The principal knows the supervisor's interest in curriculum research and invites him to help study the effect of such an innovation as large group instruction and departmentalization in the upper elementary school.

Of course the supervisor has to meet with the staff and to talk about this generally. How does the staff feel about this change? How do the children seem to be adjusting? Are parents responding in any unusual way? Do teachers have any particular difficulties in working with special groups of students, such as the exceptionally bright or slow? How do the other teachers who are not involved feel about the change? Are the children progressing academically as well as usual? Are there any signs of tension or frustration on the part of youngsters who take part in the program?

Through such questions the group may finally find itself defining a problem. For example, perhaps several major areas of professional concern can be identified: student achievement, motivation, anxiety, self-concept, and attitudes toward others. Perhaps information about each of these particular things can be obtained: parents' estimates, teachers' estimates, students' estimates, and actual attainment. The design for the study then looks something like this:

	Parents' Estimates	Teachers' Estimates	Students' Estimates	Actual Attainment
Achievement in Reading				
Achievement in Science				
Achievement in English				
Achievement in Social Studies				
Achievement in Arithmetic				
Concept of Self				
Concept of Others				
General Anxiety				
Test Anxiety				
Motivation Toward School				

With this kind of blank design, the problem is selecting or devising ways of collecting data about each of the designated areas. If parents', students', and teachers' reactions about each of these things are obtained, and compared with actual attainments in the various areas of youngster's achievement and growth, the next step is to determine ways of making valid observations in each area defined. The supervisor might devise an interview schedule to ask selected parents certain questions about their child's progress—how he seems to be adjusting to the new situation, whether or not he seems to be making satisfactory progress in each of the academic areas, whether he displays any unusual nervous habits or behaviors, how much he seems to like school and tries to do well in his studies, etc. From these interviews, the supervisor might arrive at some precise determination of parental feeling about the total program and their youngster's participation in it. Or, he might make up a questionnaire so that responses to these same areas of interest were elicited anonymously from all parents who had children involved.

Interview or questionnaire data could also be collected from teachers and children about their attitudes and estimates of the effectiveness regarding the program. In addition, students and teachers could be observed in actual learning situations according to standardized observational procedures, making inferences about both students' and teachers' feelings as reflected in their classroom behavior.

To compare estimated with actual attainments among the youngsters participating in the new program, established measuring devices to determine levels of achievement, anxiety, motivation, and attitudes toward self and others could be used. If studying comparable groups would provide meaningful comparative data, this could also be done. The supervisor could also accumulate information relative to frequency of problems referred to the principal's office, extent and type of parental complaint, extent of student illness reported to the school nurse, and similar data.

The principal and teachers in this study are doing more than asking questions—they are asserting biases, exploring new procedures, struggling with traditional concepts in nontraditional situations. The inherent features of the design provide genuine opportunities for professional growth. Why should we use this achievement test rather than that one? Will a word association test be as good a measure of self-other concept as psychological evaluations? What kinds of instruments are available for ascertaining students' motivational levels? How many parents have complained about the new setup thus far this year? What are their major objections? Have any parents expressed special satisfaction with the new arrangement? What do they like most about it? What if there are major discrepancies between teachers' judgments and students' actual accomplishments? What questions can we ask parents to provide us with accurate information about their child's behavior? Should we share the findings of our study with parents and others when we are done? How much of the variation can be attributed to the fact that everybody involved is making a special effort to study the entire situation carefully and precisely? Will changing teachers in the middle of the year upset our data?

When teachers look long and hard at what they are doing, especially when they are trying to make observations as valid and as objective as possible, they enjoy a professional stimulus not possible through exhortation or admonition of any kind. Significant changes are possible because they have helped shape the nature of the investigation, have assisted in collecting the information, and will talk through and argue about the conclusions.

Curriculum research has a way of helping even the most obstinate teacher to explore his innermost feelings and convictions about educational method and teaching technique. By providing data, the focus of attention shifts from the teachers themselves to other aspects within the educational situation. Change becomes possible for the teachers because it is based upon the facts. Whatever the conclusions, all persons involved in the study will probably feel good about the decision and about themselves because they will have been allowed to maintain their professional integrity. The curriculum research bulletin described in the following paragraphs might be the kind of ultimate report available after a study of the questions already outlined.

A Study of the Effectiveness of Departmentalization and Large Group Instruction in One Elementary School

The Problem

What is the effect of modified departmentalization and large group instruction upon students in the upper elementary grades? How will such an organizational pattern affect youngsters' academic achievement? Will it materially influence their attitudes toward themselves and others? How will such an organization affect their motivation and their anxiety levels? Will parents accept such an innovation? Finally, what will teachers' reactions be?

The Procedures

In an endeavor to answer these questions, a three phase study was initiated in one Riverside elementary school. To begin with, fifth and sixth grade students were placed in an organizational structure which included some time spent in large groups and some time spent in small groups. Second, these students' progress was studied intensively during one academic year. Third, parents' and teachers' reactions were assessed. The design of the study was such that students, parents, and teachers all estimated how the youngsters were progressing in several different phases of their development, and then objective measures of this development were taken for purposes of comparison.

Organizing Students for Instructional Purposes. First, all of the fifth and sixth grade students in one elementary school were administered the Sequential Test of Educational Progress (STEP Tests)—Form 4A, in the areas of mathematics, reading, science, social studies, and writing. The students were then grouped into four sections per grade level according to their achievement scores in mathematics. The lowest 20 per cent were placed together in a group that spent three hours each day in a core-type class with one teacher and three hours per day in a large group situation. The remaining pupils in each grade level were divided into three groups of approximately 25 students each, and received instruction each day in English (spelling, penmanship), reading, and mathematics for one hour each from three different teachers. The other three hours of the instructional day were spent in a large group of approximately 90 students. One teacher and one aide taught science, social studies, music, art, and physical education in this large group situation.

It should be mentioned that there were two different teachers for the large group during the year; one the first semester and another the second semester.

Studying Students' Progress. Several efforts were made to study students' progress and development during the academic year. The STEP Test—Form 4B, was again administered to all students in the final week of school to compare with the initial testing from the previous fall. The Junior Index of Motivation was given to every pupil involved in the study and was also administered to students in several nearby schools for comparative purposes. Each student was tested with the Sarason Test Anxiety scale and the General Anxiety Scale, and again, youngsters in other nearby schools were similarly measured. Bills' Index of Adjustment Values, a measure of a student's concept of self and others, was also administered to all pupils in the study and to a comparable group in another school. Finally, a questionnaire-type instrument (Appendix C) was given to all students included in the project to determine their attitudes and feelings in each of the areas under study: achievement, motivation, anxiety, and self-other concept. There were 87 fifth grade pupils and 98 sixth graders included in this study.

Parent and Teacher Reaction. Parents' attitudes and feelings were ascertained by mailing questionnaires (Appendix D) twice during the school year to every home which had a fifth or sixth grade youngster in this particular school. These questionnaires were structured to assess areas of feeling comparable to that being measured in the students' questionnaires and other scales. In every case, parents were asked to estimate their youngster's progress in the various academic areas, social development, anxiety level, and motivation.

During the month of January, 172 questionnaires were mailed and 107 were returned. During May, 173 were mailed and 73 were returned, a 52.17 per cent response.

Teachers' attitudes were studied by a series of responses on three different occasions to a questionnaire-type instrument (Appendix E). Questions were included which related to their feelings about their success in helping motivate children, teaching skills and attitudes, and aiding children to achieve academically.

The Results

Academic Achievement. Table 25 describes the mean scores of students tested in the fall and spring of their fifth grade in school on the Sequential Tests of Educational Progress (STEP Tests). Since several months of instruction intervened between the fall and spring testing, progress was expected in

every instance. The difference between spring and fall test means should have
been significant statistically, and the spring mean should have been higher.
Eighteen of the 20 comparisons made in Table 25 were in the expected direction, and 14 were statistically significant. Greatest gains were made in mathematics and social studies. There was no significant growth among the more
able students in either English or science, though less able youngsters made
expected progress in these two fields.

Table 25

Comparison of Different Groups of Fifth Grade Students' Academic Progress During School Year

Group	N	Subject	Fall Mean	Spring Mean	t
High	22	English	274	275	.00
High Average	25		261	261	.00
Low Average	24		252	262	3.98*
Low	16		241	248	2.67*
High	22	Math	—	—	—
High Average	25		249	258	6.03*
Low Average	24		242	254	3.97*
Low	16		239	252	6.84*
High	22	Reading	268	286	5.94*
High Average	25		258	273	3.44*
Low Average	24		251	254	1.03*
Low	16		242	252	3.61*
High	22	Science	271	278	1.75
High Average	25		261	268	1.91
Low Average	24		255	262	3.18*
Low	16		242	256	4.68*
High	22	Social	261	275	4.44*
High Average	25	Studies	253	266	6.42*
Low Average	24		248	258	5.46*
Low	16		243	249	2.22*

* Significant at .05 level of confidence.

Table 26 describes the mean scores of students tested in the fall and spring of their sixth grade in school on the Sequential Tests of Educational Progress (STEP Tests). Again, since there were several months of instructional time between the administration of the two tests, progress was expected in every instance. Eighteen of the 20 observations reflect this progress, and 16 indicate statistically significant growth. Like the fifth graders, the more able sixth grade students did not show significant growth in the area of English.

Table 26

Comparison of Different Groups of Sixth Grade Students' Academic Progress During School Year

Group	N	Subject	Fall Mean	Spring Mean	t
High	26	English	281	276	1.31
High Average	25		267	268	.35
Low Average	22		255	261	2.09*
Low	25		243	251	2.10*
High	26	Math	265	269	2.22*
High Average	25		262	265	2.03*
Low Average	22		251	259	4.35*
Low	25		242	248	2.21*
High	26	Reading	278	287	2.21*
High Average	25		267	277	2.77*
Low Average	22		258	257	.28
Low	25		238	249	2.15*
High	26	Science	270	280	2.64*
High Average	25		264	272	3.15*
Low Average	22		258	259	.32
Low	25		245	254	2.30*
High	26	Social Studies	266	276	4.20*
High Average	25		259	269	4.22*
Low Average	22		255	261	3.03*
Low	25		246	253	2.88*

* Significant at .05 level of confidence.

Anxiety. Table 27 describes the results obtained with Sarason's two anxiety scales for the experimental school and a comparable school. The General
Anxiety Scale purports to measure the degree to which youngsters evidence
a generalized fear or anxiousness; the Test Anxiety Scale assesses reaction
to testing situations, the extent to which they are afraid of examinations.
School A is the experimental school.

Table 27

Comparison of Mean Anxiety Scores of
Upper Elementary Students from Two
Riverside Schools

Instrument	N	School A 172	School B 61	t
General Anxiety Scale		10.12	10.03	.10
Test Anxiety Scale		9.89	10.10	.15

These data indicate no appreciable difference in the extent to which students in the experimental project are either more or less anxious than students in a comparable school. A *t* value this small implies that we have no
assurance whatsoever that the differences between these mean scores could
not have occurred by chance.

Motivation. Table 28 describes the mean scores of students from four
different elementary schools on the Junior Index of Motivation (JIM Scale),
modified for use in this study. This instrument is designed to ascertain each
student's personal desire to do good work in school.

On this measure, the mean score of students in School A, the experimental
school, is lower than the mean score of students in any of the other schools
involved. The difference between these means is significant statistically in
two cases, with a *t* value of 4.46 between the means of Schools D and A, a *t*
value of 2.06 between Schools B and A. These data imply that pupils in the
experimental school probably functioned with less motivation toward school
than pupils in the other schools involved, for the odds that these differences
would have occurred by chance are less than one in a hundred.

Concept of Self and Others. The Index of Adjustment Values is a word
association instrument designed to measure young people's feelings about

Table 28

Comparison of Mean Motivational Scores of
Students in Four Riverside
Elementary Schools

Instrument	N	School A 172	School B	School C	School D
JIM Scale		27.02	28.04	27.48	29.44

themselves and other people. There are four possible categories of scores: (++) means that an individual has positive feelings about himself and others; (+−) means that a person thinks well of himself but less well of others; (− +) means that a youngster feels relatively inadequate himself but has a positive concept of others; and (− −) means that a person sees himself in negative terms and other people in a similar light. Table 29 notes the number of students in each of these four categories from Schools A (the experimental school) and B.

Table 29

Comparison of Number of Students Scoring
in Various Categories of Bills' Index
of Adjustment Values Test

Category	N	School A 158	School B 132	Chi Square
++		33 (20%)	66 (51%)	
+ −		62 (39%)	8 (6%)	
− +		45 (30%)	27 (20%)	93.63*
− −		18 (11%)	31 (23%)	

* Chi Square significant beyond .01 level with 3 df.

The Chi Square value of 93.63 indicates that the difference in the number of students in each category is very significant statistically. The odds that these differences would have occurred by chance are less than one time out

of a hundred. Evidently the youngsters in these two schools did see themselves differently. The most apparent discrepancy occurs in the (+ +) and
(+ −) categories, with many more pupils from School B viewing themselves
and others in positive terms; students from the experimental school think
better of themselves than they do of other people.

Students' Estimates of Progress.   The attached student questionnaire (see
Appendix C) was read to each fifth and sixth grade student in the large group
by the regular teacher during the eighth month of school. Table 30 describes
the proportion of students in each grade level who felt they were making
progress academically in the various subject areas specified.

Table 30

Proportion of Fifth and Sixth Graders Who Felt They Were Achieving Academically

Questionnaire Item	Subject Matter Area Involved	Per cent 5th Graders Estimating Satisfactory Progress	Per cent 6th Graders Estimating Satisfactory Progress
9	Science	99%	91%
10	Social Studies	86	96
11	English	81	85
12	Reading	90	87
13	Arithmetic	89	87
14	Art and Music	83	76

In general, these figures indicate most of these students apparently felt
that they were learning in these particular subject matter areas. They also
seemed especially satisfied with their progress in science and social studies,
which were taught in the large group situation, but less satisfied with their
learnings in the areas of art and music, which were also large group activities.

The two statements to elicit pupils' estimates of their general anxiety and
test anxiety levels were answered affirmatively by large numbers of students, indicating some general concern in this particular area. For instance,
52 per cent of the fifth and sixth graders agreed with the statement, "There
are many times when I feel very nervous and afraid." Likewise, 44 per cent of

the fifth graders and 58 per cent of the sixth grade students agreed with the item, "When a teacher says a test is to be given I worry."

Several questionnaire items explored students' attitudes toward school and learning. "Learning is lots of fun" was answered positively by 94 per cent of the fifth graders, but by only 78 per cent of the sixth grade pupils. There was almost unanimous agreement, however, among both fifth and sixth graders (99 per cent) that "I try to do good work in school most all the time." Also, 94 and 92 per cent of each group agreed that "Putting things together and making something new and different is very exciting." However, only 37 per cent of the fifth grade pupils and 66 per cent of the sixth grade youngsters agreed that "When children have several different teachers every day they learn better." Similarly, only 44 per cent of the fifth grade students as opposed to 73 per cent of the sixth graders agreed that "changing classes is a good way to learn." And though 96 per cent of each group agreed that "The teachers in this school are very good to me," only 81 per cent of the fifth graders and 68 per cent of the sixth graders agreed that "The teachers and students in this school get along well."

The reactions of youngsters to items designed to ascertain their feelings about themselves and others are described in Table 31.

Table 31

Proportion of Fifth and Sixth Graders Agreeing with Self-Other Concept Items

Item	Proportion 5th Graders Agreeing	Proportion 6th Graders Agreeing
The students in this school are friendly.	87%	92%
Everybody is important in this school.	95	86
There are a lot more good people in the world than bad.	97	93
Most of my friends are in my section.	28	36
I feel pretty good about myself and I can do a lot of things quite well.	71	73

These figures are somewhat contradictory to the Index of Adjustment Values data described earlier, since students here apparently feel more positively toward others than toward themselves.

Parental Estimates. Table 32 summarizes the responses of parents on the questionnaire they completed estimating their youngsters' progress in general terms (see Appendix D). That is, (+) indicates that a majority of parents felt their child was progressing *about as much or better than* he had in previous years; (−) indicates that a majority felt their child was making *about the same or less* progress than previously; and (0) means that most parents felt their child was making *about the same* progress as he had in other years. Since replies were anonymous, responses from parents of fifth and sixth grade children are reported together.

These general data indicate definite shifts in parental sentiment in a positive direction during the academic year. Out of nine changes in parents' estimates of their child's progress at year's end, every one reflects more student progress than estimated at mid-year.

Teacher Reaction. All teachers in the experimental school, grades one through six, were asked to complete a questionnaire three times during the year (see Appendix E); they described their feelings in several areas. Table 33 summarizes all of these responses in general terms. A plus sign (+) indicates that the majority of teachers felt better about the teaching process than other years; a minus sign (−) indicates the majority of teachers felt poorer about the teaching process than other years; a zero (0) means that the majority of teachers felt the same about the teaching process this year as in other years.

Teachers working in the departmentalized program did not feel as good as they had in previous years in the following areas: motivating children to learn, helping children with attitudes, getting to know their students, getting personal information concerning students, teacher to teacher relationships, availability of instructional materials, availability of resource personnel, adequate physical plant, and teacher to parent relationships.

The teachers in the large groups indicated the following areas were not as good as previous years: teaching children skills, individualizing instruction, getting to know your students, maintaining satisfactory classroom control, checking students' work, getting personal information concerning students, and testing and placing children.

During the year a change in attitude and feelings was indicated by the teachers in the departmentalized program. Table 34 shows this change. Some of these attitudinal shifts are positive and some negative.

Departmentalized teachers indicated they felt much better than ever before in teaching children skills and in individualizing instruction. However, they did not feel as successful in motivating children to learn, helping children with attitudes, teacher to teacher relationships, or teacher to parent relationships.

Table 35 indicates the feelings and attitudes of the large group teachers as indicated by the responses on the questionnaire. In the area of teaching skills, individualizing instruction, knowing students, checking papers, getting per-

Table 32

Summary of Parental Estimates of Children's
Progress in Experimental Situation

Item	General Response In:	
	January	May
Academic Achievement		
How well he is learning science.	0	+
How well he is learning social studies.	0	+
How well he is learning to write and spell correctly.	+	+
How well he is learning to read and understand his reading.	+	+
How well he is learning arithmetic.	+	+
How well he is learning art and music.	+	+
Anxiety		
How anxious or nervous he is about things in general.	−	+
How anxious or nervous he is about tests and examinations in school.	−	+
Motivation and Attitudes Toward School		
His attitude toward learning in general and school in particular.	0	+
How highly motivated he is to do good work in school.	+	+
How creative he is with ideas or objects.	+	+
His attitudes toward his teachers.	−	0
His feeling about being in different rooms and moving during the day.	+	+
How well he is adjusting to being placed in various groups for instructional purposes.	+	+
How well he is adjusting to different teachers and different rooms during the day.	+	+
His attitude toward being grouped according to an achievement test for instructional purposes.	+	+
How well he is adjusting to having several different teachers each day instead of one.	0	+
Concept of Self and Others		
His attitudes toward his friends and classmates.	+	+
How he feels toward himself.	0	+
How he feels toward other persons.	0	+

Table 33

Comparison of Total Teacher Reaction in Experimental Situation

Item	Self-Contained Teachers	Depart-mentalized Teachers	Large Group Teachers
1. Motivating children	0	—	0
2. Teaching skills	+	+	—
3. Helping attitudes	+	—	+
4. Teaching concepts	+	—	+
5. Satisfied about work	+	0	+
6. Individualizing instruction	+	+	—
7. Knowing students	+	—	—
8. Satisfactory control	—	0	—
9. Planning work	+	0	+
10. Checking students' work	+	0	—
11. Feeling good physically	+	0	0
12. Attitude toward teaching	+	0	+
13. Information about students	+	—	—
14. Teacher to teacher	+	—	+
15. Availability of materials	0	—	+
16. Testing and placing children	—	0	—
17. Resource personnel	—	—	+
18. Physical plant	—	—	+
19. Teacher to parent	+	—	+
20. Teacher to administration	+	+	+

sonal information concerning students, and testing and placing students in the large group, these teachers did not feel as good as in previous years. In the areas of maintaining satisfactory classroom control, the large group teachers originally felt it was about the same as previously, but by semester time felt that it was not as satisfactory as in previous years.

Conclusions

The purpose of this study is to determine the effect of modified departmentalization and large group instruction upon students in the upper elementary

Table 34

Attitudinal Changes Among Departmentalized Teachers During One Academic Year

Item	Fall	Winter	Spring
Motivating children to learn	0	—	—
Teaching children concepts	+	+	0
Checking students' work	+	—	0
Teacher to teacher relationships	0	—	—
Availability of resource personnel	0	0	—
Feeling satisfied about work	—	0	0
Feeling good physically	—	0	0
Teacher to parent relationship	—	0	—

grades. A careful examination of these data would seem to indicate several general conclusions. First, most of the fifth and sixth graders involved in this particular project did make satisfactory progress in the various academic areas studied, although the more able pupils made less progress in English than expected. Second, the students in this experimental situation have somewhat distorted concepts of themselves and of other persons. Third, these boys and girls also seemed to reflect lower motivational levels than other pupils in conventional situations. Fourth, although there apparently was some concern by the pupils themselves and by their parents, these students were neither more nor less anxious than young people of a similar age who were in a traditional organizational pattern. Fifth, with several exceptions, most parents apparently came to accept the organizational innovation as satisfactory by the end of the school year. Sixth, teachers evidently had certain very serious reservations about their own role in this type of organizational pattern as compared to their own experience in a self-contained program.

All things considered, the apparent advantages of large group instruction and departmentalization in the upper elementary grades seem to be counterbalanced by certain definite advantages for a conventional, self-contained classroom organizational pattern as studied in this particular school. In other words, some factors probably exert more profound effect upon students' growth and development than school organization. This problem deserves further study.

Table 35

Attitude of Large Group Teachers in
Experimental Situation

Item	Fall	Winter	Spring
1. Motivating children	0	—	0
2. Teaching skills	—	—	—
3. Helping attitudes	—	—	+
4. Teaching concepts	0	0	+
5. Satisfied about work	0	—	+
6. Individualizing instruction	—	—	—
7. Knowing students	—	—	—
8. Satisfactory control	0	—	—
9. Planning work	+	—	+
10. Checking students' work	+	—	0
11. Feeling good physically	+	—	0
12. Attitude toward teaching	+	0	+
13. Information about students	—	—	—
14. Teacher to teacher	0	—	+
15. Availability of materials	+	—	+
16. Testing and placing children	—	—	—
17. Resource personnel	+	0	+
18. Physical plant	0	—	+
19. Teacher to parent	+	+	+
20. Teacher to administration	+	+	+

A Study of Transition

Familiarity with the system to date has probably resulted in a concern for more effective transition between elementary and junior high school, and between junior high and senior high school situations. If initial problem areas for study included course content, motivation, reading, and class size, transition may appear as a peripheral concern.

Perhaps a junior high school counselor, who may serve as the teacher representative on the area council for his particular school, expresses a deep conviction about the difficulties upcoming elementary students seem to have when they first enter junior high school. How many experience difficulties in adjusting? How many overcome the problems? How long does it take for a majority of youngsters to make the transition from self-contained to departmentalized operations smoothly and satisfactorily? Will youngsters who have participated in a modified departmentalized set-up in elementary school experience fewer problems in junior high school than those who had six years in self-contained classrooms? How do parents interpret the changes? Is the junior high school doing enough to orient the new students before and after they arrive on the scene? Is their academic achievement affected? How many failing grades are received during the first grading period by new seventh grade students? What kinds of achievement records did these pupils have before? Are there ample opportunities for counselor and guidance help? Are the rules and regulations in the junior high school reasonable or excessive? How many students fail seventh grade who had successful academic records before that point in their school career? Why do these students fail? Are there some young people who never seem to adjust to being in a big junior high school which is more complicated and faster moving than their elementary school experience? What are these students like? What kind of difficulties do they have? What lies behind their inability to make the grade? Does the fault for their adjustment problems rest with the school or with these youth? What can teachers do to help induct new seventh graders into the junior high school situation?

In the area council the supervisor has an opportunity to examine these questions. He needs to find out which students attended which elementary schools to see if a particular organizational structure at that level actually reduces problems of transition or whether some educators just think it does. He must talk with many teachers and parents and seek their personal observations. To make these meaningful, however, the area council will probably need to standardize the questioning procedure or prepare them in written form. Some data would be more meaningful if obtained directly from the students themselves, so that an interview schedule could be prepared identifying those questions the council considers most pertinent.

Another angle, of course, would be to undertake an intensive study of some of the research already available. What have other researchers found new junior high school students' problems to be? What does research say about the effectiveness of the core program? Do students learn more or less in departmentalized junior high school classes than they do in self-contained classrooms? Does either organizational pattern favor young people's social acceptance or acceptance of self?

From these kinds of questions, a more precise study of some phase of the transition problem should develop naturally. The area council's first efforts may be exploratory and fairly "loose," but focusing the attention of elementary and secondary people on the topic simultaneously may be a very important step. If any clues about the overall problem become apparent, these can be pursued in greater depth in subsequent studies. Making inroads on such problems as transition should give the supervisor experience and familiarity with the factors involved so that later efforts can attain greater sophistication and additional rigor. A study in this area might look like the following:

Problems of Transition from Elementary to Junior High School

The Problem

How do the organizational patterns of elementary schools affect the transition of students into one junior high school? What do students think help them to make this transition more readily? What do parents think are the problems confronting their children as they enter the seventh grade? How do teachers feel about these problems?

The Procedures

In seeking the answers to these questions a four phase program was employed. Two questionnaires were completed by 480 students in one Riverside high school, another questionnaire was sent home to the parents, and still another was supplemented by individual counseling sessions with 35 students.

The Results

The student questionnaires were completed in English classes. In response to a question as to their liking of their elementary school, 91 per cent responded strongly in the affirmative. The students comprising the 9 per cent who did not like their schools were students who had been retained, and those who had been socially promoted. Ninety-two per cent of the parents indicated satisfaction with the elementary schools of their children.

The students indicated that their elementary schools did three things that helped them to be ready for junior high school: teacher-led classroom discussions in their sixth grade clases, the trip to a junior high school, and departmentalization of the elementary school. Forty-four per cent of these seventh graders had had experience in departmentalized schools before entering junior high school, with less than three per cent indicating that they did not like this arrangement. When asked if they like having a different teacher for each subject in junior high school, 97 per cent of the students said yes. When asked to give suggestions for things which might be done at the elementary school level, 39 per cent wrote that they felt that some experience in departmentalization would be helpful. Although of the overall group only 39 per cent stated this, it was the most frequently mentioned suggestion. The response of the parents to the question of departmentalization indicated that 73 per cent thought that limited or complete departmentalization of the sixth grade would be beneficial.

What do students like and dislike about junior high school? Students responded with a strong indication of happiness and like for their school. Twenty-five per cent stated that they liked everything, and of the things listed as disliked, 19 per cent named things characteristic of large schools, and especially of the combined junior-senior high school arrangement. This percentage represents the largest group within one similar category.

What do seventh graders indicate that they would have liked as sixth graders that would have helped their transition to be easier? Of the many things which the students named, the following is a tabulation of the most frequently chosen and the percentage of seventh graders who named the particular item:

Experience in departmentalization 39%
A discussion of rules, regulations and pro-
    cedures as stated in the handbook 28%
More homework 17%
More and harder classwork 13%
Teacher explanation about junior high and
    what will be expected of them 11%

What do parents think of the organization and equipping of the schools? The parents were asked to comment on how well they felt that the elementary and the junior high schools were equipped. Seventy-two per cent felt that the elementary school was adequately equipped, but only 57 per cent felt that the junior high school was supplied with necessary equipment. The parents' ideas of equipping a school included not only the materials used as teaching aids, but also the availability of enough classrooms, library, and physical education facilities, individual locker spaces, and school buses.

What do parents think of ability grouping of students? Parents of these children expressed favorable response to the question of their approval of ability grouping of their children. Seventy-two per cent liked the program for the elementary schools, and 90 per cent approved of the program for junior high schools.

What are parents' feelings concerning the relationship between their child's teachers and themselves? Sixty-five per cent of the responding parents indicated that they did not feel that the relationship was close, with comments that this was largely their own fault. There were indications that they ceased to maintain as close a contact with the teachers in junior high school as they had in the elementary school. Some of the parents remarked that they were glad to not have to work as hard in the PTA, expressing that they had given much time to this organization on the elementary level and felt "burned out." There were comments that they felt that a less close contact was good for the child's development of independence, preferring to wait for the teacher to take the initiative for personal contacts.

How did the students adjust academically to junior high school? Table 36 shows evidence of the students' academic achievement. These figures indicate the grades earned by the students for the first six weeks grading period expressed as the percentage of students in the seventh grade who earned the following grades by subjects.

Table 36a

Percentage of Seventh Grade Students Making Various Grades

Subject Area	A	B	C	D	E
English	10	30	27	12	4
Math	17	27	29	12	12
Science	17	29	31	13	4
Social Studies	13	26	35	16	4

What do the seventh grade teachers indicate concerning adjustment of their students into one junior high school? The 17 teachers of seventh grade students were asked to complete questionnaires regarding the academic progress of these students and to discuss problems of transition. These teachers indicate that student adjustment is completed within a two week period for 90 per cent of the students. Nine teachers believed that departmentalization of the sixth grade was helpful to the adjustment of the students into junior high school. However, eight stated that they could not find evidence from their working with the students that those with departmental experience adjusted any more readily than those without this experience. Of these eight, five indicated that they personally felt that a program of departmentalization within the upper elementary grade is beneficial in the development of a student's educational progress by enabling him to learn to work with several different instructors capable of giving the student direction from a concentrative background but these teachers were unable to give specific evidence from their present students to support this belief. (Table 36b)

Table 36b

Comparison of Grades of Students Who Had
Experienced Departmentalized Sixth Grade
or Self-Contained Sixth Grade

Subject Area	Type School Organization	A	B	C	D	E
English	Departmentalized	9	37	31	18	5
	Self-Contained	19	39	31	10	1
Math	Departmentalized	17	25	31	15	12
	Self-Contained	13	37	34	9	6
Science	Departmentalized	23	25	35	13	4
	Self-Contained	19	36	27	13	4
Social Studies	Departmentalized	28	21	38	13	3
	Self-Contained	10	25	46	16	3

What did students reveal through personal interviews?   Thirty-five students were chosen at random for individual conferences. These represented a cross-section of the seventh grade, with all but one feeder school represented (this particular school sent only eight students to the present seventh grade). The interviews lasted an average of 35 minutes for each student. Many phases of the student's outlook on elementary and junior high school were discussed. These interviews were conducted over a period of five months, beginning in October.

Several major ideas were drawn from these conferences. Students do not seem to think of this transition as much of a problem. However, they feel that a period of two weeks was sufficient in their attainment of the "feeling at home" adjustment. This period of time was supported in the reports of the teachers. The teachers feel that 90 per cent of the students are well adjusted by the end of the second week of school. There was no particularly strong correlation of feelings that students from departmentalized elementary schools adjusted to a greater degree than those who had not had this experience.

Likewise, some students apparently never will be able to adjust during the period of the first semester, and probably will have adjustment problems all during the school year. Conferences with ten of these students were conducted in addition to the conferences with the 35 previously noted. These students are very slow academically as indicated by their cumulative records. Each child had a definite reading problem. The highest reading score indicated for any of them was 5.2 on the California Test and a percentile band of 9–23 on the STEP Test.

Conclusions

From a study of the materials gathered from the students, teachers, parents, and interviews, there is no evidence at present to show any strong correlation between the organization of the elementary schools and the transition problems of students into one junior high school. There is evidence that the philosophies of these "feeder" schools are producing happy, well-adjusted seventh grade students who make the transition into the program of a departmentalized junior high school within the first two weeks of the school year. However, with 73 per cent of the responding parents indicating that they feel that at least limited departmentalization of the sixth grades would be helpful to these students and 44 per cent of the students expressing that departmentalization was a helpful experience to them, continued studies on this subject are warranted.

Summary

This chapter has provided a look at three efforts to improve program which began with questions and concerns which were primarily organizational in nature. In each case, a study was outlined to get pertinent information on a problem which arose naturally in the routine functioning of a curriculum council. These studies vary in many ways: level of sophistication, clarity of design, ultimate usefulness, and the like. The next chapter will examine similar efforts to improve program by illustrating problems which center on subject matter.

Appendix C
Student Questionnaire

1. The students in this school are friendly.
2. The teachers in this school are very good to me.
3. When children have several different teachers every day they learn better.
4. Learning is lots of fun.
5. Everybody is important in this school.
6. Most of my friends are in my section.
7. Changing classes is a good way to learn.
8. The teachers and students in this school get along well.
9. Children in this class learn a lot of different things about the earth and air and how things work.
10. This year we have learned many things about different kinds of people, and how they live.
11. This year we have a better understanding of writing and spelling and speaking correctly.
12. This year we are learning to read better and understand what we read more than ever before.
13. This year we have a better understanding of how to use numbers than ever before.
14. Painting and drawing and singing are important in this school.
15. I feel pretty good about myself and I can do a lot of things quite well.
16. There are a lot more good people in the world than there are bad.
17. I try to do good work in school most all of the time.
18. When a teacher says a test is to be given I worry.

19. There are many times when I feel very nervous and afraid.
20. Putting things together and making something new and different is very exciting.

Appendix D
Parents' Questionnaire

Directions

This year your child is part of an experimental program in classroom organization. Each year you have undoubtedly observed his attitudes and his accomplishments. We are concerned about the impact of this new educational program upon your child. Would you please help us evaluate its effectiveness by giving us your honest reaction to some questions? Please DO complete the form and send it to your child's school tomorrow, but DO NOT sign your name. Thank you.

Described below are several aspects or results of your child's educational experience. In terms of his previous experiences in other situations, would you please indicate as accurately as possible your estimate of his feelings and behavior in each of the areas listed below? Use the following scale:

1	2	3	4	5
Much poorer than	Not quite as good as	About the same as	Somewhat better than	Much better than

_____ 1. His attitude toward his friends and classmates.
_____ 2. His attitude toward his teachers.
_____ 3. His feelings about being in different rooms and moving during the day.
_____ 4. His attitude toward learning in general and school in particular.
_____ 5. His attitude toward being grouped according to an achievement test score for instructional purposes.
_____ 6. How well he is adjusting to the different teachers and different rooms during the day.
_____ 7. How well he is adjusting to being placed in various groups for instructional purposes.
_____ 8. How well he is adjusting to having several teachers each day instead of one.
_____ 9. How well he is learning science.
_____ 10. How well he is learning social studies.

_____ 11. How well he is learning to write and spell and speak correctly.
_____ 12. How well he is learning to read and understand his reading.
_____ 13. How well he is learning arithmetic.
_____ 14. How well he is learning art and music.
_____ 15. How he feels toward himself.
_____ 16. How he feels toward other persons.
_____ 17. How highly motivated he is to do good work in school.
_____ 18. How anxious or nervous he is about things in general.
_____ 19. How anxious or nervous he is about tests and examinations in school.
_____ 20. How creative he is with ideas or objects.

Appendix E
Teacher Questionnaire

_____ self contained class
_____ small group class
_____ large group class

Directions

This year your school is experimenting with different ways of organizing students for instructional purposes. These are probably new experiences for you. Realizing that it is very difficult to ask you to describe your own feelings on these matters objectively, please try to do this as best you can. Listed below are several aspects or results of the teaching process. Please attempt to describe *your own feelings* accurately about each of these matters by using the scale below.

1	2	3	4	5
Much poorer than	Not quite as good as	About the same as	Somewhat better than	Much better than

_____ 1. Motivating children to learn.
_____ 2. Teaching children skills.
_____ 3. Helping children with attitudes.
_____ 4. Teaching children concepts.
_____ 5. Feeling satisfied about your work.
_____ 6. Individualizing instruction.
_____ 7. Getting to know your students.

_____ 8. Maintaining satisfactory classroom control.

_____ 9. Planning your work.

_____ 10. Checking students' work.

_____ 11. Feeling good physically.

_____ 12. Attitude toward teaching.

_____ 13. Getting personal information concerning students.

_____ 14. Teacher to teacher relationship.

_____ 15. Availability of instructional materials.

_____ 16. Testing and placing children.

_____ 17. Availability of resource personnel.

_____ 18. Adequate physical plant.

_____ 19. Teacher to parent relationships.

_____ 20. Teacher to administration relationships.

8 Curriculum Studies Involving Content

Introduction

"Content" was one of the basic concerns identified throughout all of the early discussions. Are we using the right subject matter? Are the so-called "modern" programs in mathematics, science, structural linguistics, or generative grammar better than the subject matter we have been using in our schools? Will children learn more, better, faster, and will they forget less if we adopt PSSC physics or BSCS biology, than if we continue with the traditional programs? How will we know?

These questions are heard often in schools today. Advocates of the "new" programs usually respond, "Of course the programs are good. The best educators in the country prepared the materials and planned the exercises. Who are we to question their abilities? They have had years of experience in the field. They are recognized scholars. And the government would never provide money for a big curriculum project like that unless they were certain that the people involved knew what they were doing."

How can we find out if the new materials really are sound? Should we ask people from the nearby university whom we know and respect? What criteria have other school systems employed? How do we know for certain that the new programs will help us achieve the objectives we want to achieve? Who gave that national curriculum committee the authority to change educational objectives? How will our students do on the college boards if we adopt this program? Will parents object if they do not understand the materials and cannot help their children with their homework? How much will the new textbooks cost? Will the teachers be able to handle the program? Should we have special inservice training efforts to help them get ready if we decide to change? Are there enough consultants nearby? What do our teachers think about the new content? Are they enthusiastic or lukewarm or violently opposed? Would we put the new program in every school or just where teachers and principals accept the idea and agree to give it a good try? What is a "good try?" How long do we keep using the new materials before we decide to keep the program, and how difficult would it be to go back to the conventional curriculum if we changed our minds? What kind of information will we need before we make a decision to adopt the new program, and what kind of information will we need later when we want to decide whether we should keep it or not?

If an area council decides to undertake a study along these lines, a report such as the following one might be produced to describe the council's efforts.

A Study of Fourth Grade Children's Achievement of SMSG Mathematics in Riverside School District

The Problem

During recent years a number of curriculum groups around the country have developed instructional materials in the field of mathematics. The University of Illinois Committee on School Mathematics (UICSM), the Ball State University Mathematics Program, and the School Mathematics Study Group (SMSG) are some of the better known projects. Although these programs vary in several important ways, all are similar since they include mathematical concepts which are new to the particular level for which the materials have been prepared; all employ a reorganization of content which is designed to facilitate "discovery learning" rather than rote memorization; and all include basic changes in terminology. Textual materials are arranged so that an entirely different thought process is aimed for in the learning experience. While traditional mathematics has always relied heavily upon deductive logic and the expository approach, "modern" mathematics programs depend heavily upon intuitive thinking and inductive reasoning. The entire mental process is actually turned around. Students are led from one experience to another through a series of events aimed at enabling each youngster to "discover" the fundamental principles underlying the mathematical concepts for himself.

The question is: are these new programs "good"? The case below is a study of fourth grade children's achievement in an SMSG mathematics program as compared to a similar group of fourth grade children's achievement in a conventional mathematics program.

Do children who study SMSG mathematics material learn more than children who study conventional mathematics materials over a period of one school year? What are the attitudes of such children toward mathematics?

The Procedures

In an effort to answer these questions, five phases were involved. First, the possibility of using SMSG mathematics in the schools was suggested. Second, this proposal was considered. Third, a decision was made. Fourth, the program was implemented. Finally, an evaluation was conceptualized and effected. Each of these various phases is discussed in detail below.

SMSG Program Proposed. During January, one of the members of the national staff of the School Mathematics Study Group (SMSG) served as a consultant to our schools. He spoke to all of the school principals about the SMSG program and met with various interested groups throughout the Riverside District during a two-day visit.

Following this visit of the SMSG consultant, the principal of Pine Junior High School asked the curriculum director if he could adopt the SMSG materials in his school the following year. In the discussions which ensued, several problems became evident. Who would pay for the new books? Were the teachers prepared? Did the teachers want to use the new materials? What would happen to the junior high school students if they went into a high school program which did not employ the SMSG materials and approach?

Broadening the discussion to include a senior high school principal was a logical first step. The principal of Ridge High School was willing to entertain the possibility of adopting the new program, but he wanted his mathematics teachers to react to the idea. He was also opposed to initiating a two-track— conventional and SMSG—program which would involve scheduling and other difficulties if it could be avoided. It was decided that this possibility should be referred to the area curriculum council for further consideration.

Considering the SMSG Program. After the possibility of adopting the SMSG program had been seriously proposed, the Area Four Curriculum Council of Riverside School District formally considered the proposal. Extended discussions among parents, teachers, principals, and supervisors went on for several meetings. Special committees of mathematics teachers were appointed to review the materials carefully. Problems of articulation, inservice education, and procurement of materials were identified. Outside consultants from the state department of education and the state university met with these various groups and made their recommendations based upon their knowledge of the program and their familiarity with our special situation. Discussions were held with the superintendent and members of the Riverside Board of Education regarding the availability of special resources to guarantee that the program could get off the ground. By late spring a decision was made to adopt the SMSG program in all Area Four Curriculum Council Schools.

Deciding to Adopt the SMSG Program. The decision to adopt the SMSG program in the Area Four Schools was involved. Many people had participated in the extensive discussions, and when the decision was finally made, it was a multifaceted decision based upon those intensive considerations. Four basic commitments accompanied the decision.

First, all of the teachers in all of the Area Four Schools at several different grade levels would participate in the new program. During the course of the meetings to consider adopting the SMSG program, it became apparent that the proposal had such dimensions that for all practical purposes it should probably be resolved on an "all or none" principle. Either all of the schools in Area Four should participate completely or none of them should become involved. Because the departure is so complete and the sequence of content and experiences so different, if some youngsters used SMSG mathematics materials in some schools and some did not, the problem of coping with these varying backgrounds and experiences would simply magnify the problem which already faced mathematics teachers at the junior and senior high school levels. Ultimately, with an overwhelming majority of the teachers who would be directly involved supporting the proposed change, the decision was made to adopt the program in grades four, seven, nine and ten. Theoretically, almost all of these students in Area Four would eventually move into Ridge Senior High School, and by adopting the program at grade levels described above, continuity of experience could be assured, along with proposed expansion during subsequent years to provide for students who had SMSG backgrounds. If some schools or some teachers had been permitted to continue the conventional program, either a two-track plan would have had to develop or else students would be experiencing their mathematics program according to accidental placement or teacher whim. Frustration and confusion would inevitably occur.

Second, SMSG textbooks and teacher materials had to be procured. Because the SMSG program was "experimental," only mimeographed copies of materials were available. The textual materials were supposedly priced "at cost," but investigation revealed that the Riverside District could probably print all of the necessary textbooks themselves at considerable savings if a special printing press were purchased and if permission to reproduce the materials was obtained. Permission to reprint was granted, the press was obtained, and the production of over 3000 special textbooks got under way.

Third, special inservice education programs were inaugurated beginning with preschool planning and carrying on throughout the first semester of the school year. All fourth, seventh, ninth, and tenth grade teachers who taught mathematics and who had not previously participated in a National Science Foundation Institute for mathematics teachers participated in a two-week inservice program in the teaching of SMSG mathematics before school started and, then, met regularly three hours each week during the first semester of the school year. These inservice training sessions were conducted by the mathematics supervisor and an elementary supervisor, and those teachers who wanted college credit for the sessions were able to obtain such credit from the local college after special arrangements had been made. Every teacher was encouraged to call either of the supervisors any time a problem arose, and regular invitation and consultation was designed to provide continuing support for those teachers who were involved.

Fourth, at the outset it was decided "to give the program a good try but to evaluate it carefully." This "good try" was not defined, but it was understood that this meant that the program would not be abandoned after a few weeks or even after one year. The total proposal was to be put to a thorough examination for a considerable length of time to test its real mettle. All members of the area curriculum council agreed that this proposed curriculum change should be subjected to experimental scrutiny.

Implementing the SMSG Program. The plans regarding preparation of materials and inservice training of staff were effected, along with a program aimed at helping the community understand what was underway. With the cooperation of two nearby universities, the local news media, and the wholehearted support of the local school board and the area curriculum council, the new program started in September. Each school undertook its own program of parent education, but this was supplemented by a series of efforts emanating from the Riverside Schools' central office in the form of newspaper stories, television programs, and planned discussions with civic clubs and other interested groups. There was a lot of face-to-face communication between parents, teachers, and administrators and others. Many problems arose, of course. A sufficient number of textbooks available for the opening of school was one serious problem, but the concerted efforts of all persons involved resulted in the production of thousands of textbooks and teachers' manuals by the time school began in the fall. There were some recalcitrant teachers, many confused and even some obstinate and arrogant parents, but the commitments were honored and the total program got started with everyone working hard to give it the "good try."

Evaluating the SMSG Program. Beginning with the school year in the fall, Area Four Curriculum Council immediately began to develop plans to evaluate the newly adopted program in mathematics. The program had been initiated at different levels simultaneously, with the intention of expanding the program in subsequent years so that all students in grades four through twelve would be involved within three years. It seemed appropriate, therefore, to initiate assessment efforts in a limited way. Because of the practical problems in getting the program "off the ground" and because there was no "complete" program with continuity the first year, a limited evaluation seemed both reasonable and possible as well as theoretically justifiable. The area council might have argued that they should wait three years until the program was fully in operation and then evaluate the entire operation during the fourth or fifth year. That was too long a period to wait. Working on the basis of the commitment to evaluate which had been agreed to the previous spring, informal and formal assessment efforts were begun.

The informal assessment procedures developed naturally with the beginning of the fall school term. Questions were raised in the area curriculum council. How are the students getting along with the new mathematics materials? What are the teachers' reactions? How do the parents feel? The mathematics supervisor and the elementary supervisor, who had conducted the pre-school inservice sessions, visited the teachers utilizing the new materials regularly and made periodic reports to the curriculum council. Principals in participating schools shared their observations regarding students', parents', and teachers' feelings about the new program. The mathematics supervisor from the state department of education was invited to visit the participating schools, and he gave his impressions to the members of the area curriculum council, too. These regular reports continued throughout the first year, and all indications were that the program was being very well received. Students seemed to like the new materials and the new approaches, teachers were generally enthusiastic, and parents were apprehensive but fairly well informed and typically supportive. Isolated exceptions were identified and "checked out" by the supervisors and principals involved.

In a more formal way, the area council also appointed a subcommittee to design and accomplish a systematic objective evaluation. This group began work during the early winter months, and by March proposed a five phase evaluation rationale. The remaining portion of this study describes the results of that evaluation plan, which was adopted by the area curriculum council as a beginning effort to get feedback data about the effectiveness of the program.

The Results

In an effort to determine the effectiveness of the newly adopted SMSG mathematics program, a five-phase evaluation effort based upon two explicit assumptions was undertaken.

The assumptions were simple and practical. First, the initial evaluation must be seen as a first effort in a series of efforts which would extend over a longer period of time. Second, only the fourth grade program would be studied intensively the first year.

The five-phase effort involved the following: identifying students in the "experimental" program; selection of comparable students who might serve as a "control" group; development of evaluation instruments and procedures; making observations (testing) of all students involved; and comparing the "achievements" (broadly defined) of students from the "experimental" and "control" programs. Each of these various phases of the evaluation process is described in detail below.

Identifying Students in the SMSG Program. Having made the decision to limit the evaluation to one year in time and one grade level, the obvious question arose: should we study all of the fourth graders who were participating in the new program or sample from this group somehow? Many factors affect the success or failure of any new curriculum venture (e.g., availability of instructional materials, teachers' attitudes and skill, students' abilities, etc.) and because some of the factors should be considered and controlled, the decision was made to include all fourth grade students in participating schools on whom pertinent control-type data were available. This ultimately came to mean students in 24 classrooms from six of the Area Four Curriculum Council elementary schools. Approximately 750 youngsters were involved.

Identifying Students in "Conventional" Mathematics Program. Having decided to study the achievement of as many of the students participating in the SMSG program on whom there was sufficient control-type data available, it was then decided to identify a comparable group utilizing the "conventional" mathematics program for comparison purposes. The Area Four Curriculum Council schools were generally upper-middle class schools, so that it was necessary to identify about the same number of classroom groups from approximately the same number of schools which served similar socioeconomic areas of the district. Utimately, 21 teachers from seven different schools were identified as "control" groups. There were approximately 650 students in these teachers' classroom groups. In no case did these teachers know that they were participating in the study. In fact, these identifications were not even determined until the month of May at the end of the school year.

Development of Evaluation Instruments. All of the fourth grade teachers using the SMSG program submitted test items covering the year's work during the final month of school. Teachers using the conventional program also submitted items which they thought were appropriate for ascertaining students' progress in mathematics. The county supervisor of mathematics and two elementary supervisors selected items from each group, then developed two final testing instruments: one measured achievement in SMSG mathematics and the other measured achievement in conventional mathematics. Each of these sets of items was then divided in half, and two testing instruments prepared. (Appendix F) Each instrument contained items designed to measure achievement in SMSG mathematical concepts and skills and some designed to measure achievement in conventional mathematical concepts and skills. These were not equivalent tests at all, and eventually all of the students in both the SMSG classes and the conventional classes were tested with both achievement scales. For the purpose of this study, those items which pertained to SMSG material constituted the SMSG test; those items which pertained to the conventional mathematics constituted the conventional test.

In addition to achievement in mathematics, there was real concern about these youngsters' attitudes toward mathematics. After considerable fruitless searching and extensive thought about the matter, a simple four-item attitude scale was devised. Simply, this scale consisted of four items with three drawings of human faces each. One was a "smiling" face, one a "straight" face, and one a "frowning" face. Beneath each was a line, and each student was asked to mark an "X" which described how he felt "at reading time," "at play time," "at arithmetic time," and "at Spanish time" (which was taught by television). For the purpose of this study, only the responses to the faces which pertained to students' feelings about arithmetic were utilized. It was not known whether these items were a valid measure of fourth grade students' attitudes toward mathematics, but it was generally felt that the approach was unique and interesting and probably an appropriate indicator of how these students really felt.

Collecting Achievement and Other Data. During the final two weeks of school, all of the fourth grade children in the seven SMSG and the seven conventional program schools were tested with the three instruments described: A test of SMSG concepts and skills, a test of conventional mathematical concepts and skills, and a four-item attitudinal "faces" scale. All testing was done by teams of supervisors who visited each of the 45 classrooms and administered the various instruments under "standardized" conditions. Regular classroom teachers were not involved in the testing process in any way.

Other data on these same students' achievement as measured the previous fall by the Kuhlman-Anderson Intelligence Test and the Sequential Tests of Education Progress (STEP Tests) in Mathematics and Reading were collected from permanent record files. Complete test data were available for 588 youngsters involved in the SMSG program and for 536 of those participating in the conventional program schools.

Comparing Achievement. Table 37 describes the mean achievement scores in reading, mathematics, and IQ which were obtained from the files and which demonstrate the comparability of the SMSG and conventional groups according to their fall testing scores.

Table 37

Mean Achievement Scores of Fourth Grade Students Participating in SMSG and Conventional Mathematics Programs (Pre-Experiment Control Data)

Group	N	KA IQ	STEP Mathematics	STEP Reading
SMSG Males	285	105.2	244.2	252.2
SMSG Females	303	107.9	242.8	258.0
Conventional Males	310	105.2	241.1	248.7
Conventional Females	226	108.5	241.1	256.4

These data suggest that students in the SMSG mathematics program were generally comparable to students who participated in the conventional mathematics program when school began in the fall. That is, all of the data described above were obtained during the district wide achievement testing program which was conducted during the month of October. No statistical tests of significance of difference between mean scores was accomplished, but students in the "experimental" and "control" groups were probably comparable in terms of the ability and achievement levels which they brought to the learning year. The differences which did exist favored slightly those youngsters who were participating in the experimental program.

Table 38 describes the data which were obtained when these same students were tested with the specially devised SMSG and conventional mathematics tests at the end of the school year.

Table 38

Mean Achievement Scores

Group	N	Conventional Mathematics Test	SMSG Mathematics Test
SMSG Males	285	35.0	23.0
SMSG Females	303	35.0	24.8
Conventional Males	310	35.7	7.2
Conventional Females	226	38.3	7.6

The fourth grade students who participated in an experimental program in SMSG mathematics for one school year appeared to learn about as much conventional mathematics as students participating in a conventional program. No statistical test of the significance of difference of mean scores was made, but it would appear from inspection of the data that the mean scores of SMSG students on the conventional mathematics test were probably not significantly lower than the mean scores of students who experienced conventional mathematics programs. The differences favor students in the control groups, but the differences are slight. Because the differences in pre-experiment data on the STEP tests in mathematics and reading favor the experimental group slightly, however, these very slight differences might be important. Elaborate statistical procedures would be necessary to determine the original differences in order to make sophisticated analyses, but it was thought that such refinements were not necessarily appropriate for this beginning effort in evaluation.

The data in Table 38 also describe mean scores on the specially constructed SMSG mathematics test for students from the experimental and control groups. Obviously, these scores differ considerably. The students in the SMSG program made average scores of 23.0 and 24.8 on the SMSG test, while those in the control made average scores of 7.2 and 7.6 for males and females, respectively. No statistical tests of the significance of differences of mean scores were made, but these mean scores vary greatly and favor those youngsters who participated in the experimental program.

In other words, students who participated in the experimental SMSG mathematics program seem to have learned about as much conventional mathematics plus additional "SMSG" learnings when compared to students who participated in the conventional program.

Table 39 describes the way students from the experimental program and

Table 39

Number of Students Who Chose "Smile,"
"Straight," or "Frown" Face When
Asked How They Felt
About Arithmetic

Group	Number Choosing (smile face)	Number Choosing (straight face)	Number Choosing (frown face)	Chi Square
SMSG	191	204	243	
				20.10*
Conventional	243	168	177	

* Chi Square value significant at .001 level with 2 df.

the conventional program responded to the *special* item designed to measure attitudes toward mathematics.

The students who participated in the conventional mathematics class probably enjoyed arithmetic time more and evidently had more favorable attitudes toward mathematics than those students who participated in the experimental SMSG mathematics program. The Chi Square value of 20.10 indicates that these differences are significant statistically. In other words, such a difference would probably occur by chance less than one time in a thousand. Although it may not be particularly relevant here except as an indicator of the usefulness of this technique for measuring attitudes, it is interesting to note that when the responses of these students were compared on their feelings at "play time" and "reading time" there were no statistically significant differences (X^2 value of 4.72 and 2.53 respectively). A difference between the groups was apparent on the item relating to "Spanish time" (X^2 value of 6.40).

Conclusions

Do children who study SMSG mathematics materials learn more than children who study conventional mathematics materials over a period of one school year? Apparently they do.

What are the attitudes of such children toward mathematics? It would appear that youngsters who experienced the conventional program had more favorable attitudes toward mathematics than those involved in the experimental group.

This is the first undertaking of a series of efforts to ascertain the effectiveness of using the SMSG mathematics materials in the Riverside Schools. Future studies will investigate the effectiveness of these experimental materials when used with students at junior and senior high school levels, and over a period of time, more sophisticated evaluation techniques and instruments should enable us to obtain more precise data and better answers. For the time being, students involved in the special SMSG programs are apparently learning about as much conventional mathematics as their fellow students who are experiencing the regular program, but in addition they are also learning more. The less favorable attitudes toward mathematics, however, is definite cause for concern. Most of the teachers in the experimental group felt that their youngsters were enjoying it, but these teachers may be wrong. They may be investing so much of themselves in time and energy that they cannot possibly believe the youngsters are not as excited and enthusiastic as they are. The data in this study suggest studies must employ more refined approaches to determine students' attitudes and feelings toward the program.

The recommendation at this time must be to continue with the program but extend the evaluation efforts so that future studies will be able to provide sharper, more valid data.

Summary

The study described in this chapter involved the classical experimental model design: control certain variables, manipulate others, demonstrate the similarity of groups, and see what difference the experimental variable makes. This neat, clean approach has some utility, but many other factors are important, too. As Stufflebeam points out (1) efforts to improve program should probably employ evaluation of the context, the input, the process, and the products involved. This study of SMSG mathematics touched on some of those factors, but generally it was a product-oriented study. What was the impact of the materials upon student achievement and attitude and skill?

Nevertheless, the study revealed some important ideas. The supervisor does not need to wait until there is a sophisticated researcher on the central office staff. Errors made in statistics are much less significant than errors made in thinking. One can think out a design and identify what seem to be the crucial variables. He can work to create data collecting devices which "fit" the problem needs, checking his ideas with others.

There is no substitute for careful thinking when it comes to studying curriculum with an aim to improve it. Curriculum workers need good information, and curriculum studies are one way to satisfy that need.

Appendix F

Riverside Schools
Mathematics Achievement Test
(2 parts)

Part I

1. Work the following problems and write your answer on the line at the right:

1.	2.	3.	4.	5.
19 +20	98 +47	268 432 295	68 −40	700 −547

6.	7.	8.	9.	10.
80 −61	1962 −1492	43 × 6	4 ×38	25 × 49

11. 207
    × 21

12. 2)‾48‾

13. 3)‾56‾

14. 8)‾967‾

15. 32)‾3776‾

16. Find the average:
    $9.87
    6.42
    3.95
    7.21
    2.30

17. Find the average:
    67
    42
    93
    865

1. _____

2. _____

3. _____

4. _____

5. _____

6. _____

7. _____

8. _____

9. _____

10. _____

11. _____

12. _____

13. _____

14. _____

15. _____

16. _____

17. _____

18–19. Set N = {1,2,3,4}   and Set E = {0, 2, 4}.

    18. Write the union of Set N and Set E.   18. _____

    19. Write the intersection set for Set N and Set E.   19. _____

20. Set A = {car, boat, train, airplane}.
    Set B = {wagon, bicycle, boat}.

    What is the intersection of Set A and Set B?   20. _____

21–24. Choose the correct symbol and copy it in the answer space.

$$\neq \quad > \quad \cup \quad = \quad < \quad \{\} \quad \cap$$

21. Equals   21. _____
22. Greater than
23. Union of sets   22. _____
24. Empty set

       23. _____

25–28. Fill in the chart.   24. _____

       25. _____

Numbers Operated on	Result	Operation Used	Mathematical Sentence
16, q	20	Addition	18 − r = 12
(25)	(26)	(27)	(28)

       26. _____

       27. _____

       28. _____

29. If we add 10 to 8 we get 18. What must we do to 18 to
    UNDO this?   29. _____

30–32. Put a check by the number of the problems in which   30. _____
    you must regroup the sum in order to subtract.

       31. _____

30.	92	31.	72	32.	129	32. _____
	−46		−31		−84	

33. Make an array to illustrate this sentence.

    $4 \times 6 = 24$

33.

34. Write all the factors of 12.

34. _____

_____

_____

35. What operation will "undo" multiplication?

35. _____

36. What operation will "undo" division?

36. _____

37. Write as one number:

"One thousand, three hundreds, six tens and five ones."

37. _____

38. What number should be written in the blank?

$354 = 3$ hundreds, 5 tens, and _____ ones.

38. _____

39–41. Write as Roman Numerals:

39. _____

    39.   13   40. 16   41. 62

40. _____

41. _____

42–44. Write as Arabic Numerals:

42. _____

    42.   XXIV   43. XLI   44. XCVI

43. _____

44. _____

45–46. * * * *
        * * * *
        * * *

    45. If the above objects were grouped by base six,
        what would be the base six numeral to tell how
        many there are?   45. _____

    46. If the objects were grouped by base three what
        would be the base three numeral?   46. _____

47–49. Write in cents.

    47. 1 half dollar   47. _____

    48. 2 dimes   48. _____

    49. 2 quarters   49. _____

50–52. Complete the following:

    50. 6 years = _____ months.   50. _____

    51. 28 days = _____ weeks.   51. _____

    52. 9 feet = _____ yards.   52. _____

53–55. Which of the following are true? Write *true* or *false.*

    53. $14 > 9$ 53. _____

    54. $5 + 4 \neq 5 + 9$ 54. _____

    55. $5 + n \neq 5 + n$ 55. _____

56. Using the number line below write the products which have
    factors of 3.

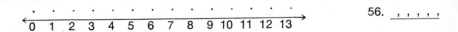

   0 1 2 3 4 5 6 7 8 9 10 11 12 13   56. _, _, _, _, _

Riverside School

Mathematics Achievement Test
(2 parts)

Part II

a.   b.   c.

1–4. Which of these faces shows how you feel at:

1. Spanish time   1. _____

2. Reading time   2. _____

3. Arithmetic time   3. _____

4. Play time   4. _____

5–7. How much of each rectangle is shaded?

5.   5. _____

6.   6. _____

7.   7. _____

8. Using fractions write *three* different names for the
shaded part of this drawing.   8. _____

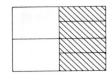

_____

_____

Complete:

9. ½ of 12 is   ?   9. _____

10. ¼ of 36 is   ?   10. _____

11. ⅟₇ of 623 is   ?   11. _____

Write as fractional numerals:

12. one third   12. _____

13. three fourths   13. _____

14. In working a problem Ellen wrote:

$3 \times 5 = n$

$(3 \times 50) + ($ $) = n$ 14. _____

What must she put in the space to show that she
distributed the multiplication of the 3?

15. Complete the following to make it true:

$5 \overline{)\ 95} = 5 \overline{)\ 30} + 5 \overline{)\ 40} + ? \overline{)\ ?}$ 15. _____

Find the missing number:

16. $8 \times 5 = n$ 16. _____

17. $3 \times n = 0$ 17. _____

18. $n = 6 \times 4$ 18. _____

19. $s = 6 \times 48$ 19. _____

20. $3 \times m = 600$ 20. _____

21. $500 + 5 = r$ 21. _____

22–25.

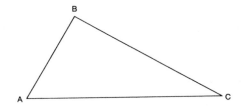

Does the above drawing suggest:

    22. A simple closed curve? (yes or no)   22. _____

    23. A triangle?   23. _____

    24. A polygon?   24. _____

    25. A quadrilateral?   25. _____

26–27. Name two line segments the figure in #22   26. _____
       suggests.
                                                          27. _____

28. What is the intersection of line MN and triangle ABC
    as shown below:

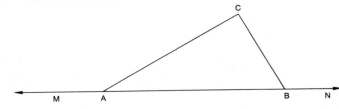

28. _____

29. Find the perimeter.

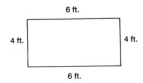

29. _____

30. Find the perimeter if we know that the triangle is isosceles.

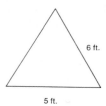

6 ft.

5 ft.

30. _____

31–33. When we say two line segments are "congruent" we mean

31. they are part of the same line. (Answer *true* or *false*)

31. _____

32. a copy of one will just fit the other.

32. _____

33. they are part of a triangle.

33. _____

34–36. How long did each activity last?

34. Stories   2:30 to 2:45

34. _____

35. Play   2:45 to 3:10

35. _____

36. Refreshments   3:10 to 3:45

36. _____

37. Write these units of measure in the order of their size, smallest first:

Yard, Mile, Inch, Foot

37.

1st _____

2nd _____

3rd _____

4th _____

38. The picture at right
suggests a set of
points called_____.   38. _____

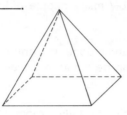

39–40. It has _____   39. _____
triangular faces and
_____ vertices.   40. _____

Look at points P and D on ray CD below.

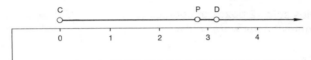

41. What is m$\overline{CP}$ to the nearest unit?   41. _____

42. What is m$\overline{CD}$ to the nearest unit?   42. _____

Work the following problems and record your answers on the answer sheet. (a) answer (b) write a
mathematical sentence that you could have used to
solve it.

43. During one week a cafeteria served lunch to 195 chil-   43. a_____
dren on Monday, 218 on Tuesday, 198 on Wednes-
day, 203 on Thursday, and 196 on Friday. How many   b_____
children were served lunch during the week?

44. In a school there are 18 classrooms. If there are   44. a_____
thirty children in each classroom, how many children
are there in the school?   b_____

45. Ellen bought one-fourth yard of ribbon. How many   45. a_____
inches of ribbon did she buy?

                                                                   b_____

46. In 1940 there were 172,172 people in Miami, Florida.   46. a_____
    During the next ten years the population increased
    to a total of 259,235. By how many people did the   b_____
    population increase?

47. "Polka for Three" is a dance done in groups of   47. a_____
    three. How many groups can be made in a class of
    thirty-two children?   b_____

48. There are 18 boys and 15 girls in Sally's room. How   48. a_____
    many children are there in her room?
                                                                      b_____

49. The children went to the circus in six buses. Forty-   49. a_____
    five children rode in each bus. How many children
    rode to the circus?   b_____

50. Each of 18 Brownies sold 12 boxes of cookies for the   50. a_____
    Girl Scouts. How many boxes were sold?
                                                                      b_____

Notes

1. Daniel Stufflebeam, "The Use and Abuse of Evaluation in Title III," *Theory Into Practice*, VI, No. 3 (June, 1967), pp. 126–133.

9 Curriculum Studies Involving Teachers

The teacher is the most powerful factor in the whole educational process. The way he works professionally makes a difference in the way children learn. What knowledge do teachers in a school system have about students? What are their attitudes toward teaching? What philosophies are represented in the staff of a school system? In what ways do these factors affect curriculum development? Can they, in fact, be measured?

The answers to these questions are clearly difficult to determine. However, to make a significant difference in curriculum development, a curriculum supervisor must address himself to these questions because the effectiveness of teaching is determined by the effectiveness of the teachers. Improved teaching requires improved teachers. Studies involving teachers can provide valuable data to serve as a basis to start.

The study described in this chapter involves a large segment of the teachers in Riverside School District. The expense of the study would have been prohibitive for the local school district, but with funds from Title 1 of the Elementary and Secondary Education Act of 1965 it became feasible. Action research of this magnitude can provide significant data for planning meaningful professional growth; these kinds of data are needed in order to make a real difference in a supervisor's effectiveness as an educational leader.

Perhaps the need to use outside consultants to develop instruments, gather data, and make objective evaluations will become apparent. This study employed a team of consultants to carry out the project.

Describing a Baseline

The Problem

Under the provisions of Title 1 of the Elementary and Secondary Education Act of 1965 funding was made available to the Riverside Public Schools for this particular project. The basic purpose of this project was to develop clearer perceptions on the part of educational personnel about unique problems relating to the education of disadvantaged children and to develop greater skill in performance of their responsibilities. To achieve this purpose, the Riverside Public Schools undertook a special inservice education effort involving the professional staff members of certain schools. To evaluate this undertaking an evaluation plan was conceptualized and implemented by the project staff. As a result of these activities, certain data about the project have been obtained. The basic purpose of this report is to describe these various activities and to review the results which are available at this time.

One of the most pressing problems in America today involves society's efforts to provide educational opportunities for children in inner-city schools. Teachers, administrators, and supervisors who serve in these schools must possess certain specialized knowledge and skills in order to employ the most effective techniques for meeting the educational and developmental needs of these children.

There were three major purposes to this project: conceptual information and understanding, situational identification, and problem solutions. Specifically, the following objectives were expected to be achieved:

(1) Provide knowledge which relates to the needs of disadvantaged pupils.
(2) Achieve more accepting attitudes toward disadvantaged pupils.
(3) Develop a design of follow-up training for individual target schools.

The Procedures

In an effort to achieve these basic objectives, two different kinds of activities were initiated: stimulus presentation and staff involvement. These were separate but inextricably related aspects of the total project. In a general way, the basic plan of the project was to provide information to certain members of the professional staff of the Riverside Public Schools and to arrange for these persons to interact among themselves and with those who provided the information to modify knowledge and attitudes there. The plan of this project presumed that making "good" information from outstanding authorities in the field readily accessible would be an important requisite for helping teachers to learn more about the problems and the situations affecting the educational development of children in inner-city schools. It was also presumed that mere presentation of information would not be enough. Some way of working with the information would be required to enable persons involved to find real meaning and personal significance in the information, so that their own experimental background and their own attitudinal structure would be changed in those directions toward more and better learning for the children they teach.

Since the basic objectives of this project were to provide knowledge, modify attitudes, and develop training experiences for those who work with children in inner-city schools, it was important to devise evaluation procedures to determine whether those objectives had been realized. What follows is a description of events in planning the evaluation, the rationale ultimately employed, and a discussion of specific measuring instruments utilized in implementing this rationale.

Planning the Evaluation. On March 28, members of the project staff met with a consultant from the state university on the problems and possibilities involved in evaluating the project. He was employed as evaluation consultant with the understanding that after visitation and consultation with many of the persons involved, he would work with colleagues on the university campus to select or devise testing instruments to provide baseline data. He spent several hours with the local staff in an effort to be as sensitive to the concerns of project members as possible before making any decisions on evaluation plans. In addition, a team of five other persons from the university setting, representing the disciplines of sociology, psychology, curriculum, instruction, and evaluation came together to form a team to assist in planning the evaluation. These persons met together on many occasions and also did extensive research individually in an effort to make the evaluation proposal valid, reliable, and workable.

The Evaluation Rationale.   In general terms, the rationale in evaluating this project involved collecting baseline descriptive data from several different groups through planned sampling process. Tests given would be employed with the notion of collecting baseline data; that is, describing what did exist at that moment in terms of teachers' knowledge, attitudes, and ways of working with children from inner-city schools.

Three assumptions prompted this decision. First, the project would probably continue in future years; therefore, baseline data collected in June could constitute appropriate pretest data for future projects. Second, if the project continued, it seemed imperative that the data collected be useful in long-range terms. Third, if the observational data collected were sufficiently descriptive, then by studying the particulars involved (i.e., response to various *items* of each of the tests), it should be possible to make inferences about precise points of competence or difficulty reflected in the areas observed.

Because this was a staff development project, it seemed reasonable to assume that most of the data collected would pertain to members of the professional staff. However, the ultimate test of any inservice education venture rests upon the extent the program manifests itself in the lives and minds of the youngsters with whom the professional staff work, so that certain data were also collected from students. The major emphasis of the evaluation effort focused, however, upon persons in professional staff capacities in the various schools participating in this project.

Faced with the need for determining precise but extensive baseline data, a problem arose regarding "how much testing time" and "what factors should be measured." Two problems were involved: the need to collect data of many kinds in order for the baseline to have meaning, but the impossibility of testing everyone with every instrument because of the unreasonable demand in terms of time.

To resolve this dilemma, a series of decisions was made aimed at collecting the largest amount of data possible but still making the least demand on people's time. By utilizing certain principles from sampling theory, the final evaluation rationale began to emerge.

It was decided that certain instruments would be utilized with students and other instruments with members of the professional staff. Further, it was assumed some of these should be primarily "objective" in nature, and others should attempt to get at the more "subjective" aspects. Also, some tests should be used with everybody, while others should only be used with certain portions of the total population involved. Finally, certain test data already available in students' or teachers' files might be added to these data to "round out" the baseline to be described.

Measuring Instruments.   In keeping with the three specific objectives of this project, measuring instruments were specially developed or deliberately selected to deal directly with each objective. In the section which follows, these tests will be described in relationship to the purpose of the project and the conditions under which they were employed.

For collecting baseline data from teachers, three different testing "packages" were prepared. These packages were distributed so that one third of the teachers in each school involved received "Package A," one third received "Package B," and one third "Package C." Each "package" contained a set of test materials to be completed by each teacher and a set of instructions. Tests were distributed by the building principal but were completed by the teachers at home. A letter was also sent from the curriculum director describing the purpose of the testing. Figure 1 describes the contents of each "package" received by the teachers.

Package A	Package B	Package C
Urban Education Information Test	Urban Education Information Test	Urban Education Information Test
Teaching Situation Reaction Test	Adjective Check List	GNC Educational Views Inventory

Figure 1. Testing Instruments Used with
Teachers and Other Professional Staff

The Urban Education Information Test (see Appendix G) was included in "Package A," "B," "C," and as such was administered to all professional staff members in all schools participating in the project and also to central office personnel. As the title implies, this test was designed to measure knowledge about various aspects of education in an urban setting. The test is a 40 item, multiple-choice-type instrument developed at a state university especially for this project. Items were prepared by a sociologist, a psychologist, and several educators familiar with the problems of urban education, and were predicated upon such publications as *Education in Depressed Areas* (1) and *Review of Educational Research* (2). Every item was checked by at least four experts and "keyed" by these same people. Every effort was made to create items factually based, unambiguous, but which would discriminate between those who were knowledgeable in the area and those who were not. It was hoped that item analysis would identify particular areas of strength and particular areas of weakness, so that future staff development programs could focus in on precise points effectively. Because the instrument was specially developed for this project, no reliability or validity data other than that already reported here were available before the instrument was used. Since that time, a comparison of the Riverside teachers' scores with a group of teachers who had completed a graduate level college course with emphasis upon urban education problems has been accomplished, lending support to the usefulness of the test as an instrument which measures "knowledge about" education in an urban setting. However, certain items of the test were also identified which obviously were not useful, and though these will be eliminated from subsequent forms of the test, this report includes data from those items as a part of the total test. This point will be discussed in more detail in the results section below.

The Teaching Situation Reaction Test (TSRT) represented the remaining portion of "Package A," and as such was administered to about one third of the teachers in the various project schools. The TSRT (see Appendix H) was originally developed for use with preservice teachers working with adolescents in a preteaching, settlement house experience in a large city. Since its development the test has undergone extensive revision and validation study. There is both an elementary and secondary teachers' form. Reliability coefficients generally exceed +.80, and several predictive studies demonstrate that the scale discriminates among teachers judged by their supervisors to be more or less effective, and among teachers whose students' cognitive and affective achievements differ. Basically, the instrument measures a teacher's capacity to cope with various kinds of complex classroom situations and includes several dimensions of classroom ability and technique: empathy, structure, sensitivity, and control, for example. High scores on the TSRT are "least desirable," and low scores reflect "more desirable" ways of handling different situations.

The Adjective Check List (see Appendix I) contains a list of 48 adjectives arranged in alphabetical order, and each teacher who completed the materials in "Package B" was asked to select 16 words that most appropriately describe the pupils in his classes. The rationale for the Adjective Check List is twofold: words are positive, neutral, or negative in tone; and the words refer to social attributes, personal or character attributes, intellectual attributes, and physical attributes. Outlined graphically, Figure 2 page 197 shows these two theoretical dimensions with the words within each cell. Even though the theoretical dimensions themselves are reasonably "clean," the placement of particular words in particular cells is obviously not precise operationally. However, the instrument has been useful in studying teachers' perceptions of their students in other situations and seemed appropriate for inclusion here.

The GNC Educational Views Inventory (3) is a 24 item scale designed to appraise the logical consistency of an individual's ideas about education. Each item consists of four substatements, and the respondent is asked to rank in order these four statements for each of the 24 items on the scale. The instrument is structured in terms of two schools of philosophical thought —the rational and the empirical. Each of the 24 items contains two substatements that represent the rational view of education and two substatements which represent the empirical view. The scoring process is accomplished so

	Positive	Neutral	Negative
S o c i a l	courteous affectionate agreeable gregarious harmonious	outgoing civil imitative informal	antagonistic rude quarrelsome disruptive
C h a r a c t e r	sincere patient considerate idealistic	realistic changeable unpredictable humble	malicious mischievous fanciful self-centered
I n t e l l e c t u a l	curious discerning creative interested	intent aware indifferent expressive	imperceptive bungling rash superficial
P h y s i c a l	dynamic vigorous neat	agile quick active animated	lazy awkward lethargic sloppy

Figure 2. Theoretical Dimensions of Adjective
Check List

that the pattern of a person's responses in rank ordering each set of four substatements produces a total score: high scores reflect a tendency toward rationalism, low scores reflect a tendency toward empiricism and would reflect an empirical rather than a rationalistic point of view. On the other hand, if he reversed that order when he ranked the substatements, it would have reflected a tendency toward rationalism rather than empiricism as a basic educational view. The GNC scale was administered to about one third of the teachers as a part of "Package C," along with the Urban Education Information Test.

Summary of Evaluation Process.   Starting with the specific purposes of this project, several persons participated in the development of an evaluation rationale aimed at procuring benchmark data about teachers, administrators, and students. There were approximately 1100 teachers involved in both the primary target and secondary target schools. All teachers completed the Urban Education Information Test. In addition, about one third of the teachers also completed the Teaching Situation Reaction Test, about one third completed the Adjective Check List, and about one third completed the GNC Educational Views Inventory. These samples were carefully selected to represent teachers from all schools and all grade levels. In the section which follows, the results of these data collecting processes will be described.

The Results

Because there were many instruments and because the data presented are somewhat involved at times (e.g., because of item analysis procedures rather than total scores), the reader may find it useful to refer to the appended test materials for greater understanding as he goes through the report. Throughout this section, three techniques will be employed. When tests have been "scored" in a conventional manner so that a "total score" was produced, mean scores of the various groups will be presented. Next, if the tests were analyzed item by item, the results of these analyses will be presented, usually in rank order form. Items of each test will be presented in descending order according to agreement, accuracy of response, or whatever seems appropriate for that particular test. Finally, generalizations about what these data mean will also be presented after a study of the data obtained with each instrument has been discussed. At the end of the report, major conclusions and overall generalizations will be drawn.

Measuring Teachers' Knowledge.   The first objective of this project was to provide knowledge related to the needs of disadvantaged pupils. To determine the existing level of knowledge about the needs of such youngsters, the Urban Education Information Test was administered to all professional staff members during the first week of June. This was a 40-item, multiple-choice-type test. Table 40 describes the mean scores for the 1186 Riverside Public School professional staff members and for one group of graduate students who had completed a college course emphasizing problems in urban education, according to the particular group of which they were a part.

It is obvious from this table that Riverside teachers score similarly, and administrative and central office staff persons score just slightly higher than teachers' groups. No check on the statistical significance of these differences was made, but it is reasonable to assume that differences among teachers' groups probably would not be significant statistically, while the difference between the teacher and administrative groups probably would be. The graduate students who had studied this kind of information in a college course made scores which were considerably higher than scores for any of the other groups. Since the basic purpose of the test was to generate baseline data, however, the information outlined in Table 41 is probably more useful.

Table 40

Mean Scores of Various Professional Groups on the Urban Education Information Test

Group	N	Mean
Primary target, elementary teachers	295	20.31
Primary target, secondary teachers	106	20.60
Secondary target, elementary teachers	392	20.89
Secondary target, secondary teachers	134	20.13
Others (did not indicate a position)	152	19.70
Administrators, elementary	16	22.50
Administrators, secondary	15	23.53
Central office	76	24.33
Graduate students	59	28.72

Table 41 describes the way in which 1074 teachers responded to each item on the Urban Education Information Test. However, these items have been arranged here in descending order, according to the extent to which these teachers agreed that one of the four possible options in each item was correct. Theoretically, the range of agreement could run from 100 per cent down to 25 per cent. That is, every teacher might indicate that choice "b," was correct; but, because there were four possible choices, if the teachers scattered their responses (disagreed as to which was the correct answer), one of the options would at least have 25 per cent agreement. The actual range for these 40 items was from 95 per cent agreement down to 29 per cent agreement. It is probably reasonable to conclude that items at the top of the list represent areas most familiar to these teachers, while those at the bottom of the list probably indicate areas in definite need of improvement. The foot-note at the end of the table explains some of the special markings which have been used.

There are several observations one might make about the data presented in Table 41. Most of the teachers who responded to the instrument agreed with the experts who "keyed" the test on about two-thirds of the items. Further, those items with disagreement suggest areas where the test should be refined or areas of teacher weakness. Only a closer study of each item and the particular data involved will resolve that problem.

For example, a careful look at item number 5 suggests that it is a poor item. "B" is the correct answer ("In comparison with middle class children, youngsters from lower class homes are more apt to experience language patterns in the home which are *more descriptive with little effort to relate concepts.*") However, the "more descriptive" is evidently not a precise phrase. Technically, it means that the language has a descriptive, rather than abstract, or concrete, rather than theoretical quality, but the particular phrasing of the possible responses only *implies* this and leaves too much to the respondent's imagination to make it a valid item.

Item 12 was poorly phrased. The statement is "definitely true," according to the best data available, but both "A" and "B" alternatives should probably be considered as "correct." Actually the item must be revised.

On the other hand, a study of the data pertaining to item 13 suggests these teachers may actually be more hopeful than realistic (in the best sense of both terms) if they assume that "there is *evidence* that *equality of educational opportunity will provide the Negro with equality regarding job opportunity*" rather than that "there is *evidence* that *education of the Negro will increase rather than decrease interpersonal tension and conflict.*" Racial prejudice and discrimination are very deep-seated phenomena, and available evidence today suggests that applying education to the problem of intergroup relations is more likely to result in increased tension than equality of job opportunity. We all *hope* that *in the long run* education will serve precisely that role, but at the moment that alternative actually represents a social hypothesis (our whole nation is committed to the idea, in fact) rather than a social fact. Un-fortunately, the "increased tension and conflict" is an indisputable fact.

Looking at the data regarding item 15, many sociologists maintain that, for the most part, "adult residents of Negro slums generally view the school as *an extension of the authority of the white community.*" This is not to say that "most" Negroes necessarily view the school that way at all, but as the question is phrased, the response of 51 per cent of the teachers maintaining that "adult residents of Negro slums generally view the school as *an avenue of opportunity for their children*" is probably not true.

Without exploring further the adequacy of particular items of the test, per-haps it would be useful now to look at the total pattern of accuracy of teacher response. The first and perhaps the most important observation one might

Table 41

Rank Ordering of Items in Terms of
Agreement with a Particular Answer of
the Urban Education Information Test
by 1074 School Teachers

Item Number	Content Measure	Proportion Choosing Option			
		A	B	C	D
9	which factor affects IQ	95	3	2	0
22	characteristics of children	2	87	8	3
25	cause of language deficiency	4	3	8	85
34	concerns of children	11	85	2	2
23	mobility of Negroes	3	12	4	81
21	Negro family life	3	9	8	80
33	culturally different groups	11	79	8	2
2	characteristics of children	6	77	8	9
6	out of school activities	14	75	6	5
32	requisites for educational success	75	13	8	4
(5)	language patterns in home	6	11	9	74
37	dropout rate	16	4	73	7
8	family structure in slum	21	2	70	7
17	community action programs	15	70	6	9
1	child's style of expression	3	17	65	15
10	Negro child's self concept	10	19	8	63
3	use of standardized tests	28	1	62	9
(13)	education and intergroup relations	61	13	7	19
18	teachers' inadequacies	21	11	61	7
24	reducing prejudice	26	11	9	54
7	characteristics of urban children	53	11	23	13
19	comparing IQ scores	25	8	51	16

Table 41 (continued)

Item Number	Content Measure	Proportion Choosing Option			
		A	B	C	D
(15)	Negroes' perception of school	19	6	51	24
16	IQ and social class	50	36	7	7
40	improving learning	19	50	19	12
11	children's motivation	49	30	17	4
28	stimulus deprivation	47	25	16	12
14	characteristics of Negroes	46	11	23	20
(12)	dropouts' chances	14	44	29	13
(38)	unemployment of Negroes	10	6	40	44
31	teachers' perceptions of students	12	21	23	44
35	improving education	43	43	13	1
(30)	Negro family life	27	10	42	21
36	Negro income	14	35	41	10
(20)	Negro childrens' achievement	16	24	41	19
(27)	deterrent to achievement	8	20	34	38
(4)	social class	26	38	15	21
(29)	use of IQ tests	25	14	37	24
(26)	curriculum change	32	18	26	24
(39)	ineffective teachers	28	23	20	29

Note: Underscored values represent choice (i.e., A, B, C, or D) which experts indicated was "correct." Item numbers in parentheses those items which a major segment of the respondent groups disagree with experts' indication of which was correct response.

make from a study of the descending order of agreement and accuracy reflected in Table 41 is that teachers evidently know more sociology and psychology than they do education. That is, items on which teachers had the greatest agreement and the most accurate responses were basically items assessing teachers' knowledge about sociological and psychological facts and principles. On the other hand, items on which there was the greatest disagreement among teachers and the least accuracy were basically items concerning educational interpretations or educational responses to particular situations. These data may simply reinforce the notion that education is *not* a science and that there are no agreed upon principles of working which are applicable in any given situation; however, this explanation does not seem to be as plausible as the one which suggests that this is really an area of teacher weakness.

For example, teachers who feel that *the first step* in curriculum modification (item 26) should begin with instructing parents or studying urban life or planning compensatory services are neither knowledgeable nor realistic about how curriculum change should occur. Curriculum change must always start with a careful assessment of precisely stated goals. "What do we want to do?" "Where do we hope to go?" "What specific behaviors are we trying to promote and develop among the boys and girls we teach?"

Item 20 suggests that teachers either do not understand the concept of grade placement (i.e., half of any *normal* group will always be *below* grade level) or they are not sufficiently knowledgeable about the precise achievements of "most" children who come from what have been primarily segregated, Negro schools in Southern states. The academic achievements of almost all of these children are typically *very* low. That is why we have finally taken major steps to abolish the reality of segregation, in fact—to assure *all* children of a greater chance to learn.

In summary, most of the 1074 teachers who responded to the Urban Education Information Test are fairly knowledgeable regarding most of the content areas measured, but several specific points of inadequacy have been identified. In general terms, it would seem reasonable to presume that what is needed now is more emphasis upon educational methodology based upon good data rather than more study of psychological or sociological generalizations.

While the Urban Education Information Test was designed to measure "knowledge about" several kinds of information pertinent to educational problems in an urban setting, the Teaching Situation Reaction Test (TSRT) was employed to get a picture of how teachers coped with particular kinds of education problems within a hypothetical classroom setting. This instrument has 48 items, and requires the respondent to rank order four options for each of the 48 situations described. The test is scored according to a key developed carefully over a period of years and empirically verified. Table 42 describes mean scores for each of the various teacher groups involved in this project.

Possible range of scores could be from 0 to 192. From these data it is apparent that teachers respond to the TSRT similarly, but those persons who work on the central office staff make slightly lower (better) scores.

There are no normative data *per se* on the TSRT, but it has been used with

Table 42

Mean Scores of Various Groups on the
Teaching Situation Reaction Test

Group	N	Mean
Primary target, elementary teachers	80	107.34
Primary target, secondary teachers	38	109.29
Secondary target, elementary teachers	122	107.18
Secondary target, secondary teachers	40	108.78
Central office staff	49	102.08

several hundred inservice teachers and preservice teachers, and something is known about how others have responded to the instrument. For example, the TSRT when administered to 106 junior high school teachers in suburban schools reported a mean score of 91.16 for that group. Only 10 scores out of the 329 reported here were as low as the mean of the total group of 106 teachers, and in this group there were 28 who had a mean TSRT score of 78.75. Not one of the 329 Riverside Public School professional staff sample had a score that low.

Other experience with the TSRT would also suggest that the scores reported here are fairly high, and "high" in this case means "less desirable." As described earlier, this instrument is designed to measure how a teacher copes with various kinds of teaching situations: how he structures the learning experience, the kind and degree of control which he employs, and the extent to which he is sensitive to various kinds of complex social interactions within a classroom setting. These high scores apparently mean that these teachers are especially concerned with the problems of control and management, but not particularly sensitive to the learning problems of specific children in an individualized way.

To get a still closer look at what the TSRT data means, an item analysis was also done on this test. Because each item of the TSRT requires the respondent to rank order in four possible options, a complete item analysis would be quite involved. Because of this, only first choice options are reported here. In other words, the number of persons who ranked option "A" first, the number who ranked "B" first, the number who ranked "C" first, and the number who ranked "D" first for each of the 48 items is described in Table 43 pages 206–207. The reader may want to refer to the particular situation described for each item by examining the instrument itself (Appendix H) as he progresses through the data. As before, items have been arranged in this table in descending order of agreement. Those items on which there was the greatest agreement about which option should be listed first are at the top of Table 43. Those items of the least agreement are at the bottom. Because the table itself is fairly long, it may be convenient simply to note that items on the first page of the table represent areas in which there was the *greatest* agreement about how to handle particular situations. Items described on the last page of the table, however, represent areas in which there was the least agreement about how to handle particular teaching situations.

Studying the data in Table 43 gives the very real impression that these Riverside teachers are very clear in their own minds about how to cope with particular classroom problems which may arise, but they are very unclear about how to plan or how to make appropriate inferences regarding what to do next after certain situations develop. For example, these teachers are fairly well agreed about handling students who are restless or rejected, how to prevent fights among students, how to maintain control during a field trip, or how to work with students who are not interested in the activites of the class. At the other end of the scale, however, these same teachers appear much less certain about how to make plans for and during the course, how to assess conflict within a group, how to use the help of other persons to improve their teaching, or how to analyze classroom events and processes with a view toward diagnosing difficulties and applying specific remedies.

To collect other data useful in making precise inferences about teachers' attitudes, the Adjective Check List was also administered to approximately one third of the teachers in the various schools. This instrument was designed to determine perceptions teachers had of their students: how did they actually see the boys and girls they taught each day?

There were no total scores for this test, but Table 44 describes the rank order listing of the 48 adjectives for each of the different teachers' groups. Each list includes the adjectives in order of the degree to which each group indicated that the various words were characteristic of the children which they taught. Those words at the top were selected more frequently, and those at the bottom less frequently. A line has also been drawn beneath that word which represents the point at which 50 per cent or more of the teachers indicated that the word was applicable to their students, and another line has been drawn at that point where 15 per cent or fewer of the teachers chose that word. Also shown in the fifth column is a similar listing by secondary school teachers from schools serving advantaged (4) neighborhoods in several large cities, as reported by Goodman. This listing may prove useful for comparative purposes.

The data in Table 44 suggest most teachers in both primary target and secondary target schools view their students as unpredictable, quarrelsome, active, mischievous, changeable, disruptive, and indifferent. On the other hand, a very large majority do not see their students as creative, patient, dynamic, civil, harmonious, intent, or idealistic. In general terms, it would

Table 43

Number of Persons Who Selected Various Options as "First Choice" For Each of 48 Items of the Teaching Situation Reaction Test

Item	Nature of Situation	Number of Persons Choosing Option			
		A	B	C	D
11	handling student restlessness	258	28	15	7
20	handling problems of social acceptance	39	8	252	8
42	making inference about perceptive students' observation	18	6	39	245
24	preventing future fights among students	12	13	45	238
17	second steps to help withdrawn girl	231	25	48	4
40	assuring good conduct during trip	18	50	237	3
33	first class meeting after parent conference	40	35	222	11
27	teaching when students not interested	34	38	220	16
13	kind of person you would try to be	48	8	45	207
25	discussing problems with teacher-counselor	8	207	21	72
9	greatest concern night before first class	54	42	7	205
43	approach after problem identified	204	19	26	59
29	planning for parents meeting at mid-term	9	87	12	200
4	personal concern before course starts	24	52	192	40
48	helping outspoken student	52	41	189	26
46	handling outspoken student	31	64	185	28
32	feeling about talking with parents	100	15	184	9
35	feelings after having a bad day	20	181	59	48
5	planning for first day's activities	112	0	172	34
12	first instructions to group	47	171	22	68
31	talking with parents first time	110	170	11	17
2	planning in light of public criticism	28	169	9	5
16	initial steps to helping a withdrawn girl	165	18	120	5
21	making inferences about student fight	27	56	157	68
19	handling students who interrupt	48	149	77	34
39	class session with students regarding trip	125	21	149	13
28	analyzing teaching when interests lag	25	46	79	148
38	planning for student field trip	145	32	83	48
3	expectations of principal regarding planning	68	27	145	68

Table 43 (continued)

Item	Nature of Situation	Number of Persons Choosing Option			
		A	B	C	D
18	making inferences about overly talkative pupils	14	130	143	21
22	approaching student who hit another	26	135	74	73
7	first information to get from students	131	55	36	86
41	handling class group during field trip	80	36	129	63
36	feelings about having a bad day	83	82	15	128
23	approaching student who had been hit	123	54	10	121
14	planning for second meeting	123	14	69	102
8	most essential planning before first class	64	121	48	75
37	making plans to analyze teaching difficulties	22	117	100	69
15	helping boys from slum area	115	64	45	84
26	planning after course underway	88	17	90	113
47	handling class with one outspoken student	78	83	110	37
44	using perceptive student's contribution	109	79	35	85
34	analyzing a bad day	61	86	109	52
6	how teacher-counselor might help	109	16	84	99
45	assessing conflict within the group	100	27	75	106
10	handling late students first day	81	78	44	105
1	initial planning for course	28	85	105	90
30	making mid-term assessment	94	74	103	37

appear that teachers in both the primary and secondary target schools in Riverside see their students in somewhat negative ways. In terms of the theoretical dimensions of the instrument, those qualities which most teachers attribute to their students which have negative connotations are social qualities rather than physical qualities or qualities of intellect or character. Those qualities which teachers do not attribute to their students are basically social or character qualities, too: harmonious, civil, idealistic, patient, and intent. It seems reasonable to conclude that these teachers are primarily concerned with their students as social beings rather than intellectual or physical beings. This is probably a very natural response, and it may be that these data reflect the fact that teachers feel that unless children's social needs are met first, their intellectual needs cannot be attended to satisfactorily. This generaliza-

Rank Order of Adjectives By Teachers

	Primary Target		Secondary Target		Higher Socioeconomic Secondary
	Elementary	Secondary	Elementary	Secondary	
50% or higher	unpredictable	disruptive	quarrelsome	disruptive	active
	quarrelsome	quarrelsome	active	changeable	interested
	active	changeable	mischievous	quarrelsome	curious
	mischievous	indifferent	unpredictable	unpredictable	courteous
	changeable	informal	disruptive	lazy	agreeable
	disruptive	gregarious	imitative	mischievous	neat
	imitative	active	changeable	antagonistic	aware
	affectionate	antagonistic	indifferent	indifferent	sincere
	indifferent	lazy	informal	rude	outgoing
	curious	mischievous	affectionate	sloppy	changeable
	antagonistic	rude	sloppy	active	expressive
	informal	lethargic	rude	imitative	imitative
	sloppy	unpredictable	antagonistic	informal	creative
	vigorous	rash	curious	lethargic	gregarious
	rude	imitative	lazy	rash	considerate
	self centered	animated	rash	gregarious	vigorous
	sincere	affectionate	awkward	imperative	informal
	rash	sloppy	gregarious	malicious	mischievous
	gregarious	malicious	outgoing	self centered	unpredictable
	imperative	self centered	lethargic	awkward	civil

lazy	sincere	sincere	expressive	animated
lethargic	neat	vigorous	animated	quick
awkward	outgoing	self centered	affectionate	affectionate
agile	expressive	interested	outgoing	harmonious
interested	awkward	imperceptive	bungling	realistic
outgoing	agile	agreeable	discerning	self centered
realistic	bungling	animated	superficial	discerning
malicious	curious	expressive	vigorous	idealistic
animated	quick	bungling	quick	dynamic
quick	superficial	malicious	courteous	intent
agreeable	realistic	considerate	curious	indifferent
expressive	courteous	realistic	agreeable	lazy
considerate	imperceptive	courteous	fanciful	agile
courteous	interested	quick	civil	awkward
humble	vigorous	agile	humble	patient
neat	agreeable	aware	idealistic	disruptive
fanciful	considerate	humble	sincere	quarrelsome
aware	fanciful	creative	realistic	rude
discerning	harmonious	harmonious	interested	superficial
creative	aware	intent	considerate	rash
bungling	humble	neat	agile	sloppy
patient	idealistic	discerning	neat	lethargic
superficial	discerning	patient	aware	antagonistic
dynamic	civil	superficial	patient	fanciful
civil	creative	fanciful	intent	imperative
harmonious	patient	civil	harmonious	humble
intent	dynamic	dynamic	dynamic	bungling
idealistic	intent	idealistic	creative	malicious

15% or
Lower

tion seems reinforced by the fact that the teachers from privileged area secondary schools as reported in Goodman's study select adjectives which more frequently refer to their students' positive intellectual qualities—curious, agreeable, outgoing. In other words, teachers serving primary or secondary target schools in Riverside evidently see their students differently than teachers who work in other kinds of socioeconomic areas. Whether this perception is accurate or distorted is obviously not evident from these data. The data in the Goodman study on inner-city schools revealed essentially the same perception of disadvantaged children (5). Whether the students actually are fundamentally different or whether the teachers have misperceived cannot be determined from the data presented here, but it does seem reasonable to assume that the perception which these teachers hold of their students focuses primarily upon their social qualities and primarily in negative ways.

The GNC Educational Views Inventory was also a measure of teachers' attitudes. Its basic philosophical positions on educational matters are ascertained with this instrument: high scores reflect philosophical realism, while low scores reflect philosophical empiricism. Or, persons who make high scores tend to agree with the philosophical pronouncements of Plato and Bagley and Hutchins; persons who make lower scores tend to agree with the philosophical pronouncements of Dewey and Bode. In terms of the scoring rationale, a theoretical midpoint would be a score of 120, with the lowest possible score 72 and the highest score possible 168. Table 45 describes the mean scores for each of the various groups of teachers who completed the inventory.

The data in this table suggest one thing, and comparisons of these scores with comparable data collected in other studies suggest another. First, differences between these various teacher groups is very small. Second, the general average of these four teacher groups is similar to those of many other teacher groups. These scores are all below the theoretical mean, and in the direction of the empiricists' point of view.

Conclusions

The basic purpose of the project was to provide inservice education which would help teachers who work with children in inner-city schools learn more about such youngsters, modify their attitudes in working with such youth, and acquire new techniques and ways of working. Because the project got off to a late start, evaluation efforts were aimed at describing a baseline rather than measuring change over a short period of time. The baseline data will hopefully constitute a useful benchmark for future comparisons, but the data collected from more than one thousand elementary and secondary

Table 45

Mean Scores of Various Teacher Groups on
the GNC Educational Views Inventory

Primary target, elementary teachers	82	103.79
Primary target, secondary teachers	21	104.10
Secondary target, elementary teachers	139	104.49
Secondary target, secondary teachers	43	105.00
Central office staff	50	93.90

school teachers in primary and secondary target areas are simply descriptive: they show what currently exists.

Teachers' knowledge, attitudes, and teaching techniques were studied by administering five different testing instruments to teachers from every school in both primary target and secondary target areas. In the sections below are described the specific conclusions, the general conclusions, and the implications reflected in the data obtained from the analyses of teachers' response to these various tests.

Specific Conclusions. Several specific conclusions are apparent from a consideration of the data described so far in this report. Each of these conclusions is set forth in simple summary form, then discussed briefly without reference to the specific data upon which it is based.

1. Teachers in primary target schools differ little from teachers in secondary target schools in terms of knowledge, attitudes, and teaching styles which were observed in this particular project. On almost every measure, mean score values and rank ordering of item analyses reflected very similar patterns of response to the various testing instruments.

2. The teachers are reasonably knowledgeable about the sociological and psychological determinants which affect inner-city children's behavior. They are aware of the social forces and the personal characteristics common to the child in the urban setting: his home life, motivations, and language development.

3. The teachers seem to have a fairly "typical" philosophy of education; they are both pragmatic and realistic, but concerned with the rudiments of education as essential tools for all American youth.

4. The teachers primarily view their students in negative ways. They also seem to see their students more in terms of their social qualities than their educational characteristics and concerns.

5. The teachers appear to be especially concerned about controlling their

students; they appear to be responding to classroom situations in relatively inflexible ways. They seem to be more concerned with "managing" children than in helping them learn.

6. The teachers seem uncertain about which educational techniques and methodology they should employ. When the problem is simple, they seem to know what to do; but, when the problem gets more complex and difficult, they appear to be less and less certain about planning and effecting an appropriate professional response.

7. The teachers do not appear to know how to use supporting services and assistance from other specialists effectively.

8. The teachers apparently view their building principal in terms of his "power" rather than his professional competence as an instructional leader.

One general conclusion seems warranted: teachers in these inner-city schools seem to adopt the behavioral patterns characteristic of the area in which they serve. The general pattern of behavior reflected by these teachers tends toward authoritarianism—restricting, controlling activities, negative perceptions of other persons, submissive acquiescence to authority figures, inaccurate perceptions of some aspects of reality, and intolerance of ambiguous situations. This pattern appears more as a tendency than actuality, but it seems sufficiently obvious to merit special attention.

The tendency would seem to be the natural result of situational factors. Confronted regularly with youngsters from lower class homes less interested in learning, these teachers, beset with learning difficulties, and less experience and skill in coping with normal educational tasks, seem to be overwhelmed by teaching situations to the point where they adopt restrictive, punitive, imposing teaching techniques and styles characteristic of many in the social group they serve. They seem to regress to the mean of the cultural situation in which they find themselves involved. To overstate the case, it is as if oppressive situations make teachers more oppressive in terms of what they do in school each day. This tendency toward authoritarian behavior must be considered an important educational problem for those concerned with developing specific proposals for inservice education and staff development. The implications of these ideas for such a program are explored here.

Implications. Three different kinds of inferences seem reasonable from the general discussion: further research is essential; inservice programs must be carefully conceptualized; and both policies and practices affecting inner-city schools must be re-examined with special care.

More baseline data are essential. Throughout this report comparisons were made with data from other situations whenever possible, but meaningful comparisons can only be made with teachers in other Riverside schools. Stated as research questions, problems such as these would seem to be especially crucial:

(a) Are there differences in the responses of teachers in target area schools from teachers in more advantaged neighborhoods to the

—Teaching Situation Reaction Test
—Adjective Check List
—GNC Educational Views Inventory
—Urban Education Information Test

(b) Do teachers who enter teaching situations in target area schools change over time on the variables measured by these instruments?

If it is true as some suggest that the best teachers for inner-city schools are those who are the least authoritarian, least dogmatic, most empathic teachers we can find, what kind of inservice program will be most likely to reverse what appears to be exactly the opposite trend? Several specific factors would certainly be involved. The program would have to be:

(a) Long-range
(b) Comprehensive
(c) Coordinated
(d) Oriented toward curriculum and methodology.

Any inservice effort that successfully helps teachers who work with youngsters in inner-city schools become less authoritarian and more skillful in teaching procedures would of necessity be both intensive and extensive in nature. No short-term, fragmented, uncoordinated effort could possibly do the job. In all probability, it should be both systematic and varied; several different approaches should be employed regularly and over a fairly long period of time. "One-shot" lectures by experts, mid-year inservice education days, or occasional faculty meetings devoted to particular problems are not enough. If the data reported here are correct and if the conclusions drawn are valid, mapping out a program designed to help teachers become different kinds of human beings with different teaching skills is a monumental chore. No incidental or piece-meal approaches to the problem will suffice. Careful planning in long-range terms is imperative.

Finally, how do present policies and practices regarding teacher employment, supervision, selection of principals, teacher transfer, allocation of resources, and availability of special services, for example, affect teachers' knowledge and attitudes and skills? What is the principal's role? Should all children be "treated the same," regardless of their sociological background or psychological need? How do teachers get special help? What motivates teachers to strive to improve? These questions are all related to existing personnel and other policies. The fundamental assumptions upon which such policies are based must be examined.

This study describes a project aimed at identifying various teacher behaviors among those who teach in inner-city Riverside schools. The baseline is neither complete nor finally accurate, but it does constitute a significant beginning. The picture described suggests that teachers in these inner-city schools have *very* difficult teaching problems, and they need help of many kinds. If it is correct, as Jackson (6) maintains, that classroom teachers make from 650 to 1000 *reactions* in their classrooms every day, then it becomes essential for teachers to develop basic reacting-styles which are positive, supportive, and democratic styles. No teacher can *rationally* respond that many times, day after day. What he needs to do is develop basic teaching styles and procedures which reflect a consistent pattern aimed along positive lines. Working in "tough" schools simply magnifies the problem. Teachers in such schools need all of the help along these lines they can possibly obtain. Inservice education is one such device.

Summary

The supervisor has the responsibility of translating data into action—they are of no value in a filing cabinet. The curriculum councils can be invaluable here. After a careful analysis of the data and study of recommendations, the next step is to move in the direction of curriculum improvement. Open discussion involving these curriculum leaders should lead to programs of action and to improvement in teaching in area schools.

Baseline data are a benchmark from which to measure the direction and amount of change in knowledge and attitudes of teachers. The effectiveness of inservice programs, administrative policies, educational practices, and assignment of personnel should have some basis for measurement. In the whole process of curriculum development, evaluation is one of its most important elements. This is no less true when considering the role of the teacher in the curriculum process.

Appendix G

Urban Education Information Test

Directions

On the pages which follow are 40 questions which pertain to education in an urban setting. Each of the questions relates to an area which has been investigated extensively by sociologists, psychologists, or educational researchers. One answer to each question is correct or most nearly correct according to the best evidence available today. Read each question carefully.

Select the answer which you feel is correct or most nearly correct, then mark your answer sheet accordingly. DO NOT MARK ON THE TEST BOOKLET.

1. In his style of self expression, the lower class child is likely to be
   (A) conceptual, abstract, and verbal.
   (B) non-verbal, conceptual, and concrete.
   (C) concrete, motoric, and non-verbal.
   (D) verbal, abstract, and motoric.

2. Compared to middle class children, which of the following statements is generally *least* true about lower class youngsters?
   (A) Their homes are more frequently broken, charged with personal conflict.
   (B) They have traveled more frequently and further from home.
   (C) They maintain essentially negative images about themselves and their future.
   (D) Their orientation focuses on present rather than future gratification.

3. The most appropriate use of standardized achievement tests with youngsters from lower class homes would probably involve
   (A) use of grade placement scores in order to group children for instructional purposes.
   (B) analysis of test results for each school in order to determine leadership qualities of principals.
   (C) analysis of test results for each child in order to determine particular learning difficulties.
   (D) comparison of grade placement scores with grades received in order to identify underachievers.

4. Which of the following statements is generally considered *least* accurate regarding the concept of social class?
   (A) American cities have two or three distinguishable social strata, whose basic styles of life can be recognized as being different.
   (B) Class membership expresses itself in social interaction patterns in the various institutions within the community.
   (C) Attitudes and values are associated with social class membership.
   (D) Education is a major vehicle by which people typically move upward in terms of social class.

5. In comparison with middle class children, youngsters from lower class homes are more apt to experience language patterns in the home which are
   (A) more descriptive with more effort to relate concepts.
   (B) more descriptive with little effort to relate concepts.
   (C) less descriptive with more effort to relate concepts.
   (D) less descriptive with little effort to relate concepts.

6. Which statement provides the strongest basis for assuming that a teacher should be concerned about the children's activities outside the school?
   (A) Most parents are too busy to take proper care of their children.

    (B) The child learns many things through his out-of-school experience.

    (C) The child may learn bad habits unless he is supervised.

    (D) The school should control the child's out-of-school experience in order to assure maximum learning.

7. In comparison with children from rural areas, children from urban areas are

    (A) more intelligent and more verbal.

    (B) more intelligent but less verbal.

    (C) less intelligent but more verbal.

    (D) less intelligent and less verbal.

8. In a Negro slum, the *major* deficiency in family structure affecting children is

    (A) too many children in a family.

    (B) inadequacy of the mother figure.

    (C) inadequacy of the father figure.

    (D) lack of love for the children.

9. Which of the following factors probably exerts the greatest influence upon any child's IQ score?

    (A) cultural background.

    (B) geographical region.

    (C) race.

    (D) sex.

10. In comparison with girls in Negro families, boys in Negro families generally have

    (A) more positive self concepts and more opportunity to identify with a desirable "model" of the same sex.

    (B) more positive self concepts but less opportunity to identify with a desirable "model" of the same sex.

    (C) less positive self concepts but more opportunity to identify with a desirable "model" of the same sex.

    (D) less positive self concepts and less opportunity to identify with a desirable "model" of the same sex.

11. Among lower class youngsters in the middle school years, motivation to learn in school could probably best be described as a function of each child's

    (A) self concept and his sense of values.

    (B) reading ability and his concept of other people.

    (C) sense of worth and his long range vocational objectives.

    (D) early start in school and father's vocation.

12. "A typical Negro high school graduate is less apt to find a job and be able to keep it than a typical white high school drop out." In statistical terms, this statement is

    (A) definitely true.

    (B) probably true.

(C) probably false.
(D) definitely false.
13. In applying education to the problems of intergroup relations, there is evidence that
(A) equality in educational opportunity will provide the Negro with equality regarding job opportunity.
(B) Spanish speaking persons, Negroes, and Indians all place little faith in education to solve their problems.
(C) the "melting pot" concept of cultural assimilation has proven applicable to Negroes, Italians, and Chinese.
(D) education of the Negro will increase rather than decrease interpersonal tension and conflict.
14. Which of the following statements is false?
(A) Negroes are more musical than white persons.
(B) Negroes maintain social class distinctions within their own group.
(C) Negroes as a group have school achievement levels which are lower than whites.
(D) Negroes life expectancy rates are lower than whites.
15. Adult residents of Negro slums generally view the school as
(A) an extension of the authority of the white community.
(B) as the only center of culture in the slums.
(C) an avenue of opportunity for their children.
(D) an agency which cares for children during the day.
16. Research indicates that the relationship of IQ and social class typically shows up in correlations which are
(A) positive and significant.
(B) positive but not significant.
(C) negative and significant.
(D) negative but not significant.
17. Neighborhood community action programs in slum areas tend to be ineffective primarily because
(A) the efforts lack financial support.
(B) the efforts lack neighborhood leadership.
(C) antagonistic outside groups defeat the efforts.
(D) neighborhood groups work in terms of selfish interest.
18. Studies of teachers who work in schools which serve lower class youth generally show that such teachers are *least* competent in the area of
(A) disciplining.
(B) grading.
(C) motivating.
(D) organizing.
19. When the average IQ of children from lower class homes is compared to the average IQ of children from middle class homes, the difference is generally *less* between

    (A) girls and more between boys.
    (B) boys and more between girls.
    (C) younger children and more between older children.
    (D) older children and more between younger children.

20. Approximately what proportion of Negro children coming from essentially a segregated school in the South would normally fall below grade level in terms of reading achievement on a standardized test?
    (A) 30%
    (B) 50%
    (C) 70%
    (D) 90%

21. Lower class Negro family life is probably best described as
    (A) patriarchal and stable.
    (B) patriarchal and unstable.
    (C) matriarchal and stable.
    (D) matriarchal and unstable.

22. Children in a school which serves predominantly lower class neighborhoods are most often characterized by
    (A) high motivation and high truancy.
    (B) high truancy and low achievement.
    (C) low achievement and high self-esteem.
    (D) high self-esteem and low truancy.

23. The Negroes who are particularly anxious to move into the predominantly all-white suburban communities are generally
    (A) Southern born, poorly educated, dark skinned, older persons.
    (B) Southern born, well educated, light skinned, younger persons.
    (C) Northern born, poorly educated, dark skinned, older persons.
    (D) Northern born, well educated, light skinned, younger persons.

24. From a sociological point of view, prejudice and race conflict can be reduced greatly by
    (A) developing cultural pluralism.
    (B) providing protective legislation for minority groups' human rights.
    (C) re-establish ethnocentrism and a basic way of life.
    (D) remedying social abuses and reducing conflict.

25. Language deficiency is a well-known problem among culturally disadvantaged pupils. This problem is most often related to
    (A) bilingualism in the home.
    (B) school absenteeism.
    (C) lack of readiness to learn language skills.
    (D) lack of models for correct speech in the home.

26. Curriculum modification is essential to improve the academic performance of children from depressed urban areas. What would be *the first step* in curriculum modification?
    (A) curriculum reappraisal in depth in terms of precisely stated goals

(B) instruction of parents on how to work with their children at home
(C) identification of unique aspects of urban life which can be incorporated into educational programs
(D) planning of compensatory services and experiences
27. Many experts on urban education maintain that the greatest deterrent to high achievement by disadvantaged pupils is
(A) low intelligence.
(B) dislike for academic work.
(C) low level of expected achievement by teachers.
(D) broken home background.
28. Many lower class children have been deprived of an opportunity to respond to many varieties of stimuli to which they are capable of responding. The most probable consequence of this deprivation is:
(A) difficulty in learning.
(B) hostile attitude toward school.
(C) personality disorder.
(D) no important consequence.
29. Which description of intelligence tests is most appropriate as they are generally used with lower class children during the elementary school years?
(A) They succeed in measuring capabilities which will become of critical importance later in life, and *do* detect intellectual deficits at the most appropriate time for remediation.
(B) They succeed in measuring capabilities which will become of critical importance later in life, but *do not* detect intellectual deficits at the most appropriate time for remediation.
(C) They fail in measuring capabilities which will become of critical importance later in life, but *do* detect intellectual deficits at the most appropriate time for remediation.
(D) They fail in measuring capabilities which will become of critical importance later in life, and *do not* detect intellectual deficits at the most appropriate time for remediation.
30. Research indicates that Negro family life is generally
(A) more authoritarian and more punitive than white family life.
(B) more authoritarian but less punitive than white family life.
(C) less authoritarian but more punitive than white family life.
(D) less authoritarian and less punitive than white family life.
31. In comparison with teachers who work in schools which serve predominantly middle class neighborhoods, teachers who work in schools which serve predominantly lower class neighborhoods generally see their students
(A) equally capable and no more troublesome.
(B) equally capable but more troublesome.

(C) less capable but no more troublesome.

(D) less capable but more troublesome.

32. The two factors which are most essential for the successful education of lower class children are

(A) belief in their educability and worth as individuals.

(B) experienced teachers and adequate facilities.

(C) special counseling personnel and special curriculum materials.

(D) extensive vocational training and adequate job placement.

33. If two culturally different peoples meet on a continuing basis, the result has generally been

(A) complete assimilation of one group by the other group.

(B) partial assimilation of each group by the other group.

(C) segregation of the two groups.

(D) continual discord and violence.

34. In comparison with middle class children, lower class children are typically more concerned about the

(A) immediate and the abstract.

(B) immediate and the concrete.

(C) future and the abstract.

(D) future and the concrete.

35. More effective teaching, better instructional materials, and more dynamic leadership in lower class schools generally result in changes in children which are as follows:

(A) raising of IQ scores, raising of standardized achievement scores, and reducing truancy and dropout rate.

(B) maintaining of IQ scores, raising of standardized achievement scores, and raising students' expectations and aspirations.

(C) raising level of grades received from teachers, maintaining standardized achievement scores, and reducing dropout rate.

(D) maintaining standardized achievement scores, reducing parent-teacher cooperation, and reducing dropout rate.

36. For many years the average income level of Negro males in the United States has been about _____ of the average income level of white males.

(A) one eighth

(B) one fourth

(C) one half

(D) three fourths

37. Research studies confirm the fact that the dropout rate is generally greater among

(A) girls than among boys.

(B) middle class students than among lower class students.

(C) students in the cities than among students in the rural areas.

(D) students in the North than among students in the South.

38. The unemployment rate for the Negro male in the United States is generally about _____ the unemployment rate of the white male in this country
    (A) one half
    (B) the same as
    (C) two times
    (D) three times
39. Which of the following is most likely to be characteristic of the *ineffective* teacher working with children from lower class backgrounds?
    (A) differential treatment of the students in his class
    (B) concern with expectations of high achievement from his pupils
    (C) emphasis upon the control of the immediate situation
    (D) helps children only after they have "helped themselves"
40. The one factor which would probably produce the most positive improvement in the learning of children from economically disadvantaged areas is
    (A) changing the organizational pattern of the school.
    (B) changing the attitudes of the professional staff who work in the school.
    (C) adopting the "modern" curriculum programs which are being developed.
    (D) maintaining year-round schools.

Appendix H

Teaching Situation Reaction Test
Revised April, 1965

Directions

The case example that follows has been planned to measure your ability to work through some of the problems of handling a classroom group. You will be given certain information about a classroom group and the working situation. You will then be asked to respond to a number of questions. This will be repeated through a series of problem situations. The case study has been designed so that you can respond regardless of your teaching subject field. You do not need technical subject matter knowledge to take this test.

You are asked to indicate your first, second, third, and fourth choice under each question by inserting respectively the numbers 1, 2, 3, 4, in the spaces provided on the answer sheets under (a), (b), (c), and (d). The most desirable choice could be labeled 1 and the least desirable 4. For example if your first choice was response (c), your second choice was response (a), your third choice was response (b), and your fourth choice was response (d), you would record your responses on the answer sheet as follows:

(a) (b) (c) (d)
 2   3   1   4
__   __   __   __

Please do not write on the test booklet

NOTE: For further information about this test write to Dr. James K. Duncan, College of Education, The Ohio State University, Columbus, Ohio 43210.

The Situation:

You have been employed by a school system which is engaged in a series of experimental studies. One of these studies involves an experimental class designed to improve pupils' general adjustment to their environment. A heterogeneous group (physically, mentally, socially) of twenty-five 13- to 14-year-old youngsters have signed up for this class entitled "Teen Topics" because they thought that it would be interesting.

The class is scheduled to meet the last period of the day on Tuesday and Thursday during the second semester. Arrangements have been made so that the class might take trips and students might have an opportunity to meet informally with the teacher after class.

Around the first of November your principal calls you in to tell you that, if you are interested, you have been chosen to teach the experimental class. You were chosen because of your background in adolescent psychology and your interest in helping youngsters with minor problems of adjustment typical of the young adolescent. You believe that the most efficient learner is the student who is relatively free from personal problems and thus can direct his attention to conventional school learning uninhibited by his personal concerns. You agree to take the class and believe that by being informed of your new teaching responsibility this early in the year that you will have adequate time to plan for the course.

Your principal has given you pretty much of a "free hand" to develop the content of the course and the activities in which the student will be engaged. A good supply of instructional materials (e.g., books on the adolescent and descriptions of similar programs in other schools) has been made available to you. There will be no direct supervision of your work, but an evaluation by students and yourself will be requested at the middle and close of the semester. Studies will also be made of the gain in personal adjustment evidenced by a selected number of your students. You do know the names of the students who have signed up for your course, but you do not know which students in the class have been chosen to be studied and will not know until the end of the semester. An experienced teacher-counselor has been asked by the principal to help you when and if you ask for help. The teacher-counselor knows each of the youngsters who have signed up for your class.

The Group:

Some of the youngsters who have signed up for the course know each other very well, having gone through school together. Three do not know anyone else in the group. Others are only casually acquainted. Members of the group have a variety of interests and abilities, and they represent many levels of competence and come from a variety of socio-economic backgrounds. The quality of their personality adjustment varies, but none is seriously maladjusted.

A. You have about eight weeks plus the Christmas vacation to plan for your class.
   1. When you begin planning the course you would:
      (a) Ask your teacher-counselor what he thinks should be in the course.
      (b) Examine the materials available to you and determine how they might be used by members of the class.
      (c) Read through the copies of publications describing other school programs of similar nature and draw ideas from them.
      (d) Interview a randomly selected group of the young people signed up for the course and set your own tentative objectives based on these interviews.
   2. During early December an important local civic group comes out against teaching sex education in the schools. Your planning had included some sex education. At this report in your planning you would:
      (a) Continue planning as you have been.
      (b) Ask the principal if you should include any sex education in your course.
      (c) Remove the lessons dealing with sex education.

    (d) Find ways to get the sex education material across without caus-
        ing an issue.
  3. About three weeks before your class is scheduled to meet for the first
     time, your principal asks you to come in and talk with him about the
     course. You would hope that your principal would:
    (a) Say that if there was anything that he could do to be of help that
        you should feel free to call on him.
    (b) Indicate to you what he would hope the course would accomplish
        during the semester.
    (c) Encourage you to talk about the purposes of your course as you
        see them after several weeks of planning.
    (d) Make specific suggestions to help you in your planning, and en-
        courage you to drop in for further suggestions if you need help.
  4. The weekend before the course is to start it would be natural for you
     to feel:
    (a) Concern that your planning has been inappropriate.
    (b) Anxious to get started and prove your ability to handle this rather
        difficult assignment.
    (c) Hopeful that the course will prove of real value to the students.
    (d) Confident knowing you have done the best you could under the
        circumstances.
B. You will have your first meeting with the group tomorrow.
  5. It will be important that you have planned for:
    (a) students to get well acquainted with each other
    (b) explaining your grading system
    (c) activities that catch student interest
    (d) explaining your complete program for the semester
  6. The teacher-counselor drops by your room and asks if he can be of
     help. You would ask him for:
    (a) his opinion about what you have planned for tomorrow
    (b) suggestions to help you make a good impression
    (c) suggestions as to what student reaction might be on the first day
    (d) nothing until you had an opportunity to meet with the group
  7. The more important personal information to gather at the first meeting
     would be:
    (a) interests of the different students
    (b) parent or guardian, home address and phone number
    (c) what they would like to do in the course
    (d) why they are taking the course
  8. Of the things you would do the evening before meeting the class, the
     most essential would be to:
    (a) become familiar with the notes for such presentation as you might
        make

   (b) become familiar with students' names and any information you have about them from their files

   (c) become familiar with the sequence and nature of any activities you may have planned

   (d) be sure any materials you were to use were available and in good condition

9. Your greatest concern on this night before the first meeting would be:
   (a) how to appear poised and at ease
   (b) how to gain control of the group
   (c) how to handle problem pupils
   (d) how to get your program moving rapidly and well

C. On meeting the group the first day a number of students come in from three to five minutes late. Following this, as you get your program underway the students get restless.

10. With the students that come in late you would:
   (a) simply acknowledge their presence and noticeably mark them present in the record book
   (b) inform them politely about the time at which the class starts
   (c) ask them politely why they were unable to get to class on time
   (d) make clear to the class as a whole and the late students in particular the standards you will maintain with regard to tardiness

11. You would handle the restlessness of the group by:
   (a) presenting your program more dynamically
   (b) asking students why they were restless
   (c) speaking to the group firmly about paying attention
   (d) picking out one or two of the worst offenders and reprimanding them

12. You would tell the group your name and:
   (a) the rules of conduct for your class
   (b) your expectations for the class
   (c) some of your personal adjustment problems at their age
   (d) some of your interests and hobbies

13. You would, by your general behavior and manner, try to present yourself as:
   (a) firm and serious but fair
   (b) efficient, orderly and business-like
   (c) friendly, sympathetic and understanding
   (d) understanding, friendly and firm

14. You would prepare for the next meeting by:
   (a) discussing with pupils what they would like to do and deciding on one or two ideas
   (b) telling them what pages to read

      (c) giving students a choice of two ideas and determining on which the majority are interested

      (d) discussing your plans for the next meeting with them

D. You have met with your class four times and have made some observations. Two boys seem particularly dirty and you have found they come from a lower class slum area. One girl seems to be withdrawn. The students do not pay any attention to her. She is a pleasant looking well dressed girl. There are four or five youngsters, apparently very good friends (both boys and girls) who do most of the talking and take most of the initiative. Students seem to continually interrupt each other and you.

  15. In the interests of the two boys from the slum area you would:

      (a) find an opportunity to discuss the matter of cleanliness with the class

      (b) speak to the boys about their need to be clean in a conference with them

      (c) inaugurate a cleanliness competition with a prize to that half of the class with the best record, putting one boy in each half

      (d) speak to the boys about their need to be clean and arrange facilities at school where they could clean up

  16. In the interest of the apparently withdrawn girl you would:

      (a) talk to her informally over a period of time to see if you could determine her difficulty

      (b) call on her regularly for contributions to the discussion

      (c) discover a skill she has and have her demonstrate for the class

      (d) have a conference with her and tell her to become involved with the class discussion and speak up

  17. To improve the relationship of the group to the apparently withdrawn girl you would:

      (a) determine who, if anyone, is friendly with her and arrange to have them work together on occasion

      (b) take the girl aside and help her see how she can establish better relations with her classmates

      (c) arrange to have her work with the group of boys and girls who take most of the initiative

      (d) allow her to work out her own problem

  18. With regard to the four or five youngsters who do most of the talking and take the initiative you would tend to believe:

      (a) they are brighter than most of the other students

      (b) they are the leaders of the class

      (c) there is considerable variation in student's ability to participate in class

      (d) they are a little too cocky and think they know more than the others

19. With regard to the tendency of class members to interrupt while others are talking you would:
   (a) tell the class politely but firmly that interruptions are impolite and should not continue
   (b) discuss the matter with the class, determining why this happens and what should be done about it
   (c) organize a system of hand raising and set rules for students' participation in discussion
   (d) set rules for student participation in discussion and firmly but fairly reprimand each person who breaks the rules

20. One of the important problems facing you now is to do something which:
   (a) will insure that no one is rejected or disliked
   (b) will result in everybody's being liked
   (c) will encourage each person's acceptance of the others
   (d) will guarantee that no one's feelings get hurt

E. At the beginning of the eighth class session (fourth week) Johnny comes into class holding on to his arm and very nearly crying. The tears are welled up in his eyes and he looks away from the others. You notice that Peter, the largest and strongest boy in the class, looks at Johnny occasionally with a sneering smile. You do not feel that you can let this pass, so you arrange to meet with Johnny and Peter separately after class.

21. You would tend to believe
   (a) that Johnny probably did something for which this was just, but maybe severe, repayment
   (b) that Peter is something of a bully
   (c) that Johnny was hit on the arm by Peter
   (d) that Johnny felt badly and Peter was quite aware of it

22. When you meet with Johnny you would:
   (a) ask him if Peter hit him and why
   (b) engage him in conversation and lead slowly into the difficulty he had that afternoon
   (c) tell him you were aware that he had some difficulty and offer your help to him
   (d) let him guide the discussion and reveal what he would about the incident

23. When you meet with Peter you would:
   (a) tell him that Johnny was upset this afternoon and you had noticed that he (Peter) was looking strange—proceed from there
   (b) make him aware that you know he had trouble with Johnny and proceed from there
   (c) make him aware that he is bigger and stronger than the other boys and that he is a bully if he picks on smaller boys
   (d) ask him if he and Johnny had had difficulty

24. To insure that this kind of thing did not happen again you would:
    (a) discuss bullying with the class
    (b) do nothing
    (c) get the two boys together to talk over the difficulty
    (d) find the cause of the trouble and work with those involved to elimi-
        nate it

F. In general your program has been moving along satisfactorily. After the
   eighth meeting you have a feeling that the students are beginning to lose
   interest. A number of students seem to be sitting through class without
   really getting involved. Others seem to stay interested and active. The
   teacher-counselor asks to see you informally over coffee.

   25. When you meet with the teacher-counselor you would:
       (a) not talk about your class or its present lack of involvement
       (b) discuss your concern with him and listen for suggestions he might
           have
       (c) speak about how satisfactory the early meetings had been
       (d) allow the teacher-counselor to orient the discussion

   26. Your planning for the next (ninth) session would include:
       (a) some new ideas that you had not tried
       (b) some clarification of the importance of students doing well in their
           work
       (c) a request for ideas from students as to how to make the class more
           interesting
       (d) ways to get more students actively doing something in class

   27. During the ninth session you would:
       (a) behave much as you had in earlier sessions
       (b) put some stress on the importance of *everybody* paying attention
           to you in class
       (c) by careful observation determine which students seemed disin-
           terested
       (d) speak pointedly to those who were not paying attention

   28. You would tend to believe the loss of interest due to:
       (a) a rather natural reaction in an elective experimental course
       (b) failure of students to realize that they must contribute much to a
           course of this kind
       (c) a rather natural group reaction to the experience of working to-
           gether on personal adjustment problems
       (d) your own failure in developing good human relationships in the
           class and stimulating the students

G. Before the mid term (eighteenth) meeting of the class you take time out
   to think about the experiences you have had. The class has been good
   some days and poor other days. You have had no word from your principal about how your work has been. The teacher-counselor has seemed
   satisfied but not very much impressed with what you are doing. You have

heard nothing about the young people who are being studied. You are asked to meet with the parents to discuss the experimental class in an informal way.

29. You would be most concerned about:
    (a) your apparent failure to impress your teacher-counselor
    (b) what you should say to the parents
    (c) the lack of reaction from your principal
    (d) what the studies of the children are showing
30. You would resolve to:
    (a) discuss your progress with the teacher-counselor
    (b) ask for an appointment with the principal to find out how he feels about your work
    (c) plan to work harder with your group
    (d) not let the present state of affairs worry you
31. When talking with the parents you would:
    (a) encourage them to ask questions about the program
    (b) tell them what the program has consisted of so far
    (c) tell them you don't know how well the program is going
    (d) impress upon them the importance of student participation in the class activities
32. In this case you would feel that parents:
    (a) ought to be told how their children are doing in this class
    (b) ought not to become involved in such an experimental program
    (c) are entitled to an opportunity to question you
    (d) ought to be referred to those in charge of the experiment
33. At your next class meeting:
    (a) you would tell students what you told their parents
    (b) you would not initiate any discussion about your visit with the parents
    (c) you would discuss briefly the parents' interest in the class
    (d) you would tell the students that you expected more cooperation from them now that their parents are involved
H. The nineteenth and twentieth class sessions are very unsatisfactory. You leave class at the end of the twentieth session with doubts in your mind as to whether students are gaining in personal and social adjustment. You can see problems with the structure and organization of the class and believe that if these could be corrected or if you had done some things differently over the past few weeks that you would not have a problem with the class.

34. At this point you would:
    (a) decide to go to class the next day and ask your students how they feel about the progress of the course
    (b) think through the problem carefully and start planning revisions for the course next year

(c) try to help yourself accept the fact that life is often filled with dis-
appointments and redouble your efforts to make your class better
in the future by spending more time in preparation and encouraging your students to work harder

(d) mention your concerns at the next meeting of your class and encourage students to talk with you after class about the progress
of the course

35. You would feel much better regarding the accuracy of your estimate
about what is wrong with the class if you:

(a) were sure that some of the students were not being difficult on
purpose to test your authority as a new teacher

(b) knew more about the expectations of your students and to what
extent they felt their expectations were being met

(c) could have a colleague in whom you could confide and in whom
you could trust, come in and observe your class and talk with you

(d) were sure of your own needs for success and the extent to which
these needs influenced your feelings

36. After the twentieth session, it would be natural for you to feel that:

(a) you wished that students accepted the fact that things that you
taught them in schools are usually good for them even though
they may not like what they are learning all of the time

(b) you would like to go out for an evening of relaxation and think
about the situation over the weekend

(c) it must have been wonderful to teach in the good old days when
students were in school because they wanted to learn

(d) things seldom go well all the time for everybody and that they
couldn't be expected to always go well for you

37. In an attempt to analyze the source of the problem you are having
with your class you would:

(a) have a conference with several of the brighter and more interested
students to see if they could give you any insight into the problem

(b) take part of the class session to share your concerns with the
class, get their reactions, and using this information, rethink the
problems

(c) ask the teacher-counselor to come in and observe the class several times and talk with you about his observations

(d) consult the records of the students to see if you could find any
clues there

I. At your twenty-fourth meeting you wish to make plans for a series of visits
to different community health and welfare agencies. You want to be sure
that the youngsters learn from the experiences and conduct themselves
properly while traveling to and from and visiting in the agencies.

38. In order to assure that all youngsters learned from their first trip you
would:

(a) assign particular things for all of them to look for and listen to
(b) ask each to write a brief commentary on the most important things they saw and heard
(c) encourage them to ask questions while they are there
(d) present them with a check sheet of items to be seen and heard and ask them to check off those that they saw or heard
39. In preparation for the first trip you would:
(a) tell them as much as you could about the agency to which they were going
(b) tell them you were sure it would be interesting and fun and let them see and hear for themselves
(c) ask them what they thought they could expect and encourage guided discussions about their expectations
(d) tell them about the most interesting things they would see and hear
40. To insure that the group conducted themselves properly you would:
(a) set out rules of conduct for them
(b) ask them to behave as young ladies and gentlemen representing their school
(c) ask them what rules of conduct they would propose and develop a code with the groups
(d) assure them that if they did not behave properly they would not go on trips in the future
41. On the trips you would:
(a) divide them into small groups with a leader responsible for each group and arrange their itinerary and meetings after you get to the agency
(b) ask the youngsters to get your permission first and on this basis allow them to pursue their own interests
(c) let the agency people take responsibility for deciding where they could go and when
(d) keep them all together as a manageable group
J. At the close of the thirtieth class session Bob, one of the most able boys, summarizes a class discussion on boy-girl relationships with "Well, we've talked all around the subject but we never get down to the important questions." The agreement of a number of the class members is evident.
42. You would tend to believe:
(a) the class members are too young to be dealing with important questions in this area
(b) you had allowed just a little too much freedom in the discussions of boy-girl relationships
(c) this simply reflects a natural desire on the part of the students to introduce some excitement into the class sessions

(d) the class could handle important questions in this area with teacher guidance and support

43. Before the thirty-first session you would:
   (a) clarify the significance and implications of Bob's statement in your own mind
   (b) determine what you will and will not allow to be discussed in class in this area
   (c) consult the principal and get direction from him
   (d) discuss the situation with the teacher-counselor with a view to getting ideas for handling the next session

44. During the thirty-first session you would:
   (a) propose a list of carefully selected questions you believe the students have in mind and begin discussions on the most manageable of these
   (b) repeat Bob's comment and draw from the class a list of what they thought should be discussed
   (c) suggest that some questions are not appropriate for discussion in school and that some of these fall in the area of boy-girl relationships
   (d) ask Bob to pick up where he left off and encourage him and other class members to clarify the directions further discussion should take

K. Your class has at last developed into a fairly cohesive unit. The discussions are more animated and everyone participates to some degree. Disagreements on ideas begin to appear and the students give evidence of intense feelings on a number of issues. George has been particularly outspoken. He has very radical ideas that seem to provoke the other students who disagree but you know that the ideas he expresses have some support from some adolescent psychologists that you consider to be the "lunatic fringe." George seldom gives in on a point.

45. You would believe that these conditions are likely to:
   (a) ultimately strengthen the group
   (b) do little but make it uncomfortable until George learns his lesson
   (c) destroy the group unity unless you intervene
   (d) make it difficult for progress to be made for some students until they learn to accept George

46. With regard to George you would:
   (a) refer him to the teacher-counselor
   (b) point out to George that he is intolerant of the views of other class members
   (c) encourage him to express his ideas in ways that would not irritate other students

    (d) politely but firmly keep him from agitating the class and if this fails, call on him less often

47. With regard to the other students you would:
    (a) encourage them in their effort to stand up to George
    (b) help them to understand what George is doing to them and why
    (c) help them to get onto topics and ideas where George could not disagree with them so forcefully
    (d) get into the discussion on their side and show George that he is wrong

48. With regard to your concern for George as a person, you would feel that:
    (a) he is developing undemocratic traits by behaving as he does, and you would hope to help him change
    (b) he does not understand how to behave in a democratic setting and may need help
    (c) he probably has never learned certain social skills necessary for democratic group behavior and the possibilities of developing such skills should be shown him
    (d) he will learn sooner or later that in a democracy some ideas are undesirable because they tend to destroy the group

Appendix I
Adjective Checklist

School _____ *Level:* Pre-Primary Primary Intermediate Jr. High Sr. High Sex: M F Teacher Class I Teacher Class II Teacher Class III Principal Assistant Principal Counselor Visiting Teacher Psychologist Supervisor, Elem. Supervisor, Sec.

A No. 2 or softer lead pencil must be used.

Not all pupils are typical, you are acquainted with the pupils in your class(es). They differ from the typical or average pupil in some general ways.

A list of forty-eight adjectives is given below. Blacken the box beside the number of those sixteen (16) words which best complete the following sentence. "The pupils I am presently teaching tend to be more _____ than the typical or average pupil." *Please check sixteen (16) choices only.*

1. Active	17. Disruptive	33. Malicious
2. Affectionate	18. Dynamic	34. Mischievous
3. Agile	19. Expressive	35. Neat
4. Agreeable	20. Fanciful	36. Outgoing
5. Animated	21. Gregarious	37. Patient
6. Antagonistic	22. Harmonious	38. Quarrelsome
7. Aware	23. Humble	39. Quick
8. Awkward	24. Idealistic	40. Rash
9. Bungling	25. Imitative	41. Realistic
10. Changeable	26. Imperceptive	42. Rude
11. Civil	27. Indifferent	43. Self Centered
12. Considerate	28. Informal	44. Sincere
13. Courteous	29. Intent	45. Sloppy
14. Creative	30. Interested	46. Superficial
15. Curious	31. Lazy	47. Unpredictable
16. Discerning	32. Lethargic	48. Vigorous

Notes

1. A. Harry Passow (ed.), *Education in Depressed Areas* (New York: Teachers College Press, 1963).

2. "Education for Socially Disadvantaged Children," Jacob T. Hunt (ed.), *Review of Educational Research,* XXXV (December, 1965).

3. D. B. Godwin, F. L. Newsome, K. A. Chandler, "A Scale to Study Logical Consistency of Ideas about Education," *Journal of Psychology,* LI (April, 1961), pp. 443–455.

4. Thomas L. Goodman, *Instructional Programs in Secondary Schools Serving Contrasting Socioeconomic Areas in Large Cities.* (Unpublished Ph.D. dissertation, The Ohio State University, 1965), p. 138.

5. *Ibid.*

6. Phillip Jackson, "The Way Teaching Is," *The Way Teaching Is* (Washington, D.C.: Association for Supervision and Curriculum Development, 1966), p. 14.

Curriculum Improvement in Principle

The last section of this book is intended as both a summative and transcending discussion of Parts I and II. In one sense it represents our efforts to generalize from the kinds of experiences which have been set forth in earlier chapters, but at the same time an attempt has been made to go beyond those experiences and generate a broader, more comprehensive concept which might be seen as the beginning dimensions of a theory of curriculum improvement. These ideas are neither complete nor adequate as theory as presently described, but they are steps in that direction.

Following in the tradition of Alexander and Saylor, Corey, Harris and Bessent, McNally and Passow, Wiles, and others, we have worked to build a set of ideas about curriculum improvement which is based on good thinking, good practice, and good data.

Much work must be done. It is not the authors' contention that the only significant curriculum improvement efforts will have to come from national government projects, outstanding scholars, or foundation-supported agencies. Such people and such groups have very important roles to play, but significant curriculum improvement must always be an ongoing effort of local schools. Practitioners working in local schools are the ones who must always be "on top" of any curriculum changes which are underway.

Ideas for modification, directions of change, proposals for variations in content, organization, evaluation, methodology can and do come from many places and in many forms. Those who hold primary responsibility for sifting and sorting, guiding and coordinating, and pulling and pushing to make these ideas operational for better curriculum for children in particular schools will always be the people who work in those particular schools. The professionals on the scene neither can nor dare avoid that responsibility. It is theirs alone. Many persons can help, but the curriculum supervisors are the ones who implement curriculum, and they are the ones who have to work at curriculum improvement every day.

The need for tough-mindedness in curriculum improvement activities demands that curriculum workers employ sound rationale in what they do. Part III outlines a rationale for curriculum improvement.

10

General Principles of Curriculum Improvement

Principles

This book describes *one* approach to curriculum improvement. Further, this description has been an effort to articulate and demonstrate this particular approach in both general and specific ways. The effective curriculum worker will rightfully see this approach as only one of many, but improving program through curriculum evaluation and curriculum research *is* an effective approach.

Now let us extrapolate from the experiences outlined in these pages those principles of curriculum improvement which might have broader utility and which seem generally applicable.

Curriculum Improvement Efforts Must Be Comprehensive

Efforts to improve curriculum must be broad enough to encompass all of the salient aspects of curriculum meaningfully. This means that a comprehensive approach is essential—all aspects of program, all grade levels, all of the people, and all geographical-sociological regions served must be involved. Efforts to improve curriculum must deal with the totality, including subject matter areas, methods and materials of instruction, organization, and evaluation, among other things.

Figure 3 is the conventional picture of curriculum as it is usually outlined in terms of vertical and horizontal organization. This matrix is a logical description of part of the totality, and our usual view of curriculum is this logical, segmented, compartmentalized view. We talk about teachers or students or materials according to the various "cells of the matrix." "Mr. Smith is a seventh grade mathematics teacher." Or, "Bill is enrolled in tenth grade English." Or, "This is a third grade science textbook." Sometimes we even say such things as "Lecture is an effective teaching method with highly motivated senior high school students, but an inappropriate technique when used with junior high school students who dislike school." Our concern with scope and sequence is simply an extension of our concern with this logical view of curriculum.

These concerns are legitimate, and all are sound. Nevertheless, someone must be concerned about the *totality* of curriculum, about *all* of the subject matter areas, *all* of the methods, *all* of the teachers, *all* of the children, *all* of the evaluation procedures, and *all* of the grade levels involved.

All of the children of *all* of the people attend schools, and program development must be conceptualized and accomplished in terms of these factors. *Every* school must be involved. *Every* teacher and *every* principal

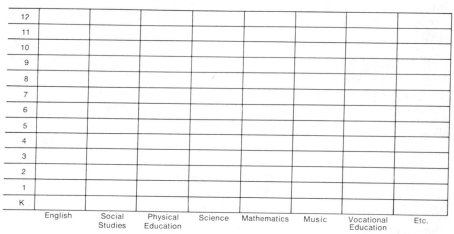

Figure 3

Conventional Curriculum Matrix

must participate in some intelligent, meaningful way. *Every* parent and *every* child should be "touched" by the efforts to improve the curriculum. Curriculum improvement efforts must be comprehensively conceived and effected. Simply, this would suggest that the context be both deep and wide:

1) All age-grade levels.
2) All subject matter areas.
3) All geographical-sociological regions.
4) All of the people who will be affected.
5) All of the assumptions which are involved.

Curriculum Improvement Efforts Must Be Systematic

One might categorize efforts to improve curriculum in terms of the degree to which they are systematic or nonsystematic. Nonsystematic efforts represent basically a short-term approach: systematic efforts represent a continuing, long-term approach. Curriculum improvement efforts must be systematic.

Unless program improvement is a regular, scheduled, continuing effort, those responsible for programs will find themselves *reacting* to demands and exigencies of the moment, rather than thoughtfully *acting* in terms of educational objectives, theoretical considerations, and professional knowledge.

Unless a planned approach to curriculum improvement extends over many months and embraces a comprehensive set of ideals and concerns, the school people will be kept busy "putting out fires."

A parent group complains about a teacher who requires his students to read what they feel is an inappropriate book. *Appoint a committee.*

A first grade teacher's group proposed the abolition of the marking system (A-B-C-D-F). *Appoint a committee.*

The federal government makes extra money available for special laboratory equipment for science and mathematics. *Assign one man for the job.*

The nearby university wants to offer a summer institute for elementary school teachers of foreign language. *Do a survey.*

One member of the school board objects to certain items on the instruments used in the district-wide standardized testing program. *Appoint a committee.*

One of the high school principals wants to offer one year of instruction in the Chinese language next year. *Approve or disapprove his plan.*

Two parents protest about their children having to walk to school along a highway without sidewalks. *Go talk with the parents.*

The business officer objects to a contracted arrangement for repairing typewriters used in typing courses. *Discuss with other staff.*

A teacher came to school intoxicated and the principal wants assistance in securing that teacher's resignation. *Go visit the teacher.*

The Dad's Club offers to raise $4,000 for a football stadium if the school board will revise its policy regarding interscholastic athletics for junior high school students. *Appoint a committee.*

These are difficult, demanding problems. Unless those who are responsible for improving curriculum employ systematic approaches, their energies will be drained in these directions. The problems involved in *maintaining* the educational system are fantastic. There are always teachers to be hired, textbooks to be selected, curriculum guides to be prepared, meetings to be held, critics to be dealt with, telephones to be answered, salesmen to be heard, reports to be filed, proposals to be prepared, etc. If people responsible for program improvement let it happen, these "demands" will take *all* of their time. They may actually feel that they are performing an important role. Perhaps they are, but it is certainly not the role of curriculum improvement. Bringing about intelligent and meaningful change in education demands premeditation, action, and a planned approach.

This means that the calendars of those who are affected must be set months in advance. The person responsible for coordinating and providing leadership in program development must see to it that he regularly "schedules" himself out of the office on projects involving particular teachers, schools, or groups. If he is committed to work on curriculum improvement, he can postpone the immediate "demand" which will inevitably arise.

Curriculum Improvement Efforts Must Be Democratic

Since John Dewey's *Democracy in Education* was published over fifty years ago, American educators have talked about, advocated, and argued through the problems and possibilities involved in employing the concepts of democracy in education (1). It seems trite to suggest that the efforts to improve curriculum must be democratic. But they must be.

Unless a supervisor devises a democratic structure, change efforts will not be lasting or effective. What is a democratic structure? An organization which is democratic has a separation of authority according to function. The policy-making group is different from the implementing group, which is also different from the evaluating or assessing group. It has a separation of authority according to the geographical domains involved. The system functions so that feedback data about the operation are funneled into the system, considered, and acted upon. In a democratic organization, the participants are representative of the total population affected, and they are actively and meaningfully involved. Their intelligence and their participation are important and valued. Communication within the organization is effective and complete; ideas get around. There is a minimum of restriction and a maximum of sharing.

Operationally, these six ideas mean deliberate efforts must be made to clarify *who* makes policy, *who* implements policy, and *who* evaluates the policy or the implementation. In terms of this book, curriculum research councils attempt to fulfill the evaluating function. Because such councils do *not* have power, they are operating from a weak position. All they can do is to try to get consideration of the evaluation data which their studies have generated.

As the idea applies to education, there appears to be a weakening of the democratic concept, since evaluation groups must always function from a "persuasive" rather than a mildly "coercive" posture. However, if people who are attempting to improve education *know* that their evaluations and feedback data appear only as recommendations, they have only *one* thing upon which they can depend: intelligence. They must sharpen their logic, check their data, review their assumptions, clarify their inferences, and make their recommendations unquestionably appropriate and sound.

Research in personality and human behavior in recent years has spelled out some of the characteristics of democratic behavior and the dimensions of personality which affect behavior (2). People who behave in democratic ways are more perceptive, more accurate in the perceptual processes, more tolerant of ambiguity, have a more positive concept of self and concept of others, and are more independent. This means that democratic people are concerned with the validity and availability of information.

They do not judge ideas according to who advances them; but rather according to the inherent logic of the idea or the data available to substantiate it. They are open to experience and to incoming data; they are sensitive, thoughtful, considerate people who respect themselves and others, and who use the power of their intelligence. The activities of democratic people are predicated upon valid information and human relationships that allow development of such information. Curriculum improvement efforts must be democratic.

Curriculum Improvement Must
Possess Integrity

Efforts to improve program must have integrity, validity, and reality. "Real" problems, "real" data, and "real" considerations must be allowed. Integrity involves *wholeness* and *truthfulness,* and curriculum improvement efforts must be characterized by these qualities. The approach must be broad enough to encompass all of the significant "pieces" which are involved. Further, it must be valid enough to generate "good" data about the operation so that the decisions made are rooted in fact (3). Working on artificial problem areas, collecting unreliable, irrelevant, and inappropriate data, or developing artificial or deceptive relationships among people struggling to improve curriculum can only result in feeble or negative improvement efforts. Attempts to "cover up" or distort or deceive anyone (parents, board members, teachers, or children) will inevitably fail.

In summary, curriculum improvement efforts must be comprehensive, systematic, democratic, and possess integrity, but to make these principles operational, the improvement effort must be predicated upon curriculum evaluation as a basis for change.

Curriculum Evaluation as a Basis
for Change

The school is a social system. Like every other social system, the school is a human undertaking designed to realize or further human goals. Curriculum is the means which schools implement to attain the goals. Evaluation is the process employed to assess both goals and means.

Graphically portrayed, the school as a social system is described below:

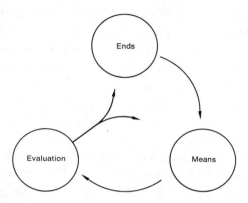

Evaluation is the relationship between ends and means. The purposes of education, what schools intend to accomplish, the goals they seek to achieve are represented by the circle labeled "ends." The subject matter selected, the organization of people and ideas, and the methodology employed are represented by the circle labeled "means." The assessment of ends and the judgment of means is represented by the circle labeled "evaluation." Curriculum evaluation is a function in its own right, but it also relates directly to educational ends and educational means.

Evaluation of Ends

In evaluation of curricular ends, three general areas of concern are paramount: philosophical acceptability, appropriateness, and attainment of ends as goals to give direction to the educational effort.

Philosophical Acceptability of Ends

In the processes of determining educational purposes, curriculum workers draw information and inspiration from three basic sources (4):

1) What is known about the nature of knowledge.
2) What is known about the nature of society.
3) What is known about the nature of the individual.

Such factors as the structure of the discipline, the facts and concepts basic to a particular body of knowledge, the methods of inquiry unique to a particular discipline, and the interrelationship of these aspects of subject matter constitute one source from which curriculum builders can draw.

A second source is what is known about the nature of society. Population patterns, cultural expectations, social values and norms, economic pressures, etc., represent this second source of information from which curriculum builders can draw.

A third source of information upon which curriculum workers can draw as they determine educational purposes is what is known about the nature of the individual. Intellectual development, past experiences, motivations, personality structure, and personal aspirations are some of the factors involved.

In an abstract sense, persons responsible for developing curriculum use these three sources of information equally. In actual practice, however, the various sources are drawn upon in varying degrees with the result that different philosophical positions are inevitably reflected in terms of the values of the persons who are involved. Three major emphases are possible. Those responsible for determining educational purposes may assume that what is known about the nature of knowledge is of primary importance, and what is known about the nature of society and the individual are of secondary importance. Such an assumption will result in educational purposes being stated primarily in subject matter terms and the curriculum will have a subject matter emphasis. On the other hand, those responsible for determining educational purposes may assume that what is known about the nature of society is primary, and what is known about the nature of knowledge and the nature of the individual are of secondary importance. That assumption would mean that educational ends would have an emphasis upon the group. Or, in determining educational purposes it may be assumed that what is known about the nature of the individual is primary and what is known about the nature of knowledge and the nature of society is of lesser importance. In that case, an entirely different set of educational purposes would emerge and these would be stated in individual or personal terms.

Each of these philosophical positions is reflected in the hierarchical ordering of curriculum sources as outlined below:

<u>Disciplines</u> Society—Individual	<u>Society</u> Disciplines—Individual	<u>Individual</u> Society—Disciplines
Assumption No. 1	Assumption No. 2	Assumption No. 3

Any implication that one set of assumptions is "good" and the others "bad" is not intended at all. What is intended is a clear delineation of the philosophical possibilities inherent in curriculum purposes with the view in mind of enabling the reader to make a more accurate assessment of curriculum ends in terms of the values implicit in the various orderings of curriculum sources as previously described. If the curriculum to be evaluated is predicated upon assumption number one, but the evaluator holds assumption number two, misunderstanding and disagreement will inevitably arise.

Appropriateness of Ends

Accepting the fact that curriculum purposes may reflect assumptions which give varying directions to the educational enterprise, questions also arise regarding the appropriateness of ends. The appropriateness question can best be discussed in terms of the three sources outlined here.

For example, are the curriculum objectives consistent with what scholars in the field say ought to be learned? Is this particular purpose worth pursuing in subject matter terms? For instance, is "learning the names of the various parts of speech" a meaningful objective from a grammarian's point of view?

Are the curriculum objectives socially acceptable? Are the objectives what society wants the schools to help children achieve? How consistent are the purposes in terms of what is known about society's needs as far as citizenship or economic sufficiency or legal requirements?

Finally, how appropriate are the ends in terms of what is known about the nature of the individuals who are involved. Can children actually learn what is intended for them to learn? In terms of what is known regarding the developmental characteristics of children, can the goal be realized? Obviously it would be inappropirate to expect a four-year-old youngster to learn to type 50 words per minute, so the question arises: "can the educational objectives be attained by all or almost all of the students who will be involved?" A curriculum purpose might be very acceptable from a social or subject matter point of view, but unrealistic and inappropriate in terms of an individual's motivational level, past experience, or physical endurance level.

Attainment of Ends

Because ends or purposes give direction to the educational effort, the question naturally arises: Were the ends achieved? Achievements, however, can be of at least two types, so curriculum evaluators must ask both questions:

> Were the intended ends achieved?
> What other achievements were gained which were not intended?

In other words, assessing the attainment of ends involves finding out what has been learned. A child may learn to spell "hippopotamus," but also learn to hate spelling. "Learning to spell" may have been the intended purpose, but "learning to hate spelling" may be an equally or more important attainment which must be evaluated and understood.

Evaluation of Means

Curriculum as a "means" includes the factual data and concepts selected, experiences contrived, methodology employed, and the organizational strategems utilized to achieve the curriculum "ends." In evaluating curriculum means, four general areas of concern seem most important: appropriateness, validity, efficiency, and effectiveness.

Appropriateness of Means

Is it appropriate to ask a thirteen-year-old to read *Ulysses?* Is it appropriate to expect an eight-year-old to comprehend "multiplication" as a concept if he has not yet learned "addition?" Is it appropriate to use first-grade reading materials to help adult illiterates learn to read? Is it appropriate to expect fourteen-year-old boys to "sit still" for ninety minutes at a time? In evaluating the appropriateness of curriculum means, questions such as the following might be posed.

Is the experience demeaning to the students involved?
Is the sequence of ideas defensible psychologically or logically or sociologically?
Are the arrangements of time and space and staff consistent with the physiological needs, motivations, and developmental levels of the students involved?

Validity of Means

Are the curriculum means truthful? Is the content accurate? Are the facts correct? Is the information complete? Is the teacher honest? Are the teacher's verbal statements to the learner consistent with the non-verbal message cues which he imparts? Does the teacher have integrity in his manner and his being?

In evaluating curriculum means, questions such as these must be asked. Is the subject matter content, the technique, or the organizational scheme what it purports to be? For example, if organizational arrangements are designed to control and restrict the students, but they are set forth as aids in facilitating student learning, deception is involved. If controversial ideas are avoided in an effort to placate certain citizens' groups, and less significant information is presented to students, deception is involved.

Asking "Do the means employed to achieve the intended curriculum ends possess validity" requires that the curriculum evaluator assess the truthfulness and the completeness or wholeness of the endeavor.

Efficiency of Means

Will the curriculum means accomplish the attainment of the intended goal within a reasonable time and for a reasonable amount of money? Efficiency involves considerations of time and money. A particular means may be both appropriate and valid, but require much too much time for efficiency reasons. A given means may be very quick to accomplish the intended objectives, but extremely costly to employ. For instance, tutorial approaches employed to teach typical children to read might be exceptionally effective, but cost twenty times as much money as is presently being spent to accomplish that end.

Effectiveness of Means

Is the desired objective realized? Do the students learn what is intended for them to learn? Are the curriculum ends actually attained? Do the arrangements of time and space and staff contribute maximally to the attainment of intended objectives? Questions such as these relate to the effectiveness of the curriculum means. Means are selected or devised to achieve particular curriculum objectives. The degree to which the objectives are realized is an indication of the effectiveness of the content, methodology, organizational arrangements, or experiences as a means to a curricular end.

Evaluation of Evaluation

Assessment of curriculum ends and means is one aspect of the educational endeavor, but the evaluation techniques and processes can be evaluated, too. In evaluating the evaluation function, four basic factors must be considered: appropriateness, efficiency, validity, and reliability.

Appropriateness of Evaluation

Does the evaluation technique violate the integrity or dignity of the individual where it is employed? Is the student forced to reveal experiences or information which degrades him or is demeaning in any way? Does the evaluation process fit his age? Is it socially acceptable? Is the technique in violation of the social norms?

Efficiency of Evaluation

Will the evaluation process produce the necessary information within the time and money limits which are available? If the evaluation technique requires an extended time period for a highly trained evaluator to accomplish with one individual (e.g., measuring a youngster's intelligence with the Wechsler Intelligence Scale for Children), it may be too inefficient for widespread use but very appropriate in special cases.

Validity of Evaluation

Does the evaluation accomplish what it purports to accomplish? The effectiveness of the evaluation process, in fact, relates directly to whether the testing procedures or observational approaches reflect an accurate picture of the reality which is involved. If the curriculum ends sought are actually attained, then it is important for the evaluation processes to indicate just that. If the evaluation devices do not accurately portray the extent to which purposes are or are not achieved, they are invalid. Likewise, if the evaluation procedures do not accurately portray the efficiency or effectiveness of the means which are being utilized, they are also invalid.

Reliability of Evaluation

Do the evaluation procedures produce information regarding the attainment of ends or the efficiency and effectiveness of means in a consistent fashion? If an evaluation technique is valid, it will be reliable, by definition, but it may be reliable without being valid, and that creates special problems. For instance, one might "say" that a foot-long ruler was actually a yard stick, then proceed to measure the length of a table several times and consistently get the very same answer, which would always be "wrong." The measuring device would be reliable, but not valid. Because it is often very difficult to determine the validity of observational devices in education, however, reliability is a useful concept of evaluation, though not as significant as validity, of course.

Special Problems in Evaluation

Two special problems exist in using curriculum evaluation as a basis for curriculum change. One involves the determination of what is ends and what is means. The other problem revolves around the nature and the interplay of the evaluation processes which have already been described:

Is the approach *comprehensive?* Is it *systematic?* Is it *democratic?* Does the approach possess *integrity?*

Ends or Means

What is ends and what is means? In curriculum efforts, as in other endeavors, ends and means are often changing, and this factor clearly complicates the evaluator's role. In temporal perspective, however, at any given point in time, ends are always ends and means are always means. In other words, any end attained may become a means to a further end, but only at some later point in time. Graphically described, the curriculum problem is one of first identifying ends "E" and then employing means "M" to achieve those particular ends:

$$M_1 \rightarrow E_1$$

Over time, however, ends achieved may become means to further ends, thus we have:

$$E_1 = M_2$$

Over an extended period of time, the curriculum effort might very well be described as follows:

$$M_3 \rightarrow E_3$$
$$\|$$
$$M_2 \rightarrow E_2$$
$$\|$$
$$M_1 \rightarrow E_1$$

and so on. In other words, what we have portrayed here is the notion that an end attained can clearly become a means to a further, "higher," and "more general" end.

In curriculum efforts, for example, we try to help children *know the meaning of particular words* (E_1) by means of *instruction in reading* (M_1) *so that* ($=$) *they will be able to read* (M_2) in order to *understand the First Amendment* (E_2) *so that* ($=$) they will be able to *use this knowledge about free speech* (M_3) to *be a good citizen* (E_3).

This logic of means and ends suggests that ends realized may become means to still futher ends, but at any given point in time they are either ends or means, not both. In evaluating curriculum, therefore, the sorting out of ends and means is both a conceptual problem and a temporal problem, but it can be done.

Summary

Improving curriculum is an involved and involving task. It takes lots of people, lots of time, lots of energy, and tremendous amounts of information. Some information is available in books and some exists in experts' minds, but most of the information which curriculum workers need is imbedded in the minds and activities and in the policies and personalities of those who work day after day to make the educational system go. To make educational programs better, one has to ferret those data out. Curriculum evaluation and curriculum research are operational tools.

The approach to the task of curriculum improvement demands breadth, organization, equalitarian relationships, and participation in decision making by all of those who are involved. And the entire endeavor must be concerned with truth.

Education is a human undertaking dedicated to the process of realizing human purposes or goals. Schooling and education have never been synonymous, and they are not today. For those who have responsibility for designing and organizing information and experiences which will help all children learn, the least that they can strive for is to guarantee that curriculum never "gets in the way" of students' significant learnings. The most that they can hope for is to make the curriculum relevant and help it "fit" the learning needs of young people in school. The signs are everywhere that the "fit" is poor today. The curriculum must be improved.

Engineers cannot solve the problem. Politicians cannot make the significant changes, nor can physicians, economists, or industrialists. Only schoolmen can find ways to help young people learn and live in creative and satisfying ways. The time to start is now. The one to act is you.

Notes

1. John Dewey, *Democracy in Education* (New York: The Macmillan Company, 1916).

2. For example, see Erich Fromm, *The Heart of Man* (New York: Harper & Row, Publishers, 1965), or T. W. Adorno, et al., *The Authoritarian Personality* (New

York: Harper & Row, Publishers, 1950), or Jack R. Frymier, *The Nature of Educational Method* (Columbus, Ohio: Charles E. Merrill Publishing Company, 1965), Chapter III.

3. For an extended discussion of this idea, see Daniel L. Stufflebeam, "Evaluation As Enlightenment for Decision Making," in Walcott H. Beatty (ed.), *Improving Educational Assessment And An Inventory of Measures of Affective Behavior* (Washington, D.C.: The Association for Supervision and Curriculum Development, 1969), pp. 41–73.

4. Ralph E. Tyler, *Basic Principles of Curriculum and Instruction* (Chicago: University of Chicago Press, 1950).

5. Virgil Herrick, *Strategies of Curriculum Development* (Columbus, Ohio: Charles E. Merrill Publishing Company, 1965), Chapter 1.

Bibliography

This listing is not intended to be an
exhaustive survey of the literature regarding
curriculum improvement. It should be
considered as illustrative of the type and
range of material which could be helpful in
this area.

Chapter 1

Curriculum Improvement in Perspective

Association for Supervision and Curriculum Development. *What Are the Sources of the Curriculum? A Symposium*. Washington, D.C.: The Association, 1962.

Bhola, H. S. "Implications of New Democratic Theory for Planned Educational Change." *Newsletter of the Conference on Strategies for Educational Change.* Columbus, Ohio: The Ohio State University, November, 1965.

Brooks, John. *The Great Leap: The Past Twenty-five Years in America*. New York: Harper and Row, Publishers, 1966.

Bruner, Jerome S. *The Process of Education*. Cambridge: Harvard University Press, 1960.

Campbell, Donald T. and Julian C. Stanley. *Experimental and Quasi-experimental Designs for Research on Teaching.* Chicago: Rand McNally and Co., 1966.

Carlson, Richard O. *Adoption of Educational Innovations.* Eugene, Ore.: Center for Advanced Study of Educational Administration, 1965.

Cowles, Milly. *Perspectives in the Education of Disadvantaged Children.* Cleveland: The World Publishing Co., 1967.

Educational Policies Commission. *Central Purpose of American Education.* Washington, D.C.: The National Education Association, 1961.

Frymier, Jack R. *Fostering Educational Change.* Columbus, Ohio: Charles E. Merrill Publishing Co., 1969.

Gilchrist, Robert S., ed. *New Curriculum Developments.* Washington, D.C.: The Association for Supervision and Curriculum Development, 1965.

Goodlad, John I. "Educational Change: A Strategy for Study and Action." *The National Elementary Principal* XLVIII, No. 5 (1969), 6–13.

———. *School Curriculum Reform in the United States.* New York: Fund for the Advancement of Education, 1964.

Guba, Egon G. "Methodological Strategies for Educational Change." A paper presented to the Conference on Strategies for Educational Change. Washington, D.C., 1965. Mimeographed.

Harris, Ben M. *Supervisory Behavior in Education.* Englewood Cliffs, N.J.: Prentice-Hall, Inc., 1963.

Harris, Lewis E. and Clyde B. Moore. *Keys to Quality: Final Booklet in the Quest for Quality Series.* Washington, D.C.: American Association of School Administrators, 1960.

Ianni, Francis A. J., "Appraisal of Changes in Education." *North Central Association Quarterly* XL, No. 2 (1965), 180–187.

Kimball, Solon T. and James E. McClellan, Jr. *Education and the New America.* New York: Random House, Inc., 1962.

Klohr, Paul R. and Jack R. Frymier. "Curriculum Development: Dynamics of Change." *Review of Educational Research* XXXIII, No. 3 (1963), 304–321.

McNally, Harold J. and A. H. Passow. *Improving the Quality of Public School Programs: Approaches to Curriculum Development.* New York: Teachers College Press, 1960.

Miles, Matthew B., ed. *Innovations in Education.* New York: Teachers College Press, 1964.

Miller, Richard I., ed. *Perspectives on Educational Change.* New York: Appleton-Century-Crofts, Inc., 1967.

Pagan, William B. *Modern Elementary Curriculum.* New York: The Dryden Press, 1966.

Rogers, Everett M. *Diffusion of Innovations.* New York: The Free Press, 1962.

Silberman, Charles E. *The Myths of Automation.* New York: Harper and Row, Publishers, 1966.

Stufflebeam, Daniel L. "The Use and Abuse of Evaluation in Title III." *Theory into Practice* VI, No. 3 (1967), 126–133.

Tyler, Ralph W. "The Function of Measurement in Improving Instruction." *Educational Measurement*. Edited by E. F. Lindquist. Washington, D.C.: American Council on Education, 1951, 47–67.

Walsh, John. "Curriculum Reform." *Science* CXLIV (1964), 642–646.

Wiles, Kimball and Robert R. Leeper, eds. *Strategy for Curriculum Change*. Washington, D.C.: Association for Supervision and Curriculum Development, 1968.

Chapter 2
Basis for Curriculum Change

Broudy, Harry S., B. Othanel Smith, and Joe R. Burnett. *Democracy and Excellence in American Secondary Education*. Chicago: Rand McNally and Co., 1964.

Corey, Stephen M. *Action Research to Improve School Practice*. New York: Teachers College Press, 1953.

Elam, Stanley, ed. *Education and the Structure of Knowledge*. Chicago: Rand McNally and Co., 1964.

Haan, Aubrey. *Elementary School Curriculum: Theory and Research*. Boston: Allyn and Bacon, Inc., 1961.

Hutchins, Robert M. "Permanence and Change." *The Center Magazine* I, No. 6 (September, 1968), 2–6.

Luckie, William Ronald. "Leader Behavior of Directors of Instruction." *Dissertation Abstracts* XXV (1964), 1690.

Manley, George J. *The Science of Educational Research*. New York: American Book Co., 1963.

Manning, Duane. *The Qualitative Elementary School*. New York: Harper and Row, Publishers, 1963.

Oscamp, Edwin. "An Investigation of the Determiners of the Curriculum in Three Elementary Schools in West Milford Township." *Dissertation Abstracts* XXIX (1968), 2153.

Phenix, Philip H. *Education and the Common Good*. New York: Harper and Row, Publishers, 1961.

Raths, Louis E., Merrill Harmin, and Sidney B. Simon. *Values and Teaching*. Columbus, Ohio: Charles E. Merrill Books, Inc., 1966.

Rodgers, Paul R. "A Study of In-Service Education Practices in Terms of Changes in Curriculum and Teaching Procedures in Selected Elementary Schools in Suburban Chicago." *Dissertation Abstracts* XXVI (1964), 4397.

Saylor, J. Galen and William M. Alexander. *Curriculum Planning for Modern Schools*. New York: Holt, Rinehart and Winston, Inc., 1966.

Shuster, Albert H. and Milton E. Ploghoft. *The Emerging Elementary Curriculum*. Columbus, Ohio: Charles E. Merrill Books, Inc., 1963.

Taba, Hilda. *Curriculum Development Theory and Practice*. New York: Harcourt, Brace and World, Inc., 1962.

Urick, Ronald and Jack R. Frymier. "Personalities, Teachers, and Curriculum Change." *Educational Leadership* XXI (1963), 107–110.

Wiley, Frank A. "A Study of Teacher Relationships Considered to Be Associated with Readiness and Non-Readiness for Curriculum Change." *Dissertation Abstracts* XXVI (1965), 5312.

Wilhelm, Fred T., ed. *Evaluation as Feedback and Guide.* Washington, D.C.: Association for Supervision and Curriculum Development, 1967.

Chapter 4

Devising a Structure for Change

American Association of School Administrators and the Association for Supervision and Curriculum Development. *Organizing for Improved Instruction.* Washington, D.C.: The Associations, 1963.

Association for Supervision and Curriculum Development. *Role of Supervisors and Curriculum Director in a Climate of Change.* Yearbook, 1965. Washington, D.C.: The Association, 1965.

Corey, Stephen M. *Helping Other People Change.* Columbus: The Ohio State University Press, 1963.

Doll, Ronald C. *Curriculum Improvement: Decision-Making and Process.* Boston: Allyn and Bacon, Inc., 1964.

———, A. Harry Passow, and Stephen Corey, *Organizing for Curriculum Improvement.* New York: Teachers College Press, 1953.

Duncan, Thomas R. "A Study of Innovative and Non-innovative Principals and Their Use of Information Sources in Curriculum Decision Making." *Dissertation Abstracts* XXIX (1968), 4512.

Farrah, George. "The Roles of Citizens Advisory Committees in Curriculum Development: A Special Case in Farmington, Michigan." *Dissertation Abstracts* XXIII (1962), 1230.

Funaro, George J. "The Confrontation Approach to Curriculum Development." *Dissertation Abstracts* XXVI (1965), 6548.

Haas, Arthur. "An Exploration of Methods of Organizing Elementary Schools for Curriculum Study." *Dissertation Abstracts* XXIII (1962), 4158.

Hillkirk, John M. "Action Research as Applied in Curriculum Development, Grades K-12, A Case Study." *Dissertation Abstracts* XXIII (1962), 3722.

McNally, Harold J. and A. Harry Passow. *Improving the Quality of Public School Programs: Approaches to Curriculum Development.* New York: Teachers College Press, 1960.

McQuigg, Robert B. "Participation in Curriculum Committees by Classroom Teachers in Selected Colorado School Systems." *Dissertation Abstracts* XXIII (1962), 3373.

Miles, Matthew B., ed. *Innovation in Education.* New York: Teachers College Press, 1964.

National Education Association, Center for the Study of Instruction. *From Book-shelves to Action: A Guide to Using the Recommendations of the NEA Project on Instruction.* Washington, D.C.: National Education Association, 1964.

Nicosia, Delores J. "An Exploratory Survey of a Process of Curricular Change in a Large Urban School System." *Dissertation Abstracts* XXIX (1968), 3777.

Oliver, Albert I. *Curriculum Improvement: A Guide to Problems, Principles, and Procedures.* New York: Dodd, Mead and Co., 1965.

Thelen, Herbert A. *Dynamics of Groups at Work.* Chicago: University of Chicago Press, 1954.

Wiles, Kimball. *The Changing Curriculum of the American High School.* Englewood Cliffs, N.J.: Prentice-Hall, Inc., 1963.

Chapter 5

Curriculum Studies Involving Community

Beach, Edward S., Jr. "The Study of a Community—Its Needs and Its Problems and Their Implications for Improvement in School Organization and Improvement." *Dissertation Abstracts* XXIX (1969), 3315.

Bernstein, Abraham. *The Education of Urban Populations.* New York: Random House, Inc., 1967.

Bloom, Benjamin, Allison Davis, and Robert D. Hess. *Compensatory Education for Cultural Deprivation.* New York: Holt, Rinehart, and Winston, Inc., 1965.

Fretwell, E. K., Jr. "Issues Facing Community Colleges Today." *Today's Education* LVII, No. 7 (1968), 46–48.

Havighurst, Robert J., Paul Hoover Bowman, Gordon P. Liddle, Charles V. Matthews, and James V. Pierce. *Growing Up in River City.* New York: John Wiley and Sons, Inc., 1962.

Henry, Jules. *Culture Against Man.* New York: Random House, Inc., 1964.

Herman, Barry E. "Winchester Community School: A Laboratory of Ideas." *Educational Leadership* XXV, No. 4 (1968), 341–342.

Keach, Everett T., Jr., Robert Fulton, and William E. Gardner. *Education and Social Crisis.* New York: John Wiley and Sons, Inc., 1967.

Kerber, August and Barbara Bommarito, eds. *The School and the Urban Crisis.* New York: Holt, Rinehart and Winston, Inc., 1965.

Larson, Richard G. "The Implementation of an Urban School Curriculum by Inner City and Outer City Primary Teachers: A Comparative Study of Deviations from Prescribed Curricula." *Dissertation Abstracts* XXIX (1968), 2040.

Levine, Daniel U. "Socio-Economic Attitudinal Correlates of Educational Viewpoint." *Journal of Experimental Education* XXXIII, No. 3 (1965), 250.

Mallery, David. *A Community-School Venture: Top Professionals Work with School Students.* Boston: National Association of Independent Schools, 1963.

Miel, Alice and Edwin Kiester, Jr. *The Shortchanged Children of Suburbia.* New York: Institute of Human Relations Press, 1967.

Moore, Wilbert E., ed. *Order and Change*. New York: John Wiley and Sons, Inc., 1967.

National Society for the Study of Education. *Social Forces Influencing American Education*. Sixth *Yearbook,* Part II. Chicago: University of Chicago Press, 1961.

Passow, A. Harry, ed. *Education in Depressed Areas*. New York: Teachers College Press, 1963.

———, Miriam Goldberg, and Abraham J. Lannebaum. *Education of the Disadvantaged*. New York: Holt, Rinehart and Winston, Inc., 1967.

Ress, Etta Schneider, ed. *Cities and Metropolitan Areas*. Mankato: Creative Educational Society, 1968.

Rubin, Louis J. *Life Skills in School and Society*. Washington, D.C.: Association for Supervision and Curriculum Development, 1969.

Weekemon, Rachel D. "Discovery in the Bronx." *Junior College Journal* XXXVI, No. 5 (1966), 76–78.

Chapter 6
Curriculum Studies Involving Students

A Guide to Research and Informed Judgment on Grouping Children. Education Briefs, No. 40. Washington, D.C.: Government Printing Office, 1964.

Benson, Ronald L. and Don H. Blocher. "Evaluation of Developmental Counseling with Groups of Low Achievers in a High School Setting." *School Counselor* XIV, No. 4, (1967), 215–220.

Berelson, Bernard and Gary A. Steiner. *Human Behavior: An Inventory of Scientific Findings*. New York: Harcourt, Brace and World, Inc., 1964.

Bloom, Benjamin S. *Stability and Change in Human Characteristics*. New York: John Wiley and Sons, Inc., 1964.

Burkey, Betty and William Asher. "A Comparison of Ninth-Grade Accelerated Students and a Group of Tenth-Grade Students in Their Ability to Comprehend Biology." *Journal of Research in Science Teaching* III (1965), 66–71.

Cantrell, Sue Rowe and Loren T. Caldwell. "A Selection and Evaluation of Physics and Chemistry Concepts to Be Used in the Seventh- and Eighth-Grade Science Program." *Science Education* XLVII, No. 3 (1963), 264–270.

Crow, Lester D., Walter I. Murray, and Hugh H. Smythe. *Educating the Culturally Disadvantaged Child*. New York: David McKay Co., Inc., 1966.

Dolan, G. Keith. "Effects of Individual Counseling on Selected Test Scores for Delayed Readers." *Personnel and Guidance Journal* XLII, No. 9 (1964), 914–919.

Doll, Ronald C. and Robert S. Fleming. *Children Under Pressure*. Columbus, Ohio: Charles E. Merrill Books, Inc., 1966.

Dunn, Lloyd M., ed. *Exceptional Children in the Schools*. New York: Holt, Rinehart and Winston, Inc., 1963.

Flavell, John H. *The Developmental Psychology of Jean Piaget*. Princeton, N.J.: D. Van Nostrand Co., Inc., 1963.

Fleming, Robert S. *Curriculum for Today's Boys and Girls*. Columbus, Ohio: Charles E. Merrill Books, Inc., 1963.

Friedlander, Bernard Z. "A Psychologist's Second Thoughts on Concepts, Curiosity, and Discovery in Teaching and Learning." *Harvard Educational Review* XXXV, No. 1 (1965), 18–38.

Frost, Joe L. and Glenn R. Hawkes, eds. *The Disadvantaged Child*. Boston: Houghton Mifflin Co., 1966.

Ginsberg, Herbert and Sylvia Opper. *Piaget's Theory of Intellectual Development: An Introduction*. Englewood Cliffs, N.J.: Prentice-Hall, Inc., 1969.

Harper, Robert J. C., Charles C. Anderson, Clifford M. Christensen, and Steven M. Hunka. *The Cognitive Processes*. Englewood Cliffs, N.J.: Prentice-Hall, Inc., 1964.

Hentoff, Nat. *Our Children Are Dying*. New York: Viking Press, Inc., 1966.

Ilg, Frances L. and Louise Bates Ames. *School Readiness*. New York: Harper and Row, Publishers, 1965.

Krumboltz, John D. and Barbara Varenhorst. "Molders of Pupil Attitudes." *Personnel and Guidance Journal* XLIII, No. 5 (1965), 443–446.

Lee, J. Murray and Doris M. Lee. *The Child and His Curriculum*. New York: Appleton-Century-Crofts, Inc., 1960.

Riessman, Frank. *The Culturally Deprived Child*. New York: Harper and Row Publishers, 1962.

Screiber, Daniel, ed. *The School Dropout*. Washington, D.C.: National Education Association, 1964.

Sears, Pauline S. and Vivian S. Sherman. *In Pursuit of Self-Esteem*. Belmont, Calif.: Wadsworth Publishing Co., 1964.

Smith, Frederick R. "The Academic Achievement of Academically Talented Students," *Journal of Educational Research* LVI, No. 5 (January, 1963), 255–259.

Torrance, E. Paul. *Education and the Creative Potential*. The Modern School Practices Series, No. 5. Minneapolis: University of Minnesota Press, 1963.

Chapter 7
Curriculum Studies Involving Organizational Factors

Alexander, William M., Vynce A. Hines, Ernest L. Bentley, R. J. Moriconi, and James D. Wells. *Independent Study in Secondary Schools*. New York: Holt, Rinehart and Winston, Inc., 1967.

—— *A Survey of Organizational Patterns of Reorganized Middle Schools*. USOE Project No. 7-D-026. Washington, D.C.: Office of Education, 1968.

——, Emmett L. Williams, Mary F. Compton, Vynce A. Hines, Dan Prescott, and Ronald Kealy. *The Emergent Middle School*. New York: Holt, Rinehart and Winston, Inc., 1969.

Brown, B. Frank. *The Appropriate Placement School: A Sophisticated Nongraded Curriculum*. West Nyack, N.Y.: Parker Publishing Co., Inc., 1965.

———. *The Nongraded High School*. Englewood Cliffs: Prentice-Hall, Inc., 1963.

Bush, Robert N. and Dwight W. Allen. *A New Design for High School Education*. New York: McGraw-Hill Book Co., Inc., 1964.

Compton, Mary F. "Middle School: Alternative to the Status Quo." *Theory into Practice* VII, No. 3 (1968), 108–110.

Cuff, William C. "Middle Schools on the March." *National Association of Secondary School Principals Bulletin* No. 316 (1967), 82–86.

Educational Research Service. *Middle Schools in Action*. Circular No. 2, Washington, D.C.: American Association of School Administration and Research Division, National Education Association, 1969.

Eichhorn, Donald H. *The Middle School*. New York: The Center for Applied Research in Education, 1966.

Eigen, Lewis D. "High School Student Reactions to Programmed Instruction." *Phi Delta Kappan* XLIV, No. 6 (1963), 282–285.

Goldberg, Miriam L., A. H. Passow, and Joseph Justman. *The Effects of Ability Grouping*. New York: Teachers College Press, 1966.

Goodlad, John I. *Planning and Organizing for Teaching*. Washington, D.C.: National Education Association, 1963.

——— and Robert H. Anderson. *The Nongraded Elementary School*. New York: Harcourt, Brace and World, Inc., 1963.

Groff, Frank H. "Effects on Academic Achievement of Excusing Elementary School Pupils from Classes to Study Instrumental Music." *Dissertation Abstracts* XXV (March, 1965), 5014–5015.

Grooms, M. Ann. *Perspectives on the Middle School*. Columbus, Ohio: Charles E. Merrill Books, Inc., 1967.

Guba, Egon G. "Elementary School Nonpromotion and Individual Potential." *Theory into Practice* IV, No. 3 (1965), 85–128.

Halliwell, Joseph W. "A Comparison of Pupil Achievement in Graded and Nongraded Primary Classrooms." *Journal of Experimental Education* XXXII (Fall, 1963), 59–64.

Halpin, Andrew W. and Don B. Croft. *Organizational Climate of Schools*. Chicago: Midwest Administration Center, University of Chicago, 1964.

Hartnett, Rodney T. and Clifford T. Stewart. "Final Examination Grades of Independent Study Students Compared with Those of Students Taught by Traditional Methods." *The Journal of Educational Research* LIX, No. 8 (1966), 356–357.

Hillson, M., ed. *Change and Innovation in Elementary School Organization*. New York: Holt, Rinehart and Winston, Inc., 1965.

Hoban, Pierce F. and Barry McManus. "How to Nongrade a Small High School." *School Management* IX, No. 9 (1965), 79–81.

Hopkins, Kenneth D. and D. Welty Lefever. "Comparative Learning and Retention of Conventional and Instructional TV Methods." *AV Communication Review* XXIII (Spring, 1965), 28–37.

Howell, Wallace J. "Influence of Curriculum Enrichment in High School Honors Group on College Board Examination Scores." *Journal on Educational Research* LIX, No. 3 (1965), 113–114.

Jacobs, James N., Althea Beery, and Judith Lernwold. "Evaluation of an Accelerated Arithmetic Program." *The Arithmetic Teacher* XII, No. 2 (1965), 113–119.

Jantzen, Victor W. "The Effectiveness of Television Teaching of American Government Compared with Regular Classes in Wichita High School South." *Dissertation Abstracts* XXIV (September–October, 1963), 1029.

Keating, Raymond F. "A Study of the Effectiveness of Language Laboratories." The Institute of Administrative Research, Teachers College, Columbia University, 1963.

Kumata, Hideya. "Two Studies in Classroom Teaching by Television." *The Impact of Educational Television.* Edited by W. Schramm. Urbana: University of Illinois Press, 1960.

Lambert, Philip, William L. Goodwin and William Wiersma. "A Comparison of Pupil Adjustment in Team and Self-Contained Organizations." *Journal of Educational Research* LVIII, No. 7 (1965), 311–314.

McNeil, John D. "Programmed Instruction versus Usual Classroom Procedures in Teaching Boys to Read." *American Educational Research Journal* I, No. 2 (1964), 113–119.

Rollins, Sidney P. "Ungraded High Schools: Why Those Who Like Them Love Them." *The Nation's Schools* LXXIII, No. 4 (1964), 110, 130.

Thelen, Herbert A. "Grouping for Teachability." *Theory into Practice* II, No. 2 (1963), 81–89.

Traweek, Melvin W. "The Relationship Between Certain Personality Variables and Achievement through Programmed Instruction." *California Journal of Educational Research* XV, No. 5 (1964), 215–220.

Wright, Grace S. and Edith S. Greer. *The Junior High School.* Bulletin 1963, No. 32, United States Office of Education. Washington, D.C.: Government Printing Office, 1963.

Chapter 8

Curriculum Studies Involving Content

Applebee, Roger K. "National Study of High School English Programs: A Record of English Teaching Today." *English Journal* LV (March, 1966), 273–281.

Bateman, Donald and Frank Zedonis. "The Effect of a Study of Transformational Grammar on the Writing of Ninth- and Tenth-Grades." *NCTE Research Report No. 6.* Champaign, Ill.: National Council of Teachers of English, 1966.

Bingham, N. Eldred. "A Study Made in Hillsborough County, Florida, to Determine What Science to Teach in the Junior High School." *Science Education* XLVII, No. 3 (1963), 226–236.

Bogle, Ruth E. "How Can Reading Be Taught to Educable Adolescents Who Have Not Learned to Read?" *English Journal* LIII (September, 1964), 467–468.

Cousins, Jack E. "The Development of Reflective Thinking in an Eighth-Grade Social Studies Class." *Bulletin of the School of Education* XXXIX, No. 3 (1963), 36–58. Bloomington, Ind.: Indiana University Press.

Cutts, Warren G. *Modern Reading Instruction.* New York: Center for Applied Research in Education, 1964.

Day, William W. "Physics and Critical Thinking: An Experimental Evaluation of PSSC and Traditional Physics in Six Areas of Critical Thinking While Controlling for Intelligence, Achievement, Course Background, and Mobility by Analysis of Covariance." *Dissertation Abstracts* XXV (1965), 4197.

Fader, Daniel N. and Elton B. McNeil. *Hooked on Books: Program and Proof.* New York: G. P. Putnam's Sons, 1966.

Fenton, Edwin. *Developing a New Curriculum.* New York: Holt, Rinehart and Winston, Inc., 1967.

Fincher, Glen E. and H. Fillmer. "Programmed Instruction in Elementary Arithmetic." *The Arithmetic Teacher* XII (January, 1965), 19–23.

Ford, G. W. and Laurence Pugno, eds. *The Structure of Knowledge and the Curriculum.* Chicago: Rand McNally and Co., 1964.

Fraser, Dorothy M. *Deciding What to Teach.* Washington, D.C.: National Education Association, 1963.

Frazier, Alexander, ed. *New Directions in Elementary English.* Champaign, Ill.: National Council of Teachers of English, 1967.

Goodlad, John I. *The Changing School Curriculum.* New York: The Fund for the Advancement of Education, 1966.

Grobman, Hulda. "High School Biology, On What Level Does It Belong?" *The Clearing House* XXXVIII, No. 8 (1964), 498–499.

Grotberg, Edith. "The Washington Report in Action," *Education* LXXXV, No. 8 (1965), 490–494.

Heath, Robert W., ed. *New Curricula.* New York: Harper and Row, Publishers, 1964.

Hunicutt, Clarence W. and William J. Iverson, eds. *Research in the Three R's.* New York: Harper and Bros., 1958.

Livingston, Howard F. "The Effect of Instruction in General Semantics on the Critical Reading Ability of Tenth-Grade Students." *Dissertation Abstracts* XXVI (1966), 3783–3784.

Ofman, William and Morton Shaevitz. "The Kinesthetic Method in Remedial Reading." *Journal of Experimental Education* XXXI, No. 3 (1963), 317–320.

Olson, Arthur V. "An Analysis of the Vocabulary of Seven Primary Reading Series." *Elementary English* XL (March, 1965), 261–264.

Palmer, Warren G. "Audio Visual Programs in Senior High Schools in Georgia, 1967–68, with Recommendations for Improvement." *Dissertation Abstracts* XXIX (1968), 1688.

Petty, Walter T. and Paul C. Bruns. "A Summary of Investigations Relating to the English Language Arts in Elementary Education: 1963." *Elementary English* XLI (February, 1964), 119–137.

Schiffman, Gilbert B. "An Investigation of the Effectiveness of Two Pedagogical Procedures in the Remediation of Remedial Retarded Readers." *Dissertation Abstracts* XXVI (1965), 1434.

Smith, Nila B. *American Reading Instruction*. Newark, Delaware: International Reading Association, 1965.

Spache, George D. *Reading in the Elementary School*. Boston: Allyn and Bacon, Inc., 1964.

Squire, James R. and Roger K. Applebee. *High School English Instruction Today*. New York: Appleton-Century-Crofts, Inc., 1968.

Stewart, John W. "Influence of Public School Music Education as Revealed by a Comparison of Forty Selected High School Music and Non-Music Students." *Dissertation Abstracts* XXII (February, 1962), 2882–2883.

Turner, Donald G. "A Comparison of the Academic Achievement in Reading and Writing by Students Enrolled in Project English Classes with that of Non-experimental Students." *Dissertation Abstracts* XXVIII (1967), 2051.

Unruh, Glenys, ed. *New Curriculum Developments*. Washington, D.C.: Association for Supervision and Curriculum Development, 1965.

White, Robert H. "The Effect of Structural Linguistics on Improving English Composition Compared to that of Prescriptive Grammar in the Absence of Grammar Instruction." *Dissertation Abstracts* XXVII (1967), 5032–5033.

Witty, Paul A., Alma Freeland, and Edith Grotberg. *The Teaching of Reading*. Boston: D. C. Heath and Co., 1966.

Chapter 9
Curriculum Studies Involving Teachers

Amidon, Edmund and Michael Giammateo. "The Verbal Behavior of Superior Teachers." *Elementary School Journal* LXV, No. 5 (1965), 283–285.

———. and Ned A. Flanders. *The Role of the Teacher in the Classroom: A Manual for Understanding and Improving Teachers' Classroom Behavior*. Minneapolis: Paul S. Amidon and Associates, Inc., 1963.

Beck, William. "Pupil Perceptions of Teacher Merit: A Factor Analysis of Five Postulated Dimensions." *Journal of Educational Research* LXI, No. 3 (1967), 127–128.

Beggs, David W., III, ed. *Team Teaching*. Indianapolis: Unified College Press, Inc., 1964.

Bellack, Arno A., ed. *Theory and Research in Teaching*. New York: Teachers College Press, 1963.

Berman, Louise M., ed. *The Nature of Teaching*. Milwaukee: School of Education, University of Wisconsin, 1963.

—— and Mary Lou Usery. *Personalized Supervision: Sources and Insights*. Washington, D.C.: Association for Supervision and Curriculum Development, 1966.

Blair, Jr., James C. "The Elementary School Media Specialist: Role Perceptions by Relevant Groups." *Dissertation Abstracts* XXIX (1968), 1061.

Brooks, Elbert D. "Effects of Alternative Techniques for Modifying Teacher Behavior." *Dissertation Abstracts* XXVIII (1967), 4521.

Brown, David L. "Level of Teacher Morale in Relation to Teacher and Principal Attitudes toward Instruction." *Dissertation Abstracts* XXVII (1966), 3651.

Cardany, Arthur T. "Selected Personal Needs of Public School Teachers and Attitudes toward In-Service Education." *Dissertation Abstracts* XXVIII (1967), 4402.

Combs, Arthur W. *The Professional Education of Teachers*. Boston: Allyn and Bacon, Inc., 1965.

Conant, James B. *The Education of American Teachers*. New York: McGraw-Hill Book Co., 1963.

Corwin, Ronald G. "Militant Professionalism, Initiative and Compliance in Public Education." *Sociology of Education* XXXVIII, No. 4 (1965), 310–331.

Dandes, Herbert M. "Psychological Health and Teaching Effectiveness." *Journal of Teacher Education* XVII, No. 3 (1966), 301–305.

Dempsey, Richard Allen. "An Analysis of Teachers' Expressed Judgments of Barriers to Curriculum Change in Relation to the Factor of Individual Readiness to Change." *Dissertation Abstracts* XXIV (1963), 3225–3226.

Gidden, Norman S. "A Scale to Measure Teacher-Student Inter-Action," *Journal of Experimental Education* XXXVI, No. 1 (1968), 52–58.

Good, Vera M. "An Examination of an In-Service Education Operation to Determine Its Potential for Effective Change in Teaching Practices." *Dissertation Abstracts* XXVI (1964), 155.

Green, James E. "The Relationship between Dogmatism of Principles and Teachers and Teachers' Morale in Twelve Selected Secondary Schools in Michigan." *Dissertation Abstracts* XXVII (1966), 3255–3256.

Huettig, Alice and John M. Newell. "Attitudes Toward Introduction of Modern Mathematics Program by Teachers With Large and Small Number of Years Experience." *The Arithmetic Teacher* XIII, No. 2 (1966), 125–128.

Jackson, Joseph. "Analysis of a Team Teaching and a Self-Contained Homeroom Experiment in Grades Five-Six." *Journal of Experimental Education* XXXII, No. 4 (1964), 317–331.

Johnston, James. "Change in Student Teacher Dogmatism." *Journal of Educational Research* LXII, No. 5 (1969), 224–226.

Klausmeier, Herbert J. and William Wiersma. "Team Teaching and Achievement." *Education* LXXXVI, No. 4 (1965), 238–242.

Lee, Walter S. "A Study of the Effectiveness of Sensitivity Training in an In-Service Teacher Training Program in Human Relations." *Dissertation Abstracts* XXVIII (1967), 1680.

McCallon, Earl L. "Interpersonal Perception Characteristics of Teachers." *Journal of Experimental Education* XXXIV, No. 3 (1966), 97–100.

Mitchell, James V. "Personality Characteristics Associated with Motives for Entering Teaching." *Phi Delta Kappan* XLVI, No. 10 (1965), 529–532.

Parker, J. Cecil and Louis J. Rubin. *Process as Content.* Chicago: Rand McNally and Co., 1966.

Raack, Marilyn L. "The Effect of an In-Service Education Program on Teacher Verbal Behavior." *Dissertation Abstracts* XXVIII (1967), 1332.

Raths, James and Robert R. Leeper, eds. *The Supervisor: Agent for Change in Teaching.* Washington, D.C.: Association for Supervision and Curriculum Development, 1966.

Shaplin, Judson T. and Henry F. Olds, Jr., eds. *Team Teaching.* New York: Harper and Row, Publishers, 1964.

Smith, B. Othanel and Milton O. Menx. *A Study of the Logic of Teaching.* Urbana, Ill.: College of Education, University of Illinois, 1963.

Sorenson, A. G., T. R. Husek, and Constance Yu. "Divergent Concepts of Teacher Role: An Approach to the Measurement of Teacher Effectiveness." *Journal of Educational Psychology* LIV, No. 6 (1963), 287–294.

Sowards, G. Wesley and Mary-Margaret Scober. *The Changing Curriculum and the Elementary Teacher.* Belmont, Calif.: Wadsworth Publishing Co., 1961.

Strom, Robert. *Teaching in the Slum School.* Columbus, Ohio: Charles E. Merrill Books, Inc., 1965.

Walberg, Herbert J. "Scholastic Aptitude, The National Teacher Examinations and Teaching Success." *Journal of Educational Research* LXI, No. 3 (1967), 129–130.

Watson, Betty J. "A Study of the Relationships among Selected Aspects of Administrative Behavior and Teacher Group Cohesiveness in the Elementary School." *Dissertation Abstracts* XXV (1965), 1463–1464.

White, J. Claude. "A Study Comparing the Effectiveness of Three Teacher In-Service Training Programs Using Selected Self-Analysis Techniques." *Dissertation Abstracts* XXVIII (1967), 2053.

Chapter 10

General Principles of Curriculum Development

Adorno, T. W., Else Frenkel-Brunswick, D. J. Levinson and R. N. Sanford in collaboration with Betty Aron, Maria H. Levinson, and W. Morrow. *The Authoritarian Personality.* New York: Harper and Bros., 1950.

Bruner, Jerome S. *Toward a Theory of Instruction.* Cambridge: Belkuad Press of Harvard University, 1966.

Dewey, John. *Democracy in Education.* New York: The Macmillan Co., 1916.

Ford, G. W. and Lawrence Pugno, eds. *Structure of Knowledge and the Curriculum.* Chicago: Rand McNally and Co., 1964.

Fromm, Erich. *The Heart of Man*. New York: Harper and Row, Publishers, 1965.

Frymier, Jack R. *The Nature of Educational Method*. Columbus, Ohio: Charles E. Merrill Books, Inc., 1965.

————, ed. "Curriculum Theory Development: Work in Progress." *Theory Into Practice* VI, No. 4 (1967), 165–211.

Gardner, John. *Self-Renewal: The Individual and the Innovative Society*. New York: Harper and Row, Publishers, 1965.

Guba, Egon G. "Planning for Educational Change." *Theory into Practice* V, No. 1 (1966).

Harris, Ben M. and Wailand Bessent in collaboration with Kenneth E. McIntyre. *In-service Education: A Guide to Better Practice*. Englewood Cliffs, N.J.: Prentice-Hall, Inc., 1969.

Herrick, Virgil. *Strategies of Curriculum Development*. Columbus, Ohio: Charles E. Merrill Books, Inc., 1965.

Kelley, Earl C. *Education for What Is Real*. New York: Harper and Bros., 1947.

Michaelis, John U., Ruth H. Grossman, and Lloyd F. Scott. *New Designs for the Elementary School Curriculum*. New York: McGraw-Hill Book Co., 1967.

Phenix, Philip H. *Realms of Meaning*. New York: McGraw-Hill Book Co., 1964.

Russell, James E. *Change and Challenge in American Education*. Boston: Houghton Mifflin Co., 1965.

Stufflebeam, Daniel L. "Evaluation as Enlightenment for Decision Making." *Improving Educational Assessment and an Inventory of Measures of Affective Behavior*. Edited by Walcott H. Beatty. Washington, D.C.: The Association for Supervision and Curriculum Development, 1968.

Trump, J. Lloyd. *Focus on Change: Guide to Better Schools*. Chicago: Rand McNally and Co., 1961.

———— and Delmas F. Miller. *Secondary School Curriculum Improvement*. Boston: Allyn and Bacon, Inc., 1968.

Tyler, Ralph E. *Basic Principles of Curriculum and Instruction*. Chicago: University of Chicago Press, 1950.

VanTil, William. *The Year 2000: Teacher Education*. Terre Haute, Ind.: Indiana State University Press, 1968.

Index